A
WODEHOUSE
BESTIARY

A
WODEHOUSE
BESTIARY

P. G. WODEHOUSE

Edited and with a Preface by
D. R. BENSEN

Foreword by
HOWARD PHIPPS, JR.

A Mariner Book
HOUGHTON MIFFLIN COMPANY
Boston • New York

First Mariner Books edition 1999
Preface copyright © 1985 by D. R. Bensen

Library of Congress Cataloging-in-Publication Data
Wodehouse, P. G. (Pelham Grenville), 1881–1975.
A Wodehouse bestiary.
1. Animals — Fiction. 2. Pekingese spaniels — Fiction.
I. Bensen, D. R. (Donald R.), date. II. Title.
PR6045.O53A6 1985 823'.912 85-7999
ISBN 0-618-00186-7 (pbk.)

Printed in the United States of America

QUM 10 9 8 7 6 5 4 3 2 1

Contents

Foreword

Fans already familiar with Wodehouse the Connoisseur of Country Houses or Wodehouse the Golfing Enthusiast have a real and unexpected treat in store for them in this remarkable anthology, which highlights a previously overlooked Wodehouse — the Keen Animal Observer, a Wodehouse worthy of a special place of honor. Since the collection contains some of his very best stories, it will also serve as a delightful introduction to his complete oeuvre as well as to his natural history.

The P. G. Wodehouse Shelter of the Bide-a-Wee Home Association in Westhampton, Long Island, was quite appropriately named to honor his warm-hearted generosity toward his dumb chums. While, of course, the shelter housed dogs and cats and not the giraffes or rhinos that live some two hours away at the Bronx Zoo, our author's interests include many wild as well as tame animals, judging by the frequent mention of well- and lesser-known fauna. Unfortunately he is sometimes unspecific, referring only to a "snake" or a "parrot," and is frequently guilty of adopting a stereotyped view of snakes, parrots, rabbits, and rats. It is clear that he knows better, for in "Unpleasantness at Bludleigh Court" he rattles off the names and habits of big game, and incidentally shows more sympathy toward the viewpoint of trophy hunters wise in animal lore than toward the saccharine opinions of the uninformed. His writings show that he understands both why zoo animals appeal to all types and ages and why millions are spent on advertising pet food.

Anyone who has been a student of animals or has lived in the country will recognize the precision and profundity of some of the zoological observations scattered throughout the Master's work. No ornithologist has transcribed more accurately the warning hiss of a large, white, active, and short-tempered swan "like a tire bursting in a nest of cobras," or ever before saw fit to ask, "Have you ever noticed how a swan's eyebrows sort of meet in the middle?" Wodehouse appears to be very sound in his observations on the prudent opossum, while shy naturalists, comfortable only when they can share their deepest interests, can understand perfectly why "Gussie, terrified by the arrival of the mood, the moonlight and the expectant Madeline all together, started talking about newts."

Considering that it was written long before the publication of Dr. George B. Schaller's authoritative study on the mountain gorilla, Wodehouse's sketch of a gorilla personality is a model of verisimilitude, and it is a constant pleasure to find him tossing off lines that deepen our appreciation of the kinship between man and nature, such as, "The magistrate looked like an owl with a dash of weasel blood in him."

Then, too, one of the most memorable animals in literature is the Berkshire sow, Empress of Blandings. The passionate care that is lavished upon her should be an example to every zoo's curatorial staff.

Besides pigs, a high proportion of the creatures in these stories are domesticated; not surprising considering the urban and bucolic scenes where the action takes place. Wodehouse himself enjoyed pets and was generally surrounded by his beloved Pekes, shepherds, boxers, dachshunds, and by his cats. "Cats are not dogs" is only one of the many thoughtful comments you will find in this book.

His pre–World War II tale "Open House" is concerned, at least in part, with a Peke named Reginald. The British six-month quarantine is a fact bearing some importance on the shape of the plot. Ironically, years later, that same quarantine, threatening to separate Wodehouse from his Peke, Wonder, caused him to delay his departure from France across the channel despite clear warnings he had received, until it was too late and he was caught by the German occupation.

I believe that Wodehouse, by helping to develop a vast and happy audience sympathetic to the most bizarre patterns of behavior, animal and human, and by encouraging a relish for the variety of life on earth, has contributed toward the goal of today's zoos, which is to preserve nature's diversity for coming generations.

Howard Phipps, Jr.
President, New York Zoological Society

Preface

The first time I met P. G. Wodehouse, he was substantially more occupied with a dachshund called Jed than with a visiting editor and publisher. As Wodehouse's attentions involved holding Jed rather as if the dog were a bolster and pulling gently at his ears, I was content to allow the animal primacy.

This Jed was, in dog years, somewhat Wodehouse's senior (98 to 80), though he had not written as many books; they were clearly close companions in spite of the disparities in age, achievement and background. All the same, dachshunds were not Wodehouse's prime enthusiasm. For him, the canine acme was the Peke. Particularly in his middle years, he seemed to wade in a sea of Pekingese; they occupy long stretches of his letters and appear in family photographs as full equals; their health and exploits are at least as constant concerns as how the new novel is going or what the tax authorities are up to. Howard Phipps has recalled in the Foreword how the conflict of the British quarantine regulations and Wodehouse's commitment to his Peke Wonder led to his being scooped up and

interned by the German army in 1940. This is sometimes crit-
icized as frivolously unforesighted, but Wodehouse shared this
lack of prescience with most of the military and political leaders of Britain and France — Belgium, Holland, Norway, and
Denmark as well, for that matter.

It will be no surprise, then, that Pekes predominate in this
assembly of animal tales — no fewer than nine, six of whom
appear in one story. There is nothing that can, or even should,
be done about that; if you want to do business with Wodehouse, the Pekes follow inevitably. Relax and enjoy them.

There is of course more to life, and fiction, than Pekes. We
can also offer a brace of versatile mongrels, Beefy Bingham's
stout-hearted Bottles and the nameless Mixer — Wodehouse's
only canine narrator — and major and minor cat characters,
including Webster, whose ecclesiastical dignity was shattered
when he proved to have paws of clay.

The menagerie also contains one each parrot, snake, swan,
rabbit (dead), gorilla (fake), canary, gnu, and pig, and some
racehorses, a heady enough variety to satisfy all but the most
demanding zoophile. True, such a selection may seem tame to
those who look for peril in their animal stories, but in quite a
few of these accounts, if Nature isn't red in tooth and claw, it's
only because of quick thinking and determined timidity on the
part of the human protagonists. Given full scope, that swan
would have terminated Bertie Wooster's non-career long before its time. And, offered the choice, would not Eustace Mulliner have preferred to face a ravening tiger than the combined
wrath of the Pekelorn Marcella Tyrrhwhitt, the canary-defend-
ing Orlando Wotherspoon, and his Aunt Georgiana, whose
cat he had just kicked? You bet he would.

In a curious way, this is not the first Wodehouse bestiary, at
least not the first bestiary to contain Wodehouses. Many me-

dieval treatises contained accounts, sometimes illustrated, of "wild men of the woods," variously called wudewasa or wode-houses. These could be distinguished from great apes chiefly by the large size of the feet and the elongated big toe. Wode-house, I believe, took a size 9, often preferring tennis shoes.

D. R. Bensen
Croton-on-Hudson

A
WODEHOUSE
BESTIARY

Unpleasantness at Bludleigh Court

THE POET who was spending the summer at the Anglers' Rest had just begun to read us his new sonnet sequence when the door of the bar-parlor opened and there entered a young man in gaiters. He came quickly in and ordered beer. In one hand he was carrying a double-barreled gun, in the other a posy of dead rabbits. These he dropped squashily to the floor, and the poet, stopping in midsentence, took one long, earnest look at the remains. Then, wincing painfully, he turned a light green and closed his eyes. It was not until the banging of the door announced the visitor's departure that he came to life again.

Mr. Mulliner regarded him sympathetically over his hot Scotch and lemon.

"You appear upset," he said.

"A little," admitted the poet. "A momentary malaise. It may be purely personal prejudice, but I confess to preferring rabbits with rather more of their contents inside them."

"Many sensitive souls in your line of business hold similar

views," Mr. Mulliner assured him. "My niece Charlotte did."

"It is my temperament," said the poet. "I dislike all dead things — particularly when, as in the case of the above rabbits, they have so obviously, so — shall I say? — blatantly made the Great Change. Give me," he went on, the greenish tinge fading from his face, "life and joy and beauty."

"Just what my niece Charlotte used to say."

"Oddly enough, that thought forms the theme of the second sonnet in my sequence — which, now that the young gentleman with the portable Morgue has left us, I will . . ."

"My niece Charlotte," said Mr. Mulliner, with quiet firmness, "was one of those gentle, dreamy, wistful girls who take what I have sometimes felt to be a mean advantage of having an ample private income to write Vignettes in Verse for the artistic weeklies. Charlotte's Vignettes in Verse had a wide vogue among the editors of London's higher-browed but less prosperous periodicals. Directly these frugal men realized that she was willing to supply unstinted vignettes gratis, for the mere pleasure of seeing herself in print, they were all over her. The consequence was that before long she had begun to move freely in the most refined literary circles, and one day, at a little luncheon at the Crushed Pansy (the Restaurant with a Soul), she found herself seated next to a godlike young man, at the sight of whom something seemed to go off inside her like a spring."

"Talking of spring . . ." said the poet.

"Cupid," proceeded Mr. Mulliner, "has always found the family to which I belong a ready mark for his bow. Our hearts are warm, our passions quick. It is not too much to say that my niece Charlotte was in love with this young man before she had finished spearing the first anchovy out of the hors d'oeuvres dish. He was intensely spiritual-looking, with a broad, white forehead and eyes that seemed to Charlotte not so much eyes as a couple of holes punched in the surface of a beautiful soul. He wrote, she learned, Pastels in Prose, and his name, if she had caught it correctly at the moment of their introduction, was Aubrey Trefusis."

Friendship ripens quickly at the Crushed Pansy (said Mr. Mulliner). The *poulet rôti au cresson* had scarcely been distributed before the young man was telling Charlotte his hopes, his fears, and the story of his boyhood. And she was amazed to find that he sprang — not from a long line of artists but from an ordinary, conventional county family of the type that cares for nothing except hunting and shooting.

"You can readily imagine," he said, helping her to Brussels sprouts, "how intensely such an environment jarred upon my unfolding spirit. My family are greatly respected in the neighborhood, but I personally have always looked upon them as a gang of blood-imbrued plug-uglies. My views on kindness to animals are rigid. My impulse, on encountering a rabbit, is to offer it lettuce. To my family, on the other hand, a rabbit seems incomplete without a deposit of small shot in it. My father, I believe, has cut off more assorted birds in their prime than any other man in the Midlands. A whole morning was spoiled for me last week by the sight of a photograph of him in the *Tatler,* looking rather severely at a dying duck. My elder brother Reginald spreads destruction in every branch of the animal kingdom. And my younger brother Wilfred is, I understand, working his way up to the larger fauna by killing sparrows with an air-gun. Spiritually, one might just as well live in Chicago as at Bludleigh Court."

"Bludleigh Court?" cried Charlotte.

"The moment I was twenty-one and came into a modest but sufficient inheritance, I left the place and went to London to lead the life literary. The family, of course, were appalled. My

Uncle Francis, I remember, tried to reason with me for hours. Uncle Francis, you see, used to be a famous big-game hunter. They tell me he has shot more gnus than any other man who ever went to Africa. In fact, until recently he virtually never stopped shooting gnus. Now, I hear, he has developed lumbago and is down at Bludleigh treating it with Riggs's Superfine Emulsion and sun-baths."

"But is Bludleigh Court your home?"

"That's right. Bludleigh Court, Lesser Bludleigh, near Goresby-on-the-Ouse, Bedfordshire."

"But Bludleigh Court belongs to Sir Alexander Bassinger."

"My name is really Bassinger. I adopted the pen-name of Trefusis to spare the family's feelings. But how do you come to know of the place?"

"I'm going down there next week for a visit. My mother was an old friend of Lady Bassinger."

Aubrey was astonished. And, being, like all writers of Pastels in Prose, a neat phrasemaker, he said what a small world it was, after all.

"Well, well, well!" he said.

"From what you tell me," said Charlotte, "I'm afraid I shall not enjoy my visit. If there's one thing I loathe, it's anything connected with sport."

"Two minds with but a single thought," said Aubrey. "Look here, I'll tell you what. I haven't been near Bludleigh for years, but if you're going there, why, dash it, I'll come too — aye, even though it means meeting my Uncle Francis."

"You will?"

"I certainly will. I don't consider it safe that a girl of your exquisite refinement and sensibility should be dumped down at an abattoir like Bludleigh Court without a kindred spirit to lend her moral stability."

"What do you mean?"

"I'll tell you." His voice was grave. "That house exercises a spell."

"A what?"

"A spell. A ghastly spell that saps the strongest humanitarian principles. Who knows what effect it might have upon you, should you go there without someone like me to stand by you and guide you in your hour of need?"

"What nonsense!"

"Well, all I can tell you is that once, when I was a boy, a high official of Our Dumb Brothers' League of Mercy arrived there lateish on a Friday night, and at two-fifteen on the Saturday afternoon he was the life and soul of an informal party got up for the purpose of drawing one of the local badgers out of an upturned barrel."

Charlotte laughed merrily.

"The spell will not affect me," she said.

"Nor me, of course," said Aubrey. "But all the same, I would prefer to be by your side, if you don't mind."

"Mind, Mr. Bassinger!" breathed Charlotte softly, and was thrilled to note that at the words and the look with which she accompanied them this man to whom — for, as I say, we Mulliners are quick workers — she had already given her heart, quivered violently. It seemed to her that in those soulful eyes of his she had seen the love-light.

Bludleigh Court, when Charlotte reached it some days later, proved to be a noble old pile of Tudor architecture, situated in rolling parkland and flanked by pleasant gardens leading to a lake with a tree-fringed boathouse. Inside, it was comfortably furnished and decorated throughout with groves of glass cases containing the goggle-eyed remnants of birds and beasts assassinated at one time or another by Sir Alexander Bassinger and his son Reginald. From every wall there peered down with an air of mild reproach selected portions of the gnus, moose, elks, zebus, antelopes, giraffes, mountain goats and wapiti which had had the misfortune to meet Colonel Sir Francis Pashley-Drake before lumbago spoiled him for the chase. The cemetery also included a few stuffed sparrows, which showed that little Wilfred was doing his bit.

The first two days of her visit Charlotte passed mostly in the society of Colonel Pashley-Drake, the Uncle Francis to whom Aubrey had alluded. He seemed to have taken a paternal fancy to her: and, lithely though she dodged down back-stairs and passages, she generally found him breathing heavily at her side. He was a red-faced, almost circular man, with eyes like a prawn's, and he spoke to her freely of lumbago, gnus and Aubrey.

"So you're a friend of my nephew?" he said, snorting twice in a rather unpleasant manner. It was plain that he disapproved of the pastel-artist. "Shouldn't see too much of him, if I were you. Not the sort of fellow I'd like any daughter of mine to get friendly with."

"You are quite wrong," said Charlotte warmly. "You have only to gaze into Mr. Bassinger's eyes to see that his morals are above reproach."

"I never gaze into his eyes," replied Colonel Pashley-Drake. "Don't like his eyes. Wouldn't gaze into them if you paid me. I maintain his whole outlook on life is morbid and unwholesome. I like a man to be a clean, strong, upstanding Englishman who can look his gnu in the face and put an ounce of lead in it."

"Life," said Charlotte coldly, "is not all gnus."

"You imply that there are also wapiti, moose, zebus and mountain-goats?" said Sir Francis. "Well, maybe you're right. All the same, I'd give the fellow a wide berth, if I were you."

"So far from doing so," replied Charlotte proudly, "I am

about to go for a stroll with him by the lake at this very moment."

And, turning away with a petulant toss of her head, she moved off to meet Aubrey, who was hurrying towards her across the terrace.

"I am so glad you came, Mr. Bassinger," she said to him as they walked together in the direction of the lake. "I was beginning to find your Uncle Francis a little excessive."

Aubrey nodded sympathetically. He had observed her in conversation with his relative and his heart had gone out to her.

"Two minutes of my Uncle Francis," he said, "is considered by the best judges a good medium dose for an adult. So you find him trying, eh? I was wondering what impression my family had made on you."

Charlotte was silent for a moment.

"How relative everything is in this world," she said pensively. "When I first met your father, I thought I had never seen anybody more completely loathsome. Then I was introduced to your brother Reginald, and I realized that, after all, your father might have been considerably worse. And, just as I was thinking that Reginald was the furthest point possible, along came your Uncle Francis, and Reginald's quiet charm seemed to leap out at me like a beacon on a dark night. Tell me," she said, "has no one ever thought of doing anything about your Uncle Francis?"

Aubrey shook his head gently.

"It is pretty generally recognized now that he is beyond the reach of human science. The only thing to do seems to be to let him go on till he eventually runs down."

They sat together on a rustic bench overlooking the water. It was a lovely morning. The sun shone on the little wavelets which the sighing breeze drove gently to the shore. A dreamy stillness had fallen on the world, broken only by the distant sound of Sir Alexander Bassinger murdering magpies, of Reginald Bassinger encouraging dogs to eviscerate a rabbit, of Wilfred busy among the sparrows, and a monotonous droning noise from the upper terrace, which was Colonel Sir Francis Pashley-Drake telling Lady Bassinger what to do with the dead gnu.

Aubrey was the first to break the silence.

"How lovely the world is, Miss Mulliner."

"Yes, isn't it!"

"How softly the breeze caresses yonder water."

"Yes, doesn't it!"

"How fragrant a scent of wildflowers it has."

"Yes, hasn't it!"

They were silent again.

"On such a day," said Aubrey, "the mind seems to turn irresistibly to Love."

"Love?" said Charlotte, her heart beginning to flutter.

"Love," said Aubrey. "Tell me, Miss Mulliner, have you ever thought of Love?"

He took her hand. Her head was bent, and with the toe of her dainty shoe she toyed with a passing snail.

"Life, Miss Mulliner," said Aubrey, "is a Sahara through which we all must pass. We start at the Cairo of the cradle and we travel on to the — er — well, we go traveling on."

"Yes, don't we!" said Charlotte.

"Afar we can see the distant goal . . ."

"Yes, can't we!"

". . . and would fain reach it."

"Yes, wouldn't we!"

"But the way is rough and weary. We have to battle through the sand-storms of Destiny, face with what courage we may the howling simoons of Fate. And very unpleasant it all is. But sometimes in the Sahara of Life, if we are fortunate, we come upon the Oasis of Love. That oasis, when I had all but lost hope, I reached at one-fifteen on the afternoon of Tuesday, the twenty-second of last month. There comes a time in the life of every man when he sees Happiness beckoning to him and must grasp it. Miss Mulliner, I have something to ask you which I have been trying to ask ever since the day when we two first met. Miss Mulliner . . . Charlotte . . . Will you be my . . . Gosh! Look at that whacking great rat! Loo-loo-loo-loo-loo-loo-loo-loo!" said Aubrey, changing the subject.

Once, in her childhood, a sportive playmate had secretly withdrawn the chair on which Charlotte Mulliner was preparing to seat herself. Years had passed, but the recollection of the incident remained green in her memory. In frosty weather she could still feel the old wound. And now, as Aubrey Bassinger suddenly behaved in this remarkable manner, she experienced the same sensation again. It was as though something blunt and heavy had hit her on the head at the exact moment when she was slipping on a banana-skin.

She stared round-eyed at Aubrey. He had released her hand, sprung to his feet, and now, armed with her parasol, was beating furiously in the lush grass at the waterside. And every little while his mouth would open, his head would go back, and uncouth sounds would proceed from his slavering jaws.

"Yoicks! Yoicks! Yoicks!" cried Aubrey.

And again,

"Tally-ho! Hard For'ard! Tally-ho!"

Presently the fever seemed to pass. He straightened himself and came back to where she stood.

"It must have got away into a hole or something," he said, removing a bead of perspiration from his forehead with the ferrule of the parasol. "The fact of the matter is, it's silly ever to go out in the country without a good dog. If only I'd had a nice, nippy terrier with me, I might have obtained some solid results. As it is, a fine rat — gone — just like that! Oh, well, that's Life, I suppose." He paused. "Let me see," he said. "Where was I?"

And then it was as though he waked from a trance. His flushed face paled.

"I say," he stammered, "I'm afraid you must think me most awfully rude."

"Pray do not mention it," said Charlotte coldly.

"Oh, but you must. Dashing off like that."

"Not at all."

"What I was going to say, when I was interrupted, was, will you be my wife?"

"Oh?"

"Yes."

"Well, I won't."

"You won't?"

"No. Never." Charlotte's voice was tense with a scorn which she did not attempt to conceal. "So this is what you were all the time, Mr. Bassinger — a secret sportsman!"

Aubrey quivered from head to foot.

"I'm not! I'm not! It was the hideous spell of this ghastly house that overcame me."

"Pah!"

"What did you say?"

"I said 'Pah'?"

"Why did you say, 'Pah'?"

"Because," said Charlotte, with flashing eyes, "I do not believe you. Your story is thin and fishy."

"But it's the truth. It was as if some hypnotic influence had gripped me, forcing me to act against all my higher inclinations. Can't you understand? Would you condemn me for a moment's passing weakness? Do you think," he cried passionately, "that the real Aubrey Bassinger would raise a hand to touch a rat, save in the way of kindness? I love rats, I tell you — love them. I used to keep them as a boy. White ones with pink eyes."

Charlotte shook her head. Her face was cold and hard.

"Good-bye, Mr. Bassinger," she said. "From this instant we meet as strangers."

She turned and was gone. And Aubrey Bassinger, covering his face with his hands, sank on the bench, feeling like a sand-bagged leper.

The mind of Charlotte Mulliner, in the days which followed the painful scene which I have just described, was torn, as you may well imagine, with conflicting emotions. For a time, as was natural, anger predominated. But after a while sadness overcame indignation. She mourned for her lost happiness.

And yet, she asked herself, how else could she have acted? She had worshiped Aubrey Bassinger. She had set him upon a pedestal, looked up to him as a great white soul. She had supposed him one who lived, far above this world's coarseness and grime, on a rarefied plane of his own, thinking beautiful thoughts. Instead of which, it now appeared, he went about the place chasing rats with parasols.

That there lurked in the atmosphere of Bludleigh Court a sinister influence that sapped the principles of the most humanitarian and sent them ravening to and fro, seeking for prey, she declined to believe. The theory was pure banana-oil. If such an influence was in operation at Bludleigh, why had it not affected her?

No, if Aubrey Bassinger chased rats with parasols, it could only mean that he was one of Nature's rat-chasers. And to such a one, cost what it might to refuse, she could never confide her heart.

Few things are more embarrassing to a highly-strung girl than to be for any length of time in the same house with a man whose love she has been compelled to decline, and Charlotte would have given much to be able to leave Bludleigh Court. But there was, it seemed, to be a garden-party on the following Tuesday, and Lady Bassinger had urged her so strongly to stay on for it that departure was out of the question.

To fill the leaden moments, she immersed herself in her work. She had a long-standing commission to supply the *Animal-Lovers' Gazette* with a poem for its Christmas number, and to the task of writing this she proceeded to devote herself. And gradually the ecstasy of literary composition eased her pain.

The days crept by. Old Sir Alexander continued to maltreat magpies. Reginald and the local rabbits fought a never-ceasing battle, they striving to keep up the birthrate, he to reduce it. Colonel Pashley-Drake maundered on about gnus he had met. And Aubrey dragged himself about the house, looking licked to a splinter. Eventually Tuesday came, and with it the garden-party.

Lady Bassinger's annual garden-party was one of the big events of the countryside. By four o'clock all that was bravest and fairest for miles around had assembled on the big lawn. But Charlotte, though she had stayed on specially to be present, was not one of the gay throng. At about the time when the first strawberry was being dipped in its cream, she was up in her room, staring with bewildered eyes at a letter which had arrived by the second post.

The *Animal-Lovers' Gazette* had turned her poem down!

Yes, turned it down flat, in spite of the fact that it had been commissioned and that she was not asking a penny for it. Accompanying the rejected manuscript was a curt note from the editor, in which he said that he feared its tone might offend his readers.

Charlotte was stunned. She was not accustomed to having her efforts rejected. This one, moreover, had seemed to her so particularly good. A hard judge of her own work, she had said to herself, as she licked the envelope, that this time, if never before, she had delivered the goods.

She unfolded the manuscript and reread it.

It ran as follows:

GOOD GNUS
(A Vignette in Verse)
by
Charlotte Mulliner

> When cares attack and life seems black,
> How sweet it is to pot a yak,
>> Or puncture hares and grizzly bears,
>> And others I could mention:
> But in my Animals "Who's Who"
> No name stands higher than the Gnu:
>> And each new gnu that comes in view
>> Receives my prompt attention.
>
> When Afric's sun is sinking low,
> And shadows wander to and fro,
>> And everywhere there's in the air
>> A hush that's deep and solemn;
> Then is the time good men and true
> With View Halloo pursue the gnu:
>> (The safest spot to put your shot
>> Is through the spinal column).

To take the creature by surprise
We must adopt some rude disguise,
 Although deceit is never sweet,
  And falsehoods don't attract us:
So, as with gun in hand you wait,
Remember to impersonate
 A tuft of grass, a mountain-pass,
  A kopje or a cactus.

A brief suspense, and then at last
The waiting's o'er, the vigil past:
 A careful aim. A spurt of flame.
  It's done. You've pulled the trigger.
And one more gnu, so fair and frail,
Has handed in its dinner-pail:
 (The females all are rather small,
  The males are somewhat bigger).

Charlotte laid the manuscript down, frowning. She chafed at the imbecility of editors. Less than ever was she able to understand what anyone could find in it to cavil at. Tone likely to offend? What did the man mean about the tone being likely to offend? She had never heard such nonsense in her life. How could the tone possibly offend? It was unexceptionable. The whole poem breathed that clean, wholesome, healthy spirit of Sport which has made England what it is. And the thing was not only lyrically perfect, but educational as well. It told the young reader, anxious to shoot gnus but uncertain of the correct procedure, exactly what he wanted to know.

She bit her lip. Well, if this Animal-Lovers bird didn't know a red-hot contribution when he saw one, she would jolly well find somebody else who did — and quick, too. She . . .

At this moment, something occurred to distract her thoughts. Down on the terrace below, little Wilfred, complete with air-gun, had come into her line of vision. The boy was creeping along in a quiet, purposeful manner, obviously intent on the chase; and it suddenly came over Charlotte Mulliner in a wave that here she had been in this house all this time and never once had thought of borrowing the child's weapon and having a plug at something with it.

The sky was blue. The sun was shining. All Nature seemed to call to her to come out and kill things.

She left the room and ran quickly down the stairs.

And what of Aubrey, meanwhile? Grief having slowed him up on his feet, he had been cornered by his mother and marched off to hand cucumber sandwiches at the garden-party. After a brief spell of servitude, however, he had contrived to escape and was wandering on the terrace, musing mournfully, when he observed his brother Wilfred approaching. And at the same moment Charlotte Mulliner emerged from the house and came hurrying in their direction. In a flash, Aubrey perceived that here was a situation which, shrewdly handled, could be turned greatly to his advantage. Affecting to be unaware of Charlotte's approach, he stopped his brother and eyed the young thug sternly.

"Wilfred," he said, "where are you going with that gun?"

The boy appeared embarrassed.

"Just shooting."

Aubrey took the weapon from him and raised his voice slightly. Out of the corner of his eye he had seen that Charlotte was now well within hearing.

"Shooting, eh?" he said. "Shooting? I see. And have you never been taught, wretched child, that you should be kind to the animals that crave your compassion? Has no one ever told you that he prayeth best who loveth best all things both great and small? For shame, Wilfred, for shame!"

Charlotte had come up, and was standing there, looking at them inquiringly.

"What's all this about?" she asked.

Aubrey started dramatically.

"Miss Mulliner! I was not aware that you were there. All this? Oh, nothing. I found this lad here on his way to shoot sparrows with his air-gun, and I am taking the thing from him. It may seem to you a high-handed action on my part. You may consider me hyper-sensitive. You may ask, Why all this fuss about a few birds? But that is Aubrey Bassinger. Aubrey Bassinger will not lightly allow even the merest sparrow to be placed in jeopardy. Tut, Wilfred," he said. "Tut! Cannot you see now how wrong it is to shoot the poor sparrows?"

"But I wasn't going to shoot sparrows," said the boy. "I was going to shoot Uncle Francis while he is having his sun-bath."

"It is also wrong," said Aubrey, after a slight hesitation, "to shoot Uncle Francis while he is having his sun-bath."

Charlotte Mulliner uttered an impatient exclamation. And Aubrey, looking at her, saw that her eyes were glittering with a strange light. She breathed quickly through her delicately-chiseled nose. She seemed feverish, and a medical man would have been concerned about her blood-pressure.

"Why?" she demanded vehemently. "Why is it wrong? Why shouldn't he shoot his Uncle Francis while he is having his sun-bath?"

Aubrey stood for a moment, pondering. Her razor-like feminine intelligence had cut cleanly to the core of the matter. After all, now that she put it like that, why not?

"Think how it would tickle him up."

"True," said Aubrey, nodding. "True."

"And his Uncle Francis is precisely the sort of man who

ought to have been shot at with air-guns incessantly for the last thirty years. The moment I met him, I said to myself, 'That man ought to be shot at with air-guns.' "

Aubrey nodded again. Her girlish enthusiasm had begun to infect him.

"There is much in what you say," he admitted.

"Where is he?" asked Charlotte, turning to the boy.

"On the roof of the boathouse."

Charlotte's face clouded.

"H'm!" she said. "That's awkward. How is one to get at him?"

"I remember Uncle Francis telling me once," said Aubrey, "that, when you went shooting tigers, you climbed a tree. There are plenty of trees by the boathouse."

"Admirable!"

For an instant there came to disturb Aubrey's hearty joy in the chase a brief, faint flicker of prudence.

"But . . . I say . . . Do you really think . . . Ought we . . . ?"

Charlotte's eyes flashed scornfully.

"Infirm of purpose," she said. "Give me the air-gun."

"I was only thinking . . ."

"Well?"

"I suppose you know he'll have practically nothing on?"

Charlotte Mulliner laughed lightly.

"He can't intimidate *me*," she said. "Come! Let us be going."

Up on the roof of the boathouse, the beneficent ultra-violet rays of the afternoon sun pouring down on his globular surface, Colonel Sir Francis Pashley-Drake lay in that pleasant half-waking, half-dreaming state that accompanies this particular form of lumbago-treatment. His mind flitted lightly from one soothing subject to another. He thought of elks he had shot in Canada, of moufflon he had shot in the Grecian Archipelago, of giraffes he had shot in Nigeria. He was just on the point of thinking of a hippopotamus which he had shot in Egypt, when the train of his meditations was interrupted by a soft popping sound not far away. He smiled affectionately. So little Wilfred was out with his air-gun, eh?

A thrill of quiet pride passed through Colonel Pashley-Drake. He had trained the lad well, he felt. With a garden-party in progress, with all the opportunities it offered for quiet gorging, how many boys of Wilfred's age would have neglected their shooting to hang round the tea-table and stuff themselves with cakes. But this fine lad . . .

Ping! There it was again. The boy must be somewhere quite close at hand. He wished he could be at his side, giving him kindly advice. Wilfred, he felt, was a young fellow after his own heart. What destruction he would spread among the really worthwhile animals when he grew up and put aside childish things and exchanged his air-gun for a Winchester repeater.

Sir Francis Pashley-Drake started. Two inches from where he lay a splinter of wood had sprung from the boathouse roof. He sat up, feeling a little less affectionate.

"Wilfred!"

There was no reply.

"Be careful, Wilfred, my boy. You nearly . . ."

A sharp, agonizing twinge caused him to break off abruptly. He sprang to his feet and began to address the surrounding landscape passionately in one of the lesser-known dialects of the Congo Basin. He no longer thought of Wilfred with quiet pride. Few things so speedily modify an uncle's love as a nephew's air-gun bullet in the fleshy part of the leg. Sir Francis Pashley-Drake's plans for this boy's future had undergone in one brief instant a complete change. He no longer desired to stand beside him through his formative years, teaching him the secrets of shikari. All he wanted to do was to get close enough to him to teach him with the flat of his right hand to be a bit more careful where he pointed his gun.

He was expressing a synopsis of these views in a mixture of Urdu and Cape Dutch, when the words were swept from his lips by the sight of a woman's face, peering from the branches of a nearby tree.

Colonel Pashley-Drake reeled where he stood. Like so many outdoor men, he was the soul of modesty. Once, in Bechuanaland, he had left a native witch dance in a marked manner because he considered the chief's third supplementary wife insufficiently clad. An acute consciousness of the sketchiness of his costume overcame him. He blushed brightly.

"My dear young lady . . ." he stammered.

He had got thus far when he perceived that the young woman was aiming at him something that looked remarkably like an air-gun, her tongue protruding thoughtfully from the corner of her mouth, and had closed one eye and with the other was squinting tensely along the barrel.

Colonel Sir Francis Pashley-Drake did not linger. In all England there was probably no man more enthusiastic about shooting: but the fascination of shooting as a sport depends almost wholly on whether you are at the right or wrong end of the gun. With an agility which no gnu, unless in the very pink of condition, could have surpassed, he sprang to the side of the roof and leaped off. There was a clump of reeds not far from the boathouse. He galloped across the turf and dived into them.

Charlotte descended from her tree. Her expression was petulant. Girls nowadays are spoiled, and only too readily become peevish when baulked of their pleasures.

"I had no idea he was so nippy," she said.

"A quick mover," agreed Aubrey. "I imagine he got that way from dodging rhinoceroses."

"Why can't they make these silly guns with two barrels? A single barrel doesn't give a girl a chance."

Nestling among the reeds, Colonel Sir Francis Pashley-Drake, in spite of the indignation natural to a man in his position, could not help feeling a certain complacency. The old woodcraft of the hunter had stood him, he felt, in good stead. Not many men, he told himself, would have had the initiative and swift intelligence to act so promptly in the face of peril.

He was aware of voices close by.

"What do we do now?" he heard Charlotte Mulliner say.

"We must think," said the voice of his nephew Aubrey.

"He's in there somewhere."

"Yes."

"I hate to see a fine head like that get away," said Charlotte, and her voice was still querulous. "Especially after I winged him. The very next poem I write is going to be an appeal to air-gun manufacturers to use their intelligence, if they have any, and turn out a line with two barrels."

"I shall write a Pastel in Prose on the same subject," agreed Aubrey.

"Well, what shall we do?"

There was a short silence. An insect of unknown species crept up Colonel Pashley-Drake and bit him in the small of the back.

"I'll tell you what," said Aubrey. "I remember Uncle Francis mentioning to me once that when wounded zebus take cover by the reaches of the Lower Zambesi, the sportsman dispatches a native assistant to set fire to . . ."

Sir Francis Pashley-Drake emitted a hollow groan. It was drowned by Charlotte's cry of delight.

"Why, of course! How clever you are, Mr. Bassinger."

"Oh no," said Aubrey modestly.

"Have you matches?"

"I have a cigarette-lighter."

"Then would it be bothering you too much to go and set light to those reeds — about there would be a good place — and I'll wait here with the gun."

"I should be charmed."

"I hate to trouble you."

"No trouble, I assure you," said Aubrey. "A pleasure."

Three minutes later the revelers on the lawn were interested to observe a sight rare at the better class of English garden-party. Out of a clump of laurel bushes that bordered the smoothly mown turf there came charging a stout, pink gentleman of middle age who hopped from side to side as he ran. He was wearing a loin-cloth, and seemed in a hurry. They had just time to recognize in this newcomer their hostess's brother, Colonel Sir Francis Pashley-Drake, when he snatched a cloth from the nearest table, draped it round him, and with a quick leap took refuge behind the portly form of the Bishop of Stortford, who was talking to the local Master of Hounds about the difficulty he had in keeping his vicars off the incense.

Charlotte and Aubrey had paused in the shelter of the laurels. Aubrey, peering through this zareba, clicked his tongue regretfully.

"He's taken cover again," he said. "I'm afraid we shall find it difficult to dig him out of there. He's gone to earth behind a bishop."

Receiving no reply, he turned.

"Miss Mulliner!" he exclaimed. "Charlotte! What is the matter?"

A strange change had come over the girl's beautiful face since he had last gazed at it. The fire had died out of those lovely eyes, leaving them looking like those of a newly-awak-ened somnambulist. She was pale, and the tip of her nose quivered.

"Where am I?" she murmured.

"Bludleigh Court, Lesser Bludleigh, Goresby-on-the-Ouse, Bedfordshire. Telephone 28 Goresby," said Aubrey quickly.

"Have I been dreaming? Or did I really . . . Ah, yes, yes!" she moaned, shuddering violently. "It all comes back to me. I shot Sir Francis with the air-gun!"

"You certainly did," said Aubrey, and would have gone on to comment with warm approbation on the skill she had shown, a skill which — in an untrained novice — had struck him as really remarkable. But he checked himself. "Surely," he said, "you are not letting the fact disturb you? It's the sort of thing that might have happened to anyone."

She interrupted him.

"How right you were, Mr. Bassinger, to warn me against the spell of Bludleigh. And how wrong I was to blame you for borrowing my parasol to chase a rat. Can you ever forgive me?"

"Charlotte!"

"Aubrey!"

"Charlotte!"

"Hush!" she said. "Listen."

On the lawn, Sir Francis Pashley-Drake was telling his story to an enthralled audience. The sympathy of the meeting, it was only too plain, was entirely with him. This shooting of a sit-ting sun-bather had stirred the feelings of his hearers deeply. Indignant exclamations came faintly to the ears of the young couple in the laurels.

"Most irregular!"

"Not done!"

"Scarcely cricket!"

And then, from Sir Alexander Bassinger, a stern "I shall require a full explanation."

Charlotte turned to Aubrey.

"What shall we do?"

"Well," said Aubrey, reflecting, "I don't think we had better just go and join the party and behave as if nothing had happened. The atmosphere doesn't seem right. What I would propose is that we take a short cut through the fields to the station, hook up with the five-fifty express at Goresby, go to London, have a bit of dinner, get married and . . ."

"Yes, yes," cried Charlotte. "Take me away from this awful house."

"To the ends of the world," said Aubrey fervently. He paused. "Look here," he said suddenly. "If you move over to where I'm standing, you get the old boy plumb spang against the sky-line. You wouldn't care for just one last . . ."

"No, no!"

"Merely a suggestion," said Aubrey. "Ah well, perhaps you're right. Then let's be shifting."

Sir Roderick Comes to Lunch

❧THE BLOW FELL at precisely one forty-five (summer-time). Benson, my Aunt Agatha's butler, was offering me the fried potatoes at the moment, and such was my emotion that I lofted six of them on the sideboard with the spoon. Shaken to the core, if you know what I mean.

I've told you how I got engaged to Honoria Glossop in my efforts to do young Bingo Little a good turn. Well, on this particular morning she had lugged me round to Aunt Agatha's for lunch, and I was just saying "Death, where is thy sting?" when I realized that the worst was yet to come.

"Bertie," she said, suddenly, as if she had just remembered it, "what is the name of that man of yours — your valet?"

"Eh? Oh, Jeeves."

"I think he's a bad influence for you," said Honoria. "When we are married you must get rid of Jeeves."

It was at this point that I jerked the spoon and sent six of the best and crispest sailing on to the sideboard, with Benson gamboling after them like a dignified old retriever.

"Get rid of Jeeves!" I gasped.

"Yes. I don't like him."

"I don't like him," said Aunt Agatha.

"But I can't. I mean — why, I couldn't carry on for a day without Jeeves."

"You will have to," said Honoria. "I don't like him at all."

"I don't like him at all," said Aunt Agatha. "I never did."

Ghastly, what? I'd always had an idea that marriage was a bit of a wash-out, but I'd never dreamed that it demanded such frightful sacrifices from a fellow. I passed the rest of the meal in a sort of stupor.

The scheme had been, if I remember, that after lunch I should go off and caddy for Honoria on a shopping tour down Regent Street; but when she got up and started collecting me and the rest of her things, Aunt Agatha stopped her.

"You run along, dear," she said. "I want to say a few words to Bertie."

So Honoria legged it, and Aunt Agatha drew up her chair and started in.

"Bertie," she said, "dear Honoria does not know it, but a little difficulty has arisen about your marriage."

"By Jove! not really?" I said, hope starting to dawn.

"Oh, it's nothing at all, of course. It is only a little exasperating. The fact is, Sir Roderick is being rather troublesome."

"Thinks I'm not a good bet? Wants to scratch the fixture? Well, perhaps he's right."

"Pray do not be so absurd, Bertie. It is nothing so serious as that. But the nature of Sir Roderick's profession unfortunately makes him — over-cautious."

I didn't get it. "Over-cautious?"

"Yes. I suppose it is inevitable. A nerve specialist with his extensive practice can hardly help taking a rather warped view of humanity."

I got what she was driving at now. Sir Roderick Glossop, Honoria's father, is always called a nerve specialist, because it sounds better, but everybody knows that he's really a sort of janitor to the loony bin. I mean to say, when your uncle the Duke begins to feel the strain a bit and you find him in the blue drawing-room sticking straws in his hair, old Glossop is the first person you send for. He toddles round, gives the patient the once-over, talks about over-excited nervous systems, and recommends complete rest and seclusion and all that sort of thing. Practically every posh family in the country has called him in at one time or another, and I suppose that being in that position — I mean, constantly having to sit on people's heads while their nearest and dearest 'phone to the asylum to send round the wagon — does tend to make a chappie take what you might call a warped view of humanity.

"You mean he thinks I may be a loony, and he doesn't want a loony son-in-law?" I said.

Aunt Agatha seemed rather peeved than otherwise at my ready intelligence.

"Of course, he does not think anything so ridiculous. I told you he was simply exceedingly cautious. He wants to satisfy himself that you are perfectly normal." Here she paused, for Benson had come in with the coffee. When he had gone, she went on: "He appears to have got hold of some extraordinary story about your having pushed his son Oswald into the lake at Ditteredge Hall. Incredible of course. Even you would hardly do a thing like that."

"Well, I did sort of lean against him, you know, and he shot off the bridge."

"Oswald definitely accuses you of having pushed him into the water. That has disturbed Sir Roderick, and unfortunately it has caused him to make inquiries, and he has heard about your poor Uncle Henry."

She eyed me with a good deal of solemnity, and I took a grave sip of coffee. We were peeping into the family cupboard and having a look at the good old skeleton. My late Uncle Henry, you see, was by way of being the blot on the Wooster escutcheon. An extremely decent chappie personally, and one who had always endeared himself to me by tipping me with considerable lavishness when I was at school; but there's no doubt he did at times do rather rummy things, notably keeping eleven pet rabbits in his bedroom, and I suppose a purist might have considered him more or less off his onion. In fact, to be perfectly frank, he wound up his career, happy to the last and completely surrounded by rabbits, in some sort of a home.

"It is very absurd, of course," continued Aunt Agatha. "If any of the family had inherited poor Henry's eccentricity — and it was nothing more — it would have been Claude and Eustace, and there could not be two brighter boys."

Claude and Eustace were twins, and had been kids at school with me in my last summer term. Casting my mind back, it seemed to me that "bright" just about described them. The whole of that term, as I remembered it, had been spent in getting them out of a series of frightful rows.

"Look how well they are doing at Oxford. Your Aunt Emily had a letter from Claude only the other day, saying that they hoped to be elected shortly to a very important college club, called The Seekers."

"Seekers?" I couldn't recall any club of the name in my time at Oxford. "What do they seek?"

"Claude did not say. Truth or Knowledge, I should imagine. It is evidently a very desirable club to belong to, for Claude added that Lord Rainsby, the Earl of Datchet's son, was one of his fellow candidates. However, we are wandering from the point, which is that Sir Roderick wants to have a quiet talk with you quite alone. Now I rely on you, Bertie, to be — I won't say intelligent, but at least sensible. Don't giggle nervously; try to keep that horrible glassy expression out of your eyes; don't yawn or fidget; and remember that Sir Roderick is the president of the West London branch of the anti-gambling league, so please do not talk about horse-racing. He will lunch with you at your flat tomorrow at one-thirty. Please remember that he drinks no wine, strongly disapproves of smoking, and can only eat the simplest food, owing to an impaired digestion. Do not offer him coffee, for he considers it the root of half the nerve-trouble in the world."

"I should think a dog-biscuit and a glass of water would about meet the case, what?"

"Bertie!"

"Oh, all right. Merely persiflage."

"Now it is precisely that sort of idiotic remark that would be calculated to arouse Sir Roderick's worst suspicions. Do please try to refrain from any misguided flippancy when you are with him. He is a very serious-minded man. . . . Are you going? Well, please remember all I have said. I rely on you, and if anything goes wrong, I shall never forgive you."

"Right-ho!" I said.

And so home, with a jolly day to look forward to.

I breakfasted pretty late next morning and went for a stroll afterwards. It seemed to me that anything I could do to clear the old lemon ought to be done, and a bit of fresh air generally relieves that rather foggy feeling that comes over a fellow early in the day. I had taken a stroll in the Park, and got back as far as Hyde Park Corner, when some blighter sloshed me between the shoulder-blades. It was young Eustace, my cousin. He was arm-in-arm with two other fellows, the one on the outside being my cousin Claude and the one in the middle a pink-faced chappie with light hair and an apologetic sort of look.

"Bertie, old egg!" said young Eustace, affably.

"Hallo!" I said, not frightfully chirpily.

"Fancy running into you, the one man in London who can support us in the style we are accustomed to! By the way, you've never met old Dog-Face, have you? Dog-Face, this is my cousin Bertie. Lord Rainsby — Mr. Wooster. We've just been round to your flat, Bertie. Bitterly disappointed that you were out, but were hospitably entertained by old Jeeves. That man's a corker, Bertie. Stick to him."

"What are you doing in London?" I asked.

"Oh, buzzing round. We're just up for the day. Flying visit, strictly unofficial. We oil back on the three-ten. And now touching that lunch you very decently volunteered to stand us, which shall it be? Ritz? Savoy? Carlton? Or, if you're a member of Ciro's or the Embassy, that would do just as well."

"I can't give you lunch. I've got an engagement myself. And by Jove," I said, taking a look at my watch, "I'm late." I hailed a taxi. "Sorry."

"As man to man, then," said Eustace, "lend us a fiver."

I hadn't time to stop and argue. I unbelted the fiver and hopped into the cab. It was twenty to two when I got to the flat. I bounded into the sitting room, but it was empty.

Jeeves shimmied in.

"Sir Roderick has not yet arrived, sir."

"Good egg!" I said. "I thought I should find him smashing up the furniture." My experience is that the less you want a fellow, the more punctual he's bound to be, and I had had a vision of the old lad pacing the rug in my sitting-room, saying "He cometh not!" and generally hotting up "Is everything in order?"

"I fancy you will find the arrangements quite satisfactory, sir."

"What are you giving us?"

"Cold consommé, a cutlet, and a savory, sir. With lemon-squash, iced."

"Well, I don't see how that can hurt him. Don't go getting carried away by the excitement of the thing and start bringing in coffee."

"No, sir."

"And don't let your eyes get glassy, because if you do, you're apt to find yourself in a padded cell before you know where you are."

"Very good, sir."

There was a ring at the bell.

"Stand by, Jeeves," I said. "We're off!"

I had met Sir Roderick Glossop before, of course, but only when I was with Honoria; and there is something about Honoria which makes almost anybody you meet in the same room seem sort of undersized and trivial by comparison. I had never realized till this moment what an extraordinarily formidable old bird he was. He had a pair of shaggy eyebrows which gave his eyes a piercing look which was not at all the sort of thing a fellow wanted to encounter on an empty stomach. He was fairly tall and fairly broad, and he had the most enormous head, with practically no hair on it, which made it seem bigger and much more like the dome of St. Paul's. I suppose he must have taken about a nine or something in hats. Shows what a rotten thing it is to let your brain develop too much.

"What-ho! What-ho! What-ho!" I said, trying to strike the genial note, and then had a sudden feeling that that was just the sort of thing I had been warned not to say. Dashed difficult it is to start things going properly on an occasion like this. A fellow living in a London flat is so handicapped. I mean to say if I had been the young squire greeting the visitor in the country, I could have said "Welcome to Meadowsweet Hall!" or something zippy like that. It sounds silly to say "Welcome to Number 6A, Crichton Mansions, Berkeley Street, W.I."

"I am afraid I am a little late," he said as we sat down. "I was detained at my club by Lord Alastair Hungerford, the Duke of Ramfurline's son. His Grace, he informed me, had exhibited a renewal of the symptoms which have been causing the family so much concern. I could not leave him immediately. Hence my unpunctuality, which I trust has not discommoded you."

"Oh, not at all. So the Duke is off his rocker, what?"

"The expression which you use is not precisely the one I should have employed myself with reference to the head of perhaps the noblest family in England, but there is no doubt that cerebral excitement does, as you suggest, exist in no small degree." He sighed as well as he could with his mouth full of cutlet. "A profession like mine is a great strain, a great strain."

"Must be."

"Sometimes I am appalled at what I see around me." He stopped suddenly and sort of stiffened. "Do you keep a cat, Mr. Wooster?"

"Eh? What? Cat? No, no cat."

"I was conscious of a distinct impression that I had heard a cat mewing either in the room or very near to where we are sitting."

"Probably a taxi or something in the street."

"I fear I do not follow you."

"I mean to say, taxis squawk, you know. Rather like cats in a sort of way."

"I had not observed the resemblance," he said, rather coldly.

"Have some lemon-squash," I said. The conversation seemed to be getting rather difficult.

"Thank you. Half a glassful, if I may." The hell-brew appeared to buck him up, for he resumed in a slightly more pally manner: "I have a particular dislike for cats. But I was saying — Oh, yes. Sometimes I am positively appalled at what I see around me. It is not only the cases which come under my professional notice, painful as many of those are. It is what I see as I go about London. Sometimes it seems to me that the whole world is mentally unbalanced. This very morning, for example, a most singular and distressing occurrence took place as I was driving from my house to the club. The day being clement, I had instructed my chauffeur to open my landau-lette, and I was leaning back, deriving no little pleasure from the sunshine, when our progress was arrested in the middle of the thoroughfare by one of those blocks in the traffic which are inevitable in so congested a system as that of London."

I suppose I had been letting my mind wander a bit, for when he stopped and took a sip of lemon-squash, I had a feeling that I was listening to a lecture and was expected to say something.

"Hear, hear!" I said.

"I beg your pardon?"

"Nothing, nothing. You were saying . . ."

"The vehicles proceeding in the opposite direction had also been temporarily arrested, but after a moment they were permitted to proceed. I had fallen into a meditation when suddenly the most extraordinary thing took place. My hat was snatched abruptly from my head! And as I looked back I perceived it being waved in a kind of feverish triumph from the interior of a taxi-cab, which, even as I looked, disappeared through a gap in the traffic and was lost to sight."

I didn't laugh, but I distinctly heard a couple of my floating ribs part from their moorings under the strain.

"Must have been meant for a practical joke," I said. "What?"

This suggestion didn't seem to please the old boy.

"I trust," he said, "I am not deficient in an appreciation of
the humorous, but I confess that I am at a loss to detect anything akin to pleasantry in the outrage. The action was beyond
all question that of a mentally unbalanced subject. These mental lesions may express themselves in almost any form. The
Duke of Ramfurline, to whom I had occasion to allude just
now, is under the impression — this is in the strictest confidence — that he is a canary; and his seizure today, which so
perturbed Lord Alastair, was due to the fact that a careless
footman had neglected to bring him his morning lump of
sugar. Cases are common, again, of . . . Mr. Wooster, there *is*
a cat close at hand! It is *not* in the street! The mewing appears
to come from the adjoining room."

This time I had to admit there was no doubt about it. There
was a distinct sound of mewing coming from the next room.
I punched the bell for Jeeves, who drifted in and stood waiting
with an air of respectful devotion.

"Sir?"

"Oh, Jeeves," I said. "Cats! What about it? Are there any
cats in the flat?"

"Only the three in your bedroom, sir."

"What!"

"Cats in his bedroom!" I heard Sir Roderick whisper in a
kind of stricken way, and his eyes hit me amidships like a couple of bullets.

"What do you mean," I said, "only the three in my
bedroom?"

"The black one, the tabby, and the small lemon-colored animal, sir."

"What on earth — ?"

I charged round the table in the direction of the door. Unfortunately, Sir Roderick had just decided to edge in that direction himself, with the result that we collided in the doorway

with a good deal of force and staggered out into the hall together. He came smartly out of the clinch and grabbed an umbrella from the rack.

"Stand back!" he shouted, waving it over his head. "Stand back, sir! I am armed!"

It seemed to me that the moment had come to be soothing.

"Awfully sorry I barged into you," I said. "Wouldn't have had it happen for worlds. I was just dashing out to have a look into things."

He appeared a trifle reassured and lowered the umbrella. But just then the most frightful shindy started in the bedroom. It sounded as though all the cats in London, assisted by delegates from outlying suburbs, had got together to settle their differences once for all. A sort of augmented orchestra of cats.

"This noise is unendurable," yelled Sir Roderick. "I cannot hear myself speak."

"I fancy, sir," said Jeeves, respectfully, "that the animals may have become somewhat exhilarated as the result of having discovered the fish under Mr. Wooster's bed."

The old boy tottered.

"Fish! Did I hear you rightly?"

"Sir?"

"Did you say that there was a fish under Mr. Wooster's bed?"

"Yes, sir."

Sir Roderick gave a low moan and reached for his hat and stick.

"You aren't going?" I said.

"Mr. Wooster, I *am* going! I prefer to spend my leisure time in less eccentric society."

"But I say. Here, I must come with you. I'm sure the whole business can be explained. Jeeves, my hat."

Jeeves rallied round. I took the hat from him and shoved it on my head.

"Good heavens!"

Beastly shock it was! The bally thing had absolutely engulfed me, if you know what I mean. Even as I was putting it on I got a sort of impression that it was a trifle roomy, and no sooner had I let go of it than it settled down over my ears like a kind of extinguisher.

"I say! This isn't my hat!"

"It is *my* hat!" said Sir Roderick in about the coldest, nastiest voice I'd ever heard. "The hat which was stolen from me this morning as I drove in my car."

"But — "

I suppose Napoleon or somebody like that would have been equal to the situation, but I'm bound to say it was too much for me. I just stood there goggling in a sort of coma while the old boy lifted the hat off me and turned to Jeeves.

"I should be glad, my man," he said, "if you would accompany me a few yards down the street. I wish to ask you some questions."

"Very good, sir."

"Here, but, I say — !" I began, but he left me standing. He stalked out, followed by Jeeves. And at that moment the row in the bedroom started again, louder than ever.

I was about fed up with the whole thing. I mean, cats in your bedroom — a bit thick, what? I didn't know how the dickens they had got in, but I was jolly well resolved that they weren't going to stay picnicking there any longer. I flung open the door. I got a momentary flash of about a hundred and fifteen cats of all sizes and colors scrapping in the middle of the room, and then they all shot past me with a rush and out of the front door; and all that was left of the mob scene was the head of a whacking big fish, lying on the carpet and staring up at me in a rather austere sort of way, as if it wanted a written explanation and apology.

There was something about the thing's expression that absolutely chilled me, and I withdrew on tiptoe and shut the door. And, as I did so, I bumped into someone.

"Oh, sorry!" he said.

I spun round. It was the pink-faced chappie, Lord Something-or-other, the fellow I had met with Claude and Eustace.

"I say," he said, apologetically, "awfully sorry to bother you, but those weren't my cats I met just now legging it downstairs, were they? They looked like my cats."

"They came out of my bedroom."

"Then they *were* my cats!" he said, sadly. "Oh, dash it!"

"Did you put cats in my bedroom?"

"Your man, what's his name, did. He rather decently said I could keep them there till my train went. I'd just come to fetch them. And now they've gone! Oh, well, it can't be helped, I suppose. I'll take the hat and the fish, anyway."

I was beginning to dislike this bird.

"Did you put that bally fish there, too?"

"No, that was Eustace's. The hat was Claude's."

I sank limply into a chair.

"I say, you couldn't explain this, could you?" I said.

The chappie gazed at me in mild surprise.

"Why, don't you know all about it? I say!" He blushed profusely. "Why, if you don't know about it, I shouldn't wonder if the whole thing didn't seem rather rummy to you."

"Rummy is the word."

"It was for The Seekers, you know."

"The Seekers?"

"Rather a blood club, you know, up at Oxford, which your cousins and I are rather keen on getting into. You have to pinch something, you know, to get elected. Some sort of a souvenir, you know. A policeman's helmet, you know, or a door-knocker or something, you know. The room's decorated with the things at the annual dinner, and everybody makes speeches and all that sort of thing. Rather jolly. Well, we wanted rather to make a sort of special effort and do the thing in style, if you understand, so we came up to London to see if we couldn't pick up something here that would be a bit out of the ordinary. And we had the most amazing luck right from the start. Your cousin Claude managed to collect a quite decent top-hat out of a passing car, and your cousin Eustace got away with a really goodish salmon or something from Harrods, and I snaffled three excellent cats all in the first hour. We were fearfully braced, I can tell you. And then the difficulty was to know where to park the things till our train went. You look so beastly conspicuous, you know, tooling about London with a fish and a lot of cats. And then Eustace remembered you, and we all came on here in a cab. You were out, but your man said it would be all right. When we met you, you were in such a hurry that we hadn't time to explain. Well, I think I'll be taking the hat if you don't mind."

"It's gone."

"Gone?"

"The fellow you pinched it from happened to be the man who was lunching here. He took it away with him."

"Oh, I say! Poor old Claude will be upset. Well, how about the goodish salmon or something?"

"Would you care to view the remains?"

He seemed all broken up when he saw the wreckage.

"I doubt if the committee would accept that," he said, sadly. "There isn't a frightful lot of it left, what?"

"The cats ate the rest."

He sighed deeply.

"No cats, no fish, no hat. We've had all our trouble for nothing. I do call that hard! And on top of that — I say, I hate to ask you, but you couldn't lend me a tenner, could you?"

"A tenner? What for?"

"Well, the fact is, I've got to pop round and bail Claude and Eustace out. They've been arrested."

"Arrested!"

"Yes. You see, what with the excitement of collaring the hat and the salmon or something, added to the fact that we had rather a festive lunch, they got a bit above themselves, poor chaps, and tried to pinch a motor-lorry. Silly, of course, because I don't see how they could have got the thing to Oxford and shown it to the committee. Still, there wasn't any reasoning with them, and, when the driver started making a fuss, there was a bit of a mix-up, and Claude and Eustace are more or less languishing in Vine Street police station till I pop round and bail them out. So if you could manage a tenner — Oh, thanks, that's fearfully good of you. It would have been too bad to leave them there, what? I mean, they're both such frightfully good chaps, you know. Everybody likes them up at the 'Varsity. They're fearfully popular."

"I bet they are!" I said.

When Jeeves came back, I was waiting for him on the mat. I wanted speech with the blighter.

"Well?" I said.

"Sir Roderick asked me a number of questions, sir, respecting your habits and mode of life, to which I replied guardedly."

"I don't care about that. What I want to know is why you didn't explain the whole thing to him right at the start? A word from you would have put everything clear."

"Yes, sir."

"Now he's gone off thinking me a loony."

"I should not be surprised, from his conversation with me, sir, if some such idea had not entered his head."

I was just starting in to speak when the telephone-bell rang. Jeeves answered it.

"No, madam, Mr. Wooster is not in. No, madam, I do not know when he will return. No, madam, he left no message. Yes, madam, I will inform him." He put back the receiver.

"Mrs. Gregson, sir."

Aunt Agatha! I had been expecting it. Ever since the luncheon party had blown out a fuse, her shadow had been hanging over me, so to speak.

"Does she know? Already?"

"I gather that Sir Roderick has been speaking to her on the telephone, sir, and . . ."

"No wedding bells for me, what?"

Jeeves coughed.

"Mrs. Gregson did not actually confide in me, sir, but I fancy that some such thing may have occurred. She seemed decidedly agitated, sir."

It's a rummy thing, but I'd been so snootered by the old boy and the cats and the fish and the hat and the pink-faced chappie and all the rest of it that the bright side simply hadn't occurred to me till now. By Jove, it was like a bally weight rolling off my chest! I gave a yelp of pure relief.

"Jeeves," I said. "I believe you worked the whole thing!"

"Sir?"

"I believe you had the jolly old situation in hand right from the start."

"Well, sir, Benson, Mrs. Gregson's butler, who inadvertently chanced to overhear something of your conversation when you were lunching at the house, did mention certain of the details to me; and I confess that, though it may be a liberty to say so, I entertained hopes that something might occur to prevent the match. I doubt if the young lady was entirely suitable to you, sir."

"And she would have shot you out on your ear five minutes after the ceremony."

"Yes, sir. Benson informed me that she had expressed some such intention. Mrs. Gregson wishes you to call upon her immediately, sir."

"She does, eh? What do you advise, Jeeves?"

"I think a trip to the south of France might prove enjoyable, sir."

"Jeeves," I said, "you are right, as always. Pack the old suitcase, and meet me at Victoria in time for the boat-train. I think that's the manly, independent course, what?"

"Absolutely, sir!" said Jeeves.

Something Squishy

THERE HAD BEEN a gap for a week or so in our little circle at the Anglers' Rest, and that gap the most serious that could have occurred. Mr. Mulliner's had been the vacant chair, and we had felt his absence acutely. Inquiry on his welcome return elicited the fact that he had been down in Hertford-shire, paying a visit to his cousin Lady Wickham at her historic residence, Skeldings Hall. He had left her well, he informed us, but somewhat worried.

"About her daughter Roberta," said Mr. Mulliner.

"Delicate girl?" we asked sympathetically.

"Not at all. Physically, most robust. What is troubling my cousin is the fact that she does not get married."

A tactless Mild-and-Bitter, who was a newcomer to the bar-parlor and so should not have spoken at all, said that that was often the way with these plain girls. The modern young man, he said, valued mere looks too highly, and instead of being patient and carrying on pluckily till he was able to penetrate the unsightly exterior to the good womanly heart within . . .

"My cousin's daughter Roberta," said Mr. Mulliner with some asperity, "is not plain. Like all the Mulliners on the female side, however distantly removed from the main branch, she is remarkably beautiful. And yet she does not get married."

"A mystery," we mused.

"One," said Mr. Mulliner, "that I have been able to solve. I was privileged to enjoy a good deal of Roberta's confidence during my visit, and I also met a young man named Algernon Crufts who appears to enjoy still more and also to be friendly with some of those of the male sex in whose society she has been moving lately. I am afraid that, like so many spirited girls of today, she is inclined to treat her suitors badly. They get discouraged, and I think with some excuse. There was young Attwater, for instance . . ."

Mr. Mulliner broke off and sipped his hot Scotch and lemon. He appeared to have fallen into a reverie. From time to time, as he paused in his sipping, a chuckle escaped him.

"Attwater?" we said.

"Yes, that was the name."

"What happened to him?"

"Oh, you wish to hear the story? Certainly, certainly, by all means."

He rapped gently on the table, eyed his recharged glass with quiet satisfaction, and proceeded.

In the demeanor of Roland Moresby Attwater, that rising young essayist and literary critic, there appeared (said Mr. Mulliner), as he stood holding the door open to allow the ladies to leave his Uncle Joseph's dining-room, no outward and visible sign of the irritation that seethed beneath his mud-stained shirt-front. Well-bred and highly civilized, he knew how to wear the mask. The lofty forehead that shone above his rimless pince-nez was smooth and unruffled, and if he bared his teeth it was only in a polite smile. Nevertheless, Roland Attwater was fed to the eyebrows.

In the first place, he hated these family dinners. In the second place, he had been longing all the evening for a chance to explain that muddy shirt, and everybody had treated it with a silent tact which was simply maddening. In the third place, he knew that his Uncle Joseph was only waiting for the women to go to bring up once again the infuriating topic of Lucy.

After a preliminary fluttering, like that of hens disturbed in a barnyard, the female members of the party rustled past him in single file — his Aunt Emily; his Aunt Emily's friend, Mrs. Hughes Higham; his Aunt Emily's companion and secretary, Miss Partlett; and his Aunt Emily's adopted daughter, Lucy. The last-named brought up the rear of the procession. She was a gentle-looking girl with spaniel eyes and freckles, and as she passed she gave Roland a swift, shy glance of admiration and gratitude. It was the sort of look Ariadne might have given Theseus immediately after his turn-up with the Minotaur; and a casual observer, not knowing the facts, would have supposed that, instead of merely opening a door for her, Roland had rescued her at considerable bodily risk from some frightful doom.

Roland closed the door and returned to the table. His uncle, having pushed the port towards him, coughed significantly and opened fire.

"How did you think Lucy was looking tonight, Roland?"

The young man winced, but the fine courtly spirit which is such a characteristic of the younger members of the intelligentsia did not fail him. Instead of banging the speaker over the head with the decanter, he replied, with quiet civility:

"Splendid."

"Nice girl."

"Very."

"Wonderful disposition."

"Quite."

"And so sensible."

"Precisely."

"Very different from these shingled, cigarette-smoking young women who infest the place nowadays."

"Decidedly."

"Had one of 'em up before me this morning," said Uncle Joseph, frowning austerely over his port. Sir Joseph Moresby was by profession a metropolitan magistrate. "Charged with speeding. That's their idea of life."

"Girls," argued Roland, "will be girls."

"Not while I'm sitting at Bosher Street police-court, they won't," said his uncle, with decision. "Unless they want to pay five-pound fines and have their licenses endorsed." He sipped thoughtfully. "Look here, Roland," he said, as one struck by a novel idea, "why the devil don't you marry Lucy?"

"Well, Uncle — "

"You've got a bit of money, she's got a bit of money. Ideal. Besides, you want somebody to look after you."

"Do you suggest," inquired Roland, his eyebrows rising coldly, "that I am incapable of looking after myself?"

"Yes, I do. Why, dammit, you can't even dress for dinner, apparently, without getting mud all over your shirt-front."

Roland's cue had been long in coming, but it had arrived at a very acceptable moment.

"If you really want to know how that mud came to be on my shirt-front, Uncle Joseph," he said, with quiet dignity, "I got it saving a man's life."

"Eh? What? How?"

"A man slipped on the pavement as I was passing through Grosvenor Square on my way here. It was raining, you know, and I — "

"You walked here?"

"Yes. And just as I reached the corner of Duke Street —"

"Walked here in the rain? There you are! Lucy would never let you do a foolish thing like that."

"It began to rain after I had started."

"Lucy would never have let you start."

"Are you interested in my story, Uncle," said Roland, stiffly, "or shall we go upstairs?"

"Eh? My dear boy, of course, of course. Most interested. Want to hear the whole thing from beginning to end. You say it was raining and this fellow slipped off the pavement. And then I suppose a car or a taxi or something came along suddenly and you pulled him out of danger. Yes, go on, my boy."

"How do you mean, go on?" said Roland, morosely. He felt like a public speaker whose chairman has appropriated the cream of his speech and inserted it in his own introductory remarks. "That's all there is."

"Well, who was the man? Did he ask you for your name and address?"

"He did."

"Good! A young fellow once did something very similar to what you did, and the man turned out to be a millionaire and left him his entire fortune. I remember reading about it."

"In the *Family Herald,* no doubt?"

"Did your man look like a millionaire?"

"He did not. He looked like what he actually was — the proprietor of a small bird-and-snake shop in Seven Dials."

"Oh!" said Sir Joseph, a trifle dashed. "Well, I must tell Lucy about this," he said, brightening. "She will be tremendously excited. Just the sort of thing to appeal to a warm-hearted girl like her. Look here, Roland, why don't you marry Lucy?"

Roland came to a swift decision. It had not been his intention to lay bare his secret dreams to this pertinacious old blighter, but there seemed no other way of stopping him. He drained a glass of port and spoke crisply.

"Uncle Joseph, I love somebody else."

"Eh? What's that? Who?"

"This is, of course, strictly between ourselves."

"Of course."

"Her name is Wickham. I expect you know the family? The Hertfordshire Wickhams."

"Hertfordshire Wickhams!" Sir Joseph snorted with extraordinary violence. "Bosher Street Wickhams, you mean. If it's Roberta Wickham, a red-headed hussy who ought to be smacked and sent to bed without her supper, that's the girl I fined this morning."

"You fined her!" gasped Roland.

"Five pounds," said his uncle complacently. "Wish I could have given her five years. Menace to the public safety. How on earth did you get to know a girl like that?"

"I met her at a dance. I happened to mention that I was a critic of some small standing, and she told me that her mother wrote novels. I chanced to receive one of Lady Wickham's books for review shortly afterwards, and the — er — favorable tone of my notice apparently gave her some pleasure." Roland's voice trembled slightly, and he blushed. Only he knew what it had cost him to write eulogistically of that terrible book. "She has invited me down to Skeldings, their place in Hertfordshire, for the week-end tomorrow."

"Send her a telegram."

"Saying what?"

"That you can't go."

"But I am going." It is a pretty tough thing if a man of letters who has sold his critical soul is not to receive the reward of his crime. "I wouldn't miss it for anything."

"Don't you be a fool, my boy," said Sir Joseph. "I've known you all your life — know you better than you know yourself — and I tell you it's sheer insanity for a man like you to dream of marrying a girl like that. Forty miles an hour she was going, right down the middle of Piccadilly. The constable proved it up to the hilt. You're a quiet, sensible fellow, and you ought to marry a quiet, sensible girl. You're what I call a rabbit."

"A rabbit!"

"There is no stigma attached to being a rabbit," said Sir Joseph, pacifically. "Every man with a grain of sense is one. It simply means that you prefer a normal, wholesome life to gadding about like a — like a nonrabbit. You're going out of your class, my boy. You're trying to change your zoological species, and it can't be done. Half the divorces today are due to the fact that rabbits won't believe they're rabbits till it's too late. It is the peculiar nature of the rabbit —"

"I think we had better join the ladies, Uncle Joseph," said Roland, frostily. "Aunt Emily will be wondering what has become of us."

In spite of the innate modesty of all heroes, it was with something closely resembling chagrin that Roland discovered, on going to his club in the morning, the Press of London was unanimously silent on the subject of his last night's exploit. Not that one expected anything in the nature of publicity, of course, or even desired it. Still, if there had happened to be some small paragraph under some such title as "Gallant Behavior of an Author" or "Critical Moment for a Critic," it would have done no harm to the sale of that little book of thoughtful essays which Blenkinsop's had just put on the market.

And the fellow had seemed so touchingly grateful at the time.

Pawing at Roland's chest with muddy hands he had told him that he would never forget this moment as long as he lived. And he had not bothered even to go and call at a newspaper office.

Well, well! He swallowed his disappointment and a light lunch and returned to his flat, where he found Bryce, his manservant, completing the packing of his suit-case.

"Packing?" said Roland. "That's right. Did those socks arrive?"

"Yes, sir."

"Good!" said Roland. They were some rather special gents' half-hose from the Burlington Arcade, subtly passionate, and he was hoping much from them. He wandered to the table, and became aware that on it lay a large cardboard box. "Hullo, what's this?"

"A man left it a short while ago, sir. A somewhat shabbily-dressed person. The note accompanying it is on the mantelpiece, sir."

Roland went to the mantelpiece; and, having inspected the dirty envelope for a moment with fastidious distaste, opened it in a gingerly manner.

"The box appears to me, sir," continued Bryce, "to contain something alive. It seemed to me that I received the impression of something squirming."

"Good Lord!" exclaimed Roland, staring at the letter.

"Sir?"

"It's a snake. That fool has sent me a snake. Of all the — "

A hearty ringing at the front-door bell interrupted him. Bryce, rising from the suit-case, vanished silently. Roland continued to regard the unwelcome gift with a peevish frown.

"Miss Wickham, sir," said Bryce at the door.

The visitor, who walked springily into the room, was a girl

of remarkable beauty. She resembled a particularly good-look-ing schoolboy who had dressed up in his sister's clothes.

"Ah!" she said, cocking a bright eye at the suit-case. "I'm glad you're bustling about. We ought to be starting soon. I'm going to drive you down in the two-seater." She began a rest-less tour of the room. "Hullo!" she said, arriving at the box. "What might this be?" She shook it experimentally. "I say! There's something squishy inside!"

"Yes, it's — "

"Roland," said Miss Wickham, having conducted further experiments, "immediate investigation is called for. Inside this box there is most certainly some living organism. When you shake it it definitely squishes."

"It's all right. It's only a snake."

"Snake!"

"Perfectly harmless," he hastened to assure her. "The fool expressly states that. Not that it matters, because I'm going to send it straight back, unopened."

Miss Wickham squeaked with pleased excitement.

"Who's been sending you snakes?"

Roland coughed diffidently.

"I happened to — er — save a man's life last night. I was coming along at the corner of Duke Street — "

"Now, isn't that an extraordinary thing?" said Miss Wick-ham, meditatively. "Here have I lived all these years and never thought of getting a snake!"

"— when a man —"

"The one thing every young girl should have."

"— slipped off the pavement —"

"There are the most tremendous possibilities in a snake. The diner-out's best friend. Pop it on the table after the soup and be Society's pet."

Roland, though nothing, of course, could shake his great

love, was conscious of a passing feeling of annoyance.

"I'll tell Bryce to take the thing back to the man," he said, abandoning his story as a total loss.

"Take it back?" said Miss Wickham, amazed. "But Roland, what frightful waste! Why, there are moments in life when knowing where to lay your hands on a snake means more than words can tell." She started. "Golly! Didn't you once say that old Sir Joseph What's-his-name — the beak, you know — was your uncle? He fined me five of the best yesterday for absolutely crawling along Piccadilly. He needs a sharp lesson. He must be taught that he can't go about the place persecuting the innocent like that. I'll tell you what. Ask him to lunch here and hide the thing in his napkin! That'll make him think a bit!"

"No, no!" cried Roland, shuddering strongly.

"Roland! For my sake!"

"No, no, really!"

"And you said dozens of times that you would do anything in the world for me!" She mused. "Well, at least let me tie a string to it and dangle it out of the window in front of the next old lady that comes along."

"No, no, please! I must send it back to the man."

Miss Wickham's discontent was plain, but she seemed to accept defeat.

"Oh, all right, if you're going to refuse me every little thing! But let me tell you, my lad, that you're throwing away the laugh of a lifetime. Wantonly and callously chucking it away. Where is Bryce? Gone to earth in the kitchen, I suppose. I'll go and give him the thing while you strap the suit-case. We ought to be starting, or we shan't get there by tea-time."

"Let me do it."

"No, I'll do it."

"You mustn't trouble."

"No trouble," said Miss Wickham, amiably.

In this world, as has been pointed out in various ways by a great many sages and philosophers, it is wiser for the man who shrinks from being disappointed not to look forward too keenly to moments that promise pleasure. Roland Attwater, who had anticipated considerable enjoyment from his drive down to Skeldings Hall, soon discovered, when the car had threaded its way through the London traffic and was out in the open country, that the conditions were not right for enjoyment. Miss Wickham did not appear to share the modern girl's distaste for her home. She plainly wanted to get there as quickly as possible. It seemed to Roland that from the time they left High Barnet to the moment when, with a grinding of brakes, they drew up at the door of Skeldings Hall the two-seater had only touched Hertfordshire at odd spots.

Yet, as they alighted, Roberta Wickham voiced a certain dissatisfaction with her work.

"Forty-three minutes," she said, frowning at her watch. "I can do better than that."

"Can you?" gulped Roland. "Can you, indeed?"

"Well, we're in time for tea, anyhow. Come in and meet the mater. Forgotten Sports of the Past — Number Three, Meeting the Mater."

Roland met the mater. The phrase, however, is too mild and inexpressive and does not give a true picture of the facts. He not merely met the mater; he was engulfed and swallowed up by the mater. Lady Wickham, that popular novelist ("Strikes a singularly fresh note." — R. Moresby Attwater in the *New Examiner*), was delighted to see her guest. Welcoming Roland to her side, she proceeded to strike so many singularly fresh notes that he was unable to tear himself away till it was time to dress for dinner. She was still talking with unimpaired volubility on the subject of her books, of which Roland had been kind enough to write so appreciatively, when the gong went.

"Is it as late as that?" she said, surprised, releasing Roland, who had thought it later. "We shall have to go on with our little talk after dinner. You know your room? No? Oh, well, Claude will show you up. Claude, will you take Mr. Attwater up with you? His room is at the end of your corridor. By the way, you don't know each other, do you? Sir Claude Lynn — Mr. Attwater."

The two men bowed, but in Roland's bow there was not that heartiness which we like to see in our friends when we introduce them to fellow-guests. A considerable part of the agony which he had been enduring for the last two hours had been caused not so much by Lady Wickham's eloquence, though that had afflicted him sorely, as by the spectacle of this man Lynn, whoever he might be, monopolizing the society of Bobbie Wickham in a distant corner. There had been to him something intolerably possessive about the back of Sir Claude's neck as he bent towards Miss Wickham. It was the neck of a man who is being much more intimate and devotional than a jealous rival cares about.

The close-up which he now received of this person did nothing to allay Roland's apprehension. The man was handsome, sickeningly handsome, with just that dark, dignified, clean-cut handsomeness which attracts impressionable girls. It was, indeed, his dignity that so oppressed Roland now. There was that about Sir Claude Lynn's calm and supercilious eye that made a fellow feel that he belonged to entirely the wrong set in London and that his trousers were bagging at the knees.

"A most delightful man," whispered Lady Wickham, as Sir Claude moved away to open the door for Bobbie. "Between ourselves, the original of Captain Mauleverer, D.S.O., in my *Blood Will Tell*. Very old family, ever so much money. Plays polo splendidly. And tennis. And golf. A superb shot. Member for East Bittlesham, and I hear on all sides that he may be in the Cabinet any day."

"Indeed?" said Roland, coldly.

It seemed to Lady Wickham, as she sat with him in her study after dinner — she had stated authoritatively that he would much prefer a quiet chat in that shrine of literature to any shallow revelry that might be going on elsewhere — that Roland was a trifle distrait. Nobody could have worked harder to entertain him than she. She read him the first seven chapters of the new novel on which she was engaged, and told him in gratifying detail the plot of the rest of it, but somehow all did not seem well. The young man, she noticed, had developed a habit of plucking at his hair; and once he gave a sharp, gulping cry which startled her. Lady Wickham began to feel disappointed in Roland and was not sorry when he excused himself.

"I wonder," he said, in a rather overwrought sort of way, "if you would mind if I just went and had a word with Miss Wickham? I — I — there's something I wanted to ask her."

"Certainly," said Lady Wickham, without warmth. "You will probably find her in the billiard-room. She said something about having a game with Claude. Sir Claude is wonderful at billiards. Almost like a professional."

Bobbie was not in the billiard-room, but Sir Claude was practicing dignified cannons which never failed to come off. At Roland's entrance he looked up like an inquiring statue.

"Miss Wickham?" he said. "She left half an hour ago. I think she went to bed."

He surveyed Roland's flushed dishevelment for a moment with a touch of disapproval, then resumed his cannons. Roland, though he had that on his mind concerning which he desired Miss Wickham's counsel and sympathy, felt that it would have to stand over till the morning. Meanwhile, lest his hostess should pop out of the study and recapture him, he decided to go to bed himself.

He had just reached the passage where his haven lay when a door which had apparently been standing ajar opened and Bobbie appeared, draped in a sea-green négligée of such a caliber that Roland's heart leaped convulsively and he clutched at the wall for support.

"Oh, there you are," she said, a little petulantly. "What a time you've been!"

"Your mother was —"

"Yes, I suppose she would be," said Miss Wickham, understandingly. "Well, I only wanted to tell you about Sidney."

"Sidney? Do you mean Claude?"

"No. Sidney. The snake. I was in your room just after dinner to see if you had everything you wanted, and I noticed the box on your dressing-table."

"I've been trying to get hold of you all the evening to ask you what to do about that," said Roland, feverishly. "I was most awfully upset when I saw the beastly thing. How Bryce came to be such an idiot as to put it in the car —"

"He must have misunderstood me," said Bobbie, with a clear and childlike light shining in her hazel eyes. "I suppose he thought I said, 'Put this in the back' instead of 'Take this back.' But what I wanted to say was that it's all right."

"All right?"

"Yes. That's why I've been waiting up to see you. I thought that, when you went to your room and found the box open, you might be a bit worried."

"The box open!"

"Yes. But it's all right. It was I who opened it."

"Oh, but I say — you — you oughtn't to have done that. The snake may be roaming about all over the house."

"Oh, no, it's all right. I know where it is."

"That's good."

"Yes, it's all right. I put it in Claude's bed."

Roland Attwater clutched at his hair as violently as if he had been listening to chapter six of Lady Wickham's new novel.

"You — you — you — what?"

"I put it in Claude's bed."

Roland uttered a little whinnying sound, like a very old horse a very long way away.

"Put it in Claude's bed!"

"Put it in Claude's bed."

"But — but — but why?"

"Why not?" asked Miss Wickham, reasonably.

"But — oh, my heavens!"

"Something on your mind?" inquired Miss Wickham, solicitously.

"It will give him an awful fright."

"Jolly good for him. I was reading an article in the evening paper about it. Did you know that fear increases the secretory activity of the thyroid, suprarenal and pituitary glands? Well, it does. Bucks you up, you know. Regular tonic. It'll be like a day at the seaside for old Claude when he puts his bare foot on Sidney. Well, I must be turning in. Got that school-girl complexion to think about. Good night."

For some minutes after he had tottered to his room, Roland sat on the edge of the bed in deep meditation. At one time it seemed as if his reverie was going to take a pleasant turn. This was when the thought presented itself to him that he must have overestimated the power of Sir Claude's fascination. A girl could not, he felt, have fallen very deeply under a man's spell if she started filling his bed with snakes the moment she left him.

For an instant, as he toyed with this heartening reflection, something remotely resembling a smile played about Roland's sensitive mouth. Then another thought came to wipe the smile away — the realization that, while the broad general principle of putting snakes in Sir Claude's bed was entirely admirable, the flaw in the present situation lay in the fact that this particular snake could be so easily traced to its source. The butler, or whoever had taken his luggage upstairs, would be sure to remember carrying up a mysterious box. Probably it had squished as he carried it and was already the subject of comment in the servants' hall. Discovery was practically certain.

Roland rose jerkily from his bed. There was only one thing to be done, and he must do it immediately. He must go to Sir Claude's room and retrieve his lost pet. He crept to the door and listened carefully. No sound came to disturb the stillness of the house. He stole out into the corridor.

It was at this precise moment that Sir Claude Lynn, surfeited with cannons, put on his coat, replaced his cue in the rack, and came out of the billiard-room.

If there is one thing in this world that should be done quickly or not at all, it is the removal of one's personal snake from the bed of a comparative stranger. Yet Roland, brooding over the snowy coverlet, hesitated. All his life he had had a horror of crawling and slippery things. At his private school, while other boys had fondled frogs and achieved terms of intimacy with slow-worms, he had not been able to bring himself even to keep white mice. The thought of plunging his hand between the sheets and groping for an object of such recognized squishiness as Sidney appalled him. And even as he hesitated, there came from the corridor outside the sound of advancing footsteps.

Roland was not by nature a resourceful young man, but even a child would have known what to do in this crisis. There was a large cupboard on the other side of the room and its door had been left invitingly open. In the rapidity with which he bolted into this his Uncle Joseph would no doubt have seen further convincing evidence of his rabbit-hood. He reached it and burrowed behind a mass of hanging clothes just as Sir Claude entered the room.

It was some small comfort to Roland — and at the moment he needed what comfort he could get, however small — to find that there was plenty of space in the cupboard. And what was even better, seeing that he had had no time to close the door, it was generously filled with coats, overcoats, raincoats, and trousers. Sir Claude Lynn was evidently a man who believed in taking an extensive wardrobe with him on country-house visits, and, while he deplored the dandyism which this implied, Roland would not have had it otherwise. Nestling in the undergrowth, he peered out between a raincoat and a pair of golfing knickerbockers. A strange silence had fallen, and he was curious to know what his host was doing with himself.

At first he could not sight him; but, shifting slightly to the left, he brought him into focus, and discovered that in the interval that had passed Sir Claude had removed nearly all his clothes and was now standing before the open window, doing exercises.

It was not prudery that caused this spectacle to give Roland a sharp shock. What made him start so convulsively was the man's horrifying aspect as revealed in the nude. Downstairs, in the conventional dinner-costume of the well-dressed man,

Sir Claude Lynn had seemed robust and soldierly, but nothing in his appearance then had prepared Roland for the ghastly physique which he exhibited now. He seemed twice his previous size, as if the removal of constricting garments had caused him to bulge in every direction. When he inflated his chest, it looked like a barrel. And, though Roland in the circumstances would have preferred any other simile, there was only one thing to which his rippling muscles could be compared. They were like snakes, and nothing but snakes. They heaved and twisted beneath his skin just as Sidney was presumably even now heaving and twisting beneath the sheets.

If ever there was a man, in short, in whose bedroom one would rather not have been concealed in circumstances which might only too easily lead to a physical encounter, that man was Sir Claude Lynn; and Roland, seeing him, winced away with a shudder so violent that a coat-hanger which had been trembling on the edge of its peg fell with a disintegrating clatter.

There was a moment of complete silence; then the trousers behind which he cowered were snatched away, and a huge hand, groping like the tentacle of some dreadful marine monster, seized him painfully by the hair and started pulling.

"Ouch!" said Roland, and came out like a winkle at the end of a pin.

A modesty which Roland, who was modest himself, should have been the first to applaud had led the other to clothe himself hastily for this interview in a suit of pajamas of a stupefying mauve. In all his life Roland had never seen such a color-scheme, and in some curious way the brilliance of them seemed to complete his confusion. The result was that, instead of plunging at once into apologies and explanations, he remained staring with fallen jaw; and his expression, taken in conjunction with the fact that his hair, rumpled by the coats, appeared to be standing on end, supplied Sir Claude with a theory which seemed to cover the case. He remembered that Roland had had much the same cock-eyed look when he had come into the billiard-room. He recalled that immediately after dinner Roland had disappeared and had not joined the rest of the party in the drawing-room. Obviously the fellow must have been drinking like a fish in some secret part of the house for hours.

"Get out!" he said curtly, taking Roland by the arm with a look of disgust and leading him sternly to the door. An abstemious man himself, Sir Claude Lynn had a correct horror of excess in others. "Go and sleep it off. I suppose you can find your way to your room? It's the one at the end of the corridor, as you seem to have forgotten."

"But listen —"

"I cannot understand how a man of any decent upbringing can make such a beast of himself."

"Do listen!"

"Don't shout like that," snapped Sir Claude, severely. "Good heavens, man, do you want to wake the whole house? If you dare to open your mouth again, I'll break you into little bits."

Roland found himself out in the passage, staring at a closed door. Even as he stared it opened sharply, and the upper half of the mauve-clad Sir Claude popped out.

"No drunken singing in the corridor, mind!" said Sir Claude, sternly, and disappeared.

It was a little difficult to know what to do. Sir Claude had counseled slumber, but the suggestion was scarcely a practical one. On the other hand there seemed nothing to be gained by hanging about in the passage. With slow and lingering steps Roland moved towards his room, and had just reached it when the silence of the night was rent by a shattering scream, and the next moment there shot through the door he had left a large body. And, as Roland gazed dumbly, a voice was raised in deafening appeal.

"Shot-gun!" vociferated Sir Claude. "Help! Shot-gun! Bring a shot-gun, somebody!"

There was not the smallest room for doubt that the secretory activity of his thyroid, suprarenal and pituitary glands had been increased to an almost painful extent.

It is only in the most modern and lively country houses that this sort of thing can happen without attracting attention. So quickly did the corridor fill that it seemed to Roland as if dressing-gowned figures had shot up through the carpet. Among those present he noticed Lady Wickham in blue, her daughter Roberta in green, three male guests in bath-robes, the under-housemaid in curl-papers, and Simmons, the butler, completely and correctly clad in full afternoon costume. They were all asking what was the matter, but, as Lady Wickham's penetrating voice o'ertopped the rest, it was to her that Sir Claude turned to tell his story.

"A snake?" said Lady Wickham, interested.

"A snake."

"In your bed?"

"In my bed."

"Most unusual," said Lady Wickham, with a touch of displeasure.

Sir Claude's rolling eye, wandering along the corridor, picked out Roland as he shrank among the shadows. He pointed at him with such swift suddenness that his hostess only saved herself from a nasty blow by means of some shifty footwork.

"That's the man!" he cried.

Lady Wickham, already ruffled, showed signs of peevishness.

"My dear Claude," she said, with a certain asperity, "do come to some definite decision. A moment ago you said there was a snake in your room; now you say it was a man. Besides, can't you see that that is Mr. Attwater? What would he be doing in your room?"

"I'll tell you what he was doing. He was putting that infernal snake in my bed. I found him there."

"Found him there? In your bed?"

"In my cupboard. Hiding. I hauled him out."

All eyes were turned upon Roland. His own he turned with a look of wistful entreaty upon Roberta Wickham. A cavalier of the nicest gallantry, nothing, of course, would induce him to betray the girl; but surely she would appreciate that the moment had come for her to step forward and clear a good man's name with a full explanation.

He had been too sanguine. A pretty astonishment lit up Miss Wickham's lovely eyes. But her equally lovely mouth did not open.

"But Mr. Attwater has no snake," argued Lady Wickham. "He is a well-known man-of-letters. Well-known men-of-letters," she said, stating a pretty generally recognized fact, "do not take snakes with them when they go on visits."

A new voice joined in the discussion.

"Begging your pardon, your ladyship."

It was the voice of Simmons, grave and respectful.

"Begging your pardon, your ladyship, it is my belief that Mr. Attwater did have a serpent in his possession. Thomas, who conveyed his baggage to his room, mentioned a cardboard box that seemed to contain something alive."

From the expression of the eyes that once more raked him in his retirement, it was plain that the assembled company were of the opinion that it was Roland's turn to speak. But speech was beyond him. He had been backing slowly for some little time, and now, as he backed another step, the handle of his bedroom door insinuated itself into the small of his back. It was almost as if the thing were hinting to him that refuge that lay beyond.

He did not resist the kindly suggestion. With one quick, emotional movement he turned, plunged into his room, and slammed the door behind him.

From the corridor without came the sound of voices in debate. He was unable to distinguish words, but the general trend of them was clear. Then silence fell.

Roland sat on his bed, staring before him. He was roused from his trance by a tap on the door.

"Who's that?" he cried, bounding up. His eye was wild. He was prepared to sell his life dearly.

"It is I, sir. Simmons."

"What do you want?"

The door opened a few inches. Through the gap there came a hand. In the hand was a silver salver. On the salver lay something squishy that writhed and wriggled.

"Your serpent, sir," said the voice of Simmons.

It was the opinion of Roland Attwater that he was now entitled to the remainder of the night in peace. The hostile forces outside must now, he felt, have fired their last shot. He sat on his bed, thinking deeply, if incoherently. From time to time the clock on the stables struck the quarters, but he did not move. And then into the silence it seemed to him that some sound intruded — a small tapping sound that might have been the first tentative efforts of a very young woodpecker just starting out in business for itself. It was only after this small noise had continued for some moments that he recognized it for what it was. Somebody was knocking softly on his door.

There are moods in which even the mildest man will turn to bay, and there gleamed in Roland Attwater's eyes as he strode to the door and flung it open a baleful light. And such was his militant condition that even when he glared out and beheld Roberta Wickham, still in that green négligée, the light did not fade away. He regarded her malevolently.

"I thought I'd better come and have a word with you," whispered Miss Wickham.

"Indeed?" said Roland.

"I wanted to explain."

"Explain!"

"Well," said Miss Wickham, "you may not think there's any explanation due to you, but I really feel there is. Oh, yes, I do. You see, it was this way. Claude had asked me to marry him."

"And so you put a snake in his bed? Of course! Quite natural!"

"Well, you see, he was so frightfully perfect and immaculate and dignified and — oh, well, you've seen him for yourself, so you know what I mean. He was too darned overpowering — that's what I'm driving at — and it seemed to me that if I could only see him really human and undignified — just once — I might — well, you see what I mean?"

"And the experiment, I take it, was successful?"

Miss Wickham wriggled her small toes inside her slippers.

"It depends which way you look at it. I'm not going to marry him, if that's what you mean."

"I should have thought," said Roland, coldly, "that Sir Claude behaved in a manner sufficiently — shall I say human? — to satisfy even you."

Miss Wickham giggled reminiscently.

"He did leap, didn't he? But it's all off, just the same."

"Might I ask why?"

"Those pajamas," said Miss Wickham, firmly. "The moment

I caught a glimpse of them, I said to myself, 'No wedding bells for me!' No! I've seen too much of life to be optimistic about a man who wears mauve pajamas." She plunged for a space into maiden meditation. When she spoke again, it was on another aspect of the affair. "I'm afraid Mother is rather cross with you, Roland."

"You surprise me!"

"Never mind. You can slate her next novel."

"I intend to," said Roland, grimly, remembering what he had suffered in the study from chapters one to seven of it.

"But meanwhile I don't think you had better meet her again just yet. Do you know, I really think the best plan would be for you to go away tonight without saying good-bye. There is a very good milk-train which gets you into London at six-forty-five."

"When does it start?"

"At three-fifteen."

"I'll take it," said Roland.

There was a pause. Roberta Wickham drew a step closer.

"Roland," she said, softly, "you were a dear not to give me away. I do appreciate it so much."

"Not at all!"

"There would have been an awful row. I expect Mother would have taken away my car."

"Ghastly!"

"I want to see you again quite soon, Roland. I'm coming up to London next week. Will you give me lunch? And then we might go and sit in Kensington Gardens or somewhere where it's quiet."

Roland eyed her fixedly.

"I'll drop you a line," he said.

* * *

Sir Joseph Moresby was an early breakfaster. The hands of the clock pointed to five minutes past eight as he entered his dining room with a jaunty and hopeful step. There were, his senses told him, kidneys and bacon beyond that door. To his surprise he found that there was also his nephew Roland. The young man was pacing the carpet restlessly. He had a rumpled look, as if he had slept poorly, and his eyes were pink about the rims.

"Roland!" exclaimed Sir Joseph. "Good gracious! What are you doing here? Didn't you go to Skeldings after all?"

"Yes, I went," said Roland, in a strange, toneless voice.

"Then what —?"

"Uncle Joseph," said Roland, "you remember what we were talking about at dinner? Do you really think Lucy would have me if I asked her to marry me?"

"What! My dear boy, she's been in love with you for years."

"Is she up yet?"

"No. She doesn't breakfast till nine."

"I'll wait."

Sir Joseph grasped his hand.

"Roland, my boy —" he began.

But there was that on Roland's mind that made him unwilling to listen to set speeches.

"Uncle Joseph," he said, "do you mind if I join you in a bite of breakfast?"

"My dear boy, of course —"

"Then I wish you would ask them to fry two or three eggs and another rasher or so. While I'm waiting, I'll be starting on a few kidneys."

It was ten minutes past nine when Sir Joseph happened to go into the morning-room. He had supposed it empty, but he perceived that the large armchair by the window was occupied by his nephew Roland. He was leaning back with the air of one whom the world is treating well. On the floor beside him sat Lucy, her eyes fixed adoringly on the young man's face.

"Yes, yes," she was saying. "How wonderful! Do go on, darling."

Sir Joseph tiptoed out, unnoticed. Roland was speaking as he softly closed the door.

"Well," Sir Joseph heard him say, "it was raining, you know, and just as I reached the corner of Duke Street —"

Pig-Hoo-o-o-o-ey!

❧ THANKS TO THE PUBLICITY given to the matter by *The Bridgnorth, Shifnal, and Albrighton Argus* (with which is incorporated *The Wheat-Growers' Intelligencer and Stock Breeders' Gazetteer*), the whole world today knows that the silver medal in the Fat Pigs class at the eighty-seventh annual Shropshire Agricultural Show was won by the Earl of Emsworth's black Berkshire sow, Empress of Blandings.

Very few people, however, are aware how near that splendid animal came to missing the coveted honor.

Now it can be told.

This brief chapter of Secret History may be said to have begun on the night of the eighteenth of July, when George Cyril Wellbeloved (twenty-nine), pig-man in the employ of Lord Emsworth, was arrested by Police-Constable Evans of Market Blandings for being drunk and disorderly in the tap-room of the Goat and Feathers. On July the nineteenth, after first offering to apologize, then explaining that it had been his birthday, and finally attempting to prove an alibi, George Cyril was very properly jugged for fourteen days without the option of a fine.

On July the twentieth, Empress of Blandings, always hitherto a hearty and even a boisterous feeder, for the first time on record declined all nourishment. And on the morning of July the twenty-first, the veterinary surgeon called in to diagnose and deal with this strange asceticism was compelled to confess to Lord Emsworth that the thing was beyond his professional skill.

Let us just see, before proceeding, that we have got these dates correct:

July 18 — Birthday Orgy of Cyril Wellbeloved.
July 19 — Incarceration of Ditto.
July 20 — Pig Lays off the Vitamins.
July 21 — Veterinary Surgeon Baffled.
Right.

The effect of the veterinary surgeon's announcement on Lord Emsworth was overwhelming. As a rule, the wear and tear of our complex modern life left this vague and amiable peer unscathed. So long as he had sunshine, regular meals, and complete freedom from the society of his younger son Frederick, he was placidly happy. But there were chinks in his armor, and one of these had been pierced this morning. Dazed by the news he had received, he stood at the window of the great library of Blandings Castle, looking out with unseeing eyes.

As he stood there, the door opened. Lord Emsworth turned; and having blinked once or twice, as was his habit when confronted suddenly with anything, recognized in the handsome and imperious-looking woman who had entered his sister, Lady Constance Keeble. Her demeanor, like his own, betrayed the deepest agitation.

"Clarence," she cried, "an awful thing has happened!"

Lord Emsworth nodded dully.

"I know. He's just told me."

"What! Has he been here?"

"Only this moment left."

"Why did you let him go? You must have known I would want to see him."

"What good would that have done?"

"I could at least have assured him of my sympathy," said Lady Constance stiffly.

"Yes, I suppose you could," said Lord Emsworth, having considered the point. "Not that he deserves any sympathy. The man's an ass."

"Nothing of the kind. A most intelligent young man, as young men go."

"Young? Would you call him young? Fifty, I should have said, if a day."

"Are you out of your senses? Heacham fifty?"

"Not Heacham. Smithers."

As frequently happened to her when in conversation with her brother, Lady Constance experienced a swimming sensation in the head.

"Will you kindly tell me, Clarence, in a few simple words, what you imagine we are talking about?"

"I'm talking about Smithers. Empress of Blandings is refusing her food, and Smithers says he can't do anything about it. And he calls himself a vet!"

"Then you haven't heard? Clarence, a dreadful thing has happened. Angela has broken off her engagement to Heacham."

"And the Agricultural Show on Wednesday week!"

"What on earth has that got to do with it?" demanded Lady Constance, feeling a recurrence of the swimming sensation.

"What has it got to do with it?" said Lord Emsworth warmly. "My champion sow, with less than ten days to prepare herself for a most searching examination in competition with all the finest pigs in the county, starts refusing her food —"

"Will you stop maundering on about your insufferable pig and give your attention to something that really matters? I tell you that Angela — your niece Angela — has broken off her engagement to Lord Heacham and expresses her intention of marrying that hopeless ne'er-do-well James Belford."

"The son of old Belford, the parson?"

"Yes."

"She can't. He's in America."

"He is not in America. He is in London."

"No," said Lord Emsworth, shaking his head sagely. "You're wrong. I remember meeting his father two years ago out on the road by Meeker's twenty-acre field, and he distinctly told me the boy was sailing for America next day. He must be there by this time."

"Can't you understand? He's come back."

"Oh? Come back? I see. Come *back?*"

"You know there was once a silly sentimental sort of affair between him and Angela, but a year after he left she became engaged to Heacham, and I thought the whole thing was over and done with. And now it seems that she met this young man Belford when she was in London last week, and it has started all over again. She tells me she has written to Heacham and broken the engagement."

There was a silence. Brother and sister remained for a space plunged in thought. Lord Emsworth was the first to speak.

"We've tried acorns," he said. "We've tried skim milk. And we've tried potato-peel. But, no, she won't touch them."

Conscious of two eyes raising blisters on his sensitive skin, he came to himself with a start.

"Absurd! Ridiculous! Preposterous!" he said, hurriedly. "Breaking the engagement? Pooh! Tush! What nonsense! I'll have a word with that young man. If he thinks he can go about the place playing fast and loose with my niece and jilting her without so much as a —"

"Clarence!"

Lord Emsworth blinked. Something appeared to be wrong, but he could not imagine what. It seemed to him that in his last speech he had struck just the right note — strong, forceful, dignified.

"Eh?"

"It is Angela who has broken the engagement."

"Oh, Angela?"

"She is infatuated with this man Belford. And the point is, what are we to do about it?"

Lord Emsworth reflected.

"Take a strong line," he said, firmly. "Stand no nonsense. Don't send 'em a wedding present."

There is no doubt that, given time, Lady Constance would have found and uttered some adequately corrosive comment on this imbecile suggestion; but even as she was swelling, preparatory to giving tongue, the door opened and a girl came in.

She was a pretty girl, with fair hair and blue eyes which in their softer moments probably reminded all sorts of people of twin lagoons slumbering beneath a southern sky. This, however, was not one of those moments. To Lord Emsworth, as they met his, they looked like something out of an oxyacetylene blow-pipe; and, as far as he was capable of being disturbed by anything that was not his younger son, Frederick, he was disturbed. Angela, it seemed to him, was upset about something, and he was sorry. He liked Angela.

To ease a tense situation, he said:

"Angela, my dear, do you know anything about pigs?"

The girl laughed. One of those sharp, bitter laughs which are so unpleasant just after breakfast.

"Yes, I do. You're one."

"Me?"

"Yes, you. Aunt Constance says that if I marry Jimmy, you won't let me have my money."

"Money? Money?" Lord Emsworth was mildly puzzled. "What money? You never lent me any money."

Lady Constance's feelings found vent in a sound like an overheated radiator.

"I believe this absent-mindedness of yours is nothing but a ridiculous pose, Clarence. You know perfectly well that when poor Jane died she left you Angela's trustee."

"And I can't touch my money without your consent till I'm twenty-five."

"Well, how old are you?"

"Twenty-one."

"Then what are you worrying about?" asked Lord Emsworth, surprised. "No need to worry about it for another four years. God bless my soul, the money is quite safe. It is in excellent securities."

Angela stamped her foot. An unladylike action, no doubt, but how much better than kicking an uncle with it, as her lower nature prompted.

"I have told Angela," explained Lady Constance, "that, while we naturally cannot force her to marry Lord Heacham, we can at least keep her money from being squandered by this wastrel on whom she proposes to throw herself away."

"He isn't a wastrel. He's got quite enough money to marry

me on, but he wants some capital to buy a partnership in
a —"

"He is a wastrel. Wasn't he sent abroad because —"

"That was two years ago. And since then —"

"My dear Angela, you may argue until —"

"I'm not arguing. I'm simply saying that I'm going to marry
Jimmy, if we both have to starve in the gutter."

"What gutter?" asked his lordship, wrenching his errant
mind away from thoughts of acorns.

"Any gutter."

"Now please listen to me, Angela."

It seemed to Lord Emsworth that there was a frightful
amount of conversation going on. He had the sensation of
having become a mere bit of flotsam upon a tossing sea of
female voices. Both his sister and his niece appeared to have
much to say, and they were saying it simultaneously and for-
tissimo. He looked wistfully at the door.

It was smoothly done. A twist of the handle, and he was
where beyond those voices there was peace. Galloping gaily
down the stairs, he charged out into the sunshine.

His gaiety was not long-lived. Free at last to concentrate
itself on the really serious issues of life, his mind grew somber
and grim. Once more there descended upon him the cloud
which had been oppressing his soul before all this Heacham-
Angela-Belford business began. Each step that took him
nearer to the sty where the ailing Empress resided seemed a
heavier step than the last. He reached the sty; and, draping
himself over the rails, peered moodily at the vast expanse of
pig within.

For, even though she had been doing a bit of dieting of late,
Empress of Blandings was far from being an ill-nourished animal. She resembled a captive balloon with ears and a tail, and

was as nearly circular as a pig can be without bursting. Nevertheless, Lord Emsworth, as he regarded her, mourned and would not be comforted. A few more square meals under her belt, and no pig in all Shropshire could have held its head up in the Empress's presence. And now, just for lack of those few meals, the supreme animal would probably be relegated to the mean obscurity of an "Honorably Mentioned." It was bitter, bitter.

He became aware that somebody was speaking to him; and, turning, perceived a solemn young man in riding breeches.

"I say," said the young man.

Lord Emsworth, though he would have preferred solitude, was relieved to find that the intruder was at least one of his own sex. Women are apt to stray off into side-issues, but men are practical and can be relied on to stick to the fundamentals. Besides, young Heacham probably kept pigs himself and might have a useful hint or two up his sleeve.

"I say, I've just ridden over to see if there was anything I could do about this fearful business."

"Uncommonly kind and thoughtful of you, my dear fellow," said Lord Emsworth, touched. "I fear things look very black."

"It's an absolute mystery to me."

"To me, too."

"I mean to say, she was all right last week."

"She was all right as late as the day before yesterday."

"Seemed quite cheery and chirpy and all that."

"Entirely so."

"And then this happens — out of a blue sky, as you might say."

"Exactly. It is insoluble. We have done everything possible to tempt her appetite."

"Her appetite? Is Angela ill?"

"Angela? No, I fancy not. She seemed perfectly well a few minutes ago."

"You've seen her this morning, then? Did she say anything about this fearful business?"

"No. She was speaking about some money."

"It's all so dashed unexpected."

"Like a bolt from the blue," agreed Lord Emsworth. "Such a thing has never happened before. I fear the worst. According to the Wolff-Lehmann feeding standards, a pig, if in health, should consume daily nourishment amounting to fifty-seven thousand, eight hundred calories, these to consist of proteids, four pounds five ounces, carbohydrates, twenty-five pounds —"

"What has that go to do with Angela?"

"Angela?"

"I came to find out why Angela has broken off our engagement."

Lord Emsworth marshaled his thoughts. He had a misty idea that he had heard something mentioned about that. It came back to him.

"Ah, yes, of course. She has broken off the engagement, hasn't she? I believe it is because she is in love with someone else. Yes, now that I recollect, that was distinctly stated. The whole thing comes back to me quite clearly. Angela has decided to marry someone else. I knew there was some satisfactory explanation. Tell me, my dear fellow, what are your views on linseed meal."

"What do you mean, linseed meal?"

"Why, linseed meal," said Lord Emsworth, not being able to find a better definition. "As a food for pigs."

"Oh, curse all pigs!"

"What!" There was a sort of astounded horror in Lord Emsworth's voice. He had never been particularly fond of young Heacham, for he was not a man who took much to his juniors, but he had not supposed him capable of anarchistic sentiments like this. "What did you say?"

"I said, 'Curse all pigs!' You keep talking about pigs. I'm not interested in pigs. I don't want to discuss pigs. Blast and damn every pig in existence!"

Lord Emsworth watched him, as he strode away, with an emotion that was partly indignation and partly relief — indignation that a landowner and a fellow son of Shropshire could have brought himself to utter such words, and relief that one capable of such utterance was not going to marry into his family. He had always in his woollen-headed way been very fond of his niece Angela, and it was nice to think that the child had such solid good sense and so much cool discernment. Many girls of her age would have been carried away by the glamour of young Heacham's position and wealth, but she, divining with an intuition beyond her years that he was unsound on the subject of pigs, had drawn back while there was still time and refused to marry him.

A pleasant glow suffused Lord Emsworth's bosom, to be frozen out a few moments later as he perceived his sister Constance bearing down upon him. Lady Constance was a beautiful woman, but there were times when the charm of her face was marred by a rather curious expression, and from nursery days onward his lordship had learned that this expression meant trouble. She was wearing it now.

"Clarence," she said. "I have had enough of this nonsense of Angela and young Belford. The thing cannot be allowed to go drifting on. You must catch the two o'clock train to London."

"What! Why?"

"You must see this man Belford and tell him that, if Angela insists on marrying him, she will not have a penny for four years. I shall be greatly surprised if that piece of information does not put an end to the whole business."

Lord Emsworth scratched meditatively at the Empress's tank-like back. A mutinous expression was on his mild face.

"Don't see why she shouldn't marry the fellow," he mumbled.

"Marry James Belford?"

"I don't see why not. Seems fond of him and all that."

"You never have had a grain of sense in your head, Clarence. Angela is going to marry Heacham."

"Can't stand that man. All wrong about pigs."

"Clarence, I don't wish to have any more discussion and argument. You will go to London on the two o'clock train. You will see Mr. Belford. And you will tell him about Angela's money. Is that quite clear?"

"Oh, all right," said his lordship moodily. "All right, all right, all right."

The emotions of the Earl of Emsworth, as he sat next day facing his luncheon-guest, James Bartholomew Belford, across a table in the main dining-room of the Senior Conservative Club, were not of the liveliest and most agreeable. It was bad enough to be in London at all on such a day of golden sunshine. To be charged, while there, with the task of blighting the romance of two young people for whom he entertained a warm regard was unpleasant to a degree.

For, now that he had given the matter thought, Lord Emsworth recalled that he had always liked this boy Belford. A pleasant lad, with, he remembered now, a healthy fondness for that rural existence which so appealed to himself. By no means the sort of fellow who, in the very presence and hearing of Empress of Blandings, would have spoken disparagingly and with oaths of pigs as a class. It occurred to Lord Emsworth, as it has occurred to so many people, that the distribution of money in this world is all wrong. Why should a man like pig-despising Heacham have a rent roll that ran into the tens of thousands, while this very deserving youngster had nothing?

These thoughts not only saddened Lord Emsworth — they embarrassed him. He hated unpleasantness, and it was suddenly borne in upon him that, after he had broken the news that Angela's bit of capital was locked up and not likely to get loose, conversation with his young friend during the remainder of lunch would tend to be somewhat difficult.

He made up his mind to postpone the revelation. During the meal, he decided, he would chat pleasantly of this and that, and then, later, while bidding his guest good-bye, he would spring the thing on him suddenly and dive back into the recesses of the club.

Considerably cheered at having solved a delicate problem with such adroitness, he started to prattle.

"The gardens at Blandings," he said, "are looking particularly attractive this summer. My head gardener, Angus McAllister, is a man with whom I do not always find myself seeing eye to eye, notably in the matter of hollyhocks, on which I consider his views subversive to a degree, but there is no denying that he understands roses. The rose garden —"

"How well I remember that rose garden," said James Belford, sighing slightly and helping himself to Brussels sprouts. "It was there that Angela and I used to meet on summer mornings."

Lord Emsworth blinked. This was not an encouraging start, but the Emsworths were a fighting clan. He had another try.

"I have seldom seen such a blaze of color as was to be witnessed there during the month of June. Both McAllister and I adopted a very strong policy with the slugs and plant lice, with the result that the place was a mass of flourishing Damasks and Ayrshires and —"

"Properly to appreciate roses," said James Belford, "you want to see them as a setting for a girl like Angela. With her fair hair gleaming against the green leaves, she makes a rose garden seem a veritable Paradise."

"No doubt," said Lord Emsworth. "No doubt. I am glad you liked my rose garden. At Blandings, of course, we have the natural advantage of loamy soil, rich in plant food and humus, but, as I often say to McAllister, and on this point we have never had the slightest disagreement, loamy soil by itself is not enough. You must have manure. If every autumn a liberal mulch of stable manure is spread upon the beds and the coarser parts removed in the spring before the annual forking —"

"Angela tells me," said James Belford, "that you have forbidden our marriage."

Lord Emsworth choked dismally over his chicken. Directness of this kind, he told himself with a pang of self-pity, was the sort of thing young Englishmen picked up in America. Diplomatic circumlocution flourished only in a more leisurely civilization, and in those energetic and forceful surroundings you learned to Talk Quick and Do It Now, and all sorts of uncomfortable things.

"Er — well, yes, now you mention it, I believe some informal decision of that nature was arrived at. You see, my dear fellow, my sister Constance feels rather strongly —"

"I understand. I suppose she thinks I'm a sort of prodigal."

"No, no, my dear fellow. She never said that. Wastrel was the term she employed."

"Well, perhaps I did start out in business on those lines. But you can take it from me that when you find yourself employed on a farm in Nebraska belonging to an applejack-nourished patriarch with strong views on work and a good vocabulary, you soon develop a certain liveliness."

"Are you employed on a farm?"

"I was employed on a farm."

"Pigs?" said Lord Emsworth in a low, eager voice.

"Among other things."

Lord Emsworth gulped. His fingers clutched at the tablecloth.

"Then perhaps, my dear fellow, you can give me some advice. For the last two days my prize sow, Empress of Blandings, has declined all nourishment. And the Agricultural Show is on Wednesday week. I am distracted with anxiety."

James Belford frowned thoughtfully.

"What does your pig-man say about it?"

"My pig-man was sent to prison two days ago. Two days!" For the first time the significance of the coincidence struck him. "You don't think that can have anything to do with the animal's loss of appetite?"

"Certainly. I imagine she is missing him and pining away because he isn't there."

Lord Emsworth was surprised. He had only a distant acquaintance with George Cyril Wellbeloved, but from what he had seen of him he had not credited him with this fatal allure.

"She probably misses his afternoon call."

Again his lordship found himself perplexed. He had had no notion that pigs were such sticklers for the formalities of social life.

"His call?"

"He must have had some special call that he used when he wanted her to come to dinner. One of the first things you learn on a farm is hog-calling. Pigs are temperamental. Omit to call them, and they'll starve rather than put on the nose-bag. Call them right, and they will follow you to the ends of the earth, with their mouths watering."

"God bless my soul! Fancy that."

"A fact, I assure you. These calls vary in different parts of America. In Wisconsin, for example, the words 'Poig, Poig, Poig' bring home — in both the literal and the figurative sense — the bacon. In Illinois, I believe they call 'Burp, Burp, Burp,' while in Iowa the phrase 'Kus, Kus, Kus' is preferred. Proceeding to Minnesota, we find 'Peega, Peega, Peega' or, alternatively, 'Oink, Oink, Oink,' whereas in Milwaukee, so largely inhabited by those of German descent, you will hear the good old Teuton 'Komm Schweine, Komm Schweine.' Oh, yes, there are all sorts of pig-calls, from the Massachusetts 'Phew, Phew, Phew' to the 'Loo-ey, Loo-ey, Loo-ey' of Ohio, not counting various local devices such as beating on tin cans with axes or rattling pebbles in a suit-case. I knew a man out in Nebraska who used to call his pigs by tapping on the edge of the trough with his wooden leg."

"Did he, indeed?"

"But a most unfortunate thing happened. One evening, hearing a woodpecker at the top of a tree, they started shinning up it, and when the man came out he found them all lying there in a circle with their necks broken."

"This is no time for joking," said Lord Emsworth, pained.

"I'm not joking. Solid fact. Ask anybody out there."

Lord Emsworth placed a hand to his throbbing forehead.

"But if there is this wide variety, we have no means of knowing which call Wellbeloved . . ."

"Ah," said James Belford, "but wait. I haven't told you all. There is a master-word."

"A what?"

"Most people don't know it, but I had it straight from the

lips of Fred Patzel, the hog-calling champion of the Western States. What a man! I've known him to bring pork chops leaping from their plates. He informed me that, no matter whether an animal has been trained to answer to the Illinois 'Burp' or the Minnesota 'Oink,' it will always give immediate service in response to this magic combination of syllables. It is to the pig world what the Masonic grip is to the human. 'Oink' in Illinois or 'Burp' in Minnesota, and the animal merely raises its eyebrows and stares coldly. But go to either state and call 'Pig-hoo-o-o-ey!' . . ."

The expression on Lord Emsworth's face was that of a drowning man who sees a lifeline.

"Is that the master-word of which you spoke?"

"That's it."

"Pig —?"

"— hoo-o-o-ey."

"Pig-hoo-o-ey?"

"You haven't got it quite right. The first syllable should be short and staccato, the second long and rising into a falsetto, high but true."

"Pig-hoo-o-o-ey."

"Pig-hoo-o-o-ey."

"Pig-hoo-o-o-ey!" yodeled Lord Emsworth, flinging his head back and giving tongue in a high, penetrating tenor which caused ninety-three Senior Conservatives, lunching in the vicinity, to congeal into living statues of alarm and disapproval.

"More body to the 'hoo,' " advised James Belford.

"Pig-hoo-o-o-o-ey!"

The Senior Conservative Club is one of the few places in London where lunchers are not accustomed to getting music with their meals. White-whiskered financiers gazed bleakly at bald-headed politicians, as if asking silently what was to be done about this. Bald-headed politicians stared back at white-whiskered financiers, replying in the language of the eye that they did not know. The general sentiment prevailing was a vague determination to write to the committee about it.

"Pig-hoo-o-o-o-ey!" caroled Lord Emsworth. And as he did so, his eye fell on the clock over the mantelpiece. Its hands pointed to twenty minutes to two.

He started convulsively. The best train in the day for Market Blandings was the one which left Paddington station at two sharp. After that there was nothing till the five-five.

He was not a man who often thought, but when he did, to think was with him to act. A moment later he was scudding over the carpet, making for the door that led to the broad staircase.

Throughout the room which he had left, the decision to write in strong terms to the committee was now universal; but from the mind, such as it was, of Lord Emsworth the past, with the single exception of the word "Pig-hoo-o-o-o-ey!" had been completely blotted.

Whispering the magic syllables, he sped to the cloak-room and retrieved his hat. Murmuring them over and over again, he sprang into a cab. He was still repeating them as the train moved out of the station, and he would doubtless have gone on repeating them all the way to Market Blandings, had he not, as was his invariable practice when traveling by rail, fallen asleep after the first ten minutes of the journey.

The stopping of the train at Swindon Junction woke him with a start. He sat up, wondering, after his usual fashion on these occasions, who and where he was. Memory returned to him, but a memory that was, alas, incomplete. He remembered his name. He remembered that he was on his way home from a visit to London. But what it was that you said to a pig when inviting it to drop in for a bite of dinner, he had completely forgotten.

It was the opinion of Lady Constance Keeble, expressed verbally during dinner in the brief intervals when they were alone, and by means of silent telepathy when Beach, the butler, was adding his dignified presence to the proceedings, that her brother Clarence, in his expedition to London to put matters plainly to James Belford, had made an outstanding idiot of himself.

There had been no need whatever to invite the man Belford to lunch; but having invited him to lunch, to leave him sitting, without having clearly stated that Angela would have no money for four years, was the act of a congenital imbecile. Lady Constance had been aware ever since their childhood days that her brother had about as much sense as a —

Here Beach entered, superintending the bringing-in of the savory, and she had been obliged to suspend her remarks.

This sort of conversation is never agreeable to a sensitive man, and his lordship had removed himself from the danger zone as soon as he could manage it. He was now seated in the library, sipping port and straining a brain which Nature had never intended for hard exercise in an effort to bring back that word of magic of which his unfortunate habit of sleeping in trains had robbed him.

"Pig —"

He could remember as far as that, but of what avail was a single syllable? Besides, weak as his memory was, he could recall that the whole gist or nub of the thing lay in the syllable that followed. The "pig" was a mere preliminary.

Lord Emsworth finished his port and got up. He felt restless, stifled. The summer night seemed to call to him like some silver-voiced swineherd calling to his pig. Possibly, he thought, a breath of fresh air might stimulate his brain-cells. He wandered downstairs, and, having dug a shocking old slouch hat out of the cupboard where he hid it to keep his sister Constance from impounding and burning it, he strode heavily out into the garden.

He was pottering aimlessly to and fro in the parts adjacent to the rear of the castle when there appeared in his path a slender female form. He recognized it without pleasure. Any unbiased judge would have said that his niece Angela, standing there in the soft, pale light, looked like some dainty spirit of the Moon. Lord Emsworth was not an unbiased judge. To him, Angela merely looked like Trouble. The march of civilization has given the modern girl a vocabulary and an ability to use it which her grandmother never had. Lord Emsworth would not have minded meeting Angela's grandmother a bit.

"Is that you, my dear?" he said nervously.

"Yes."

"I didn't see you at dinner."

"I didn't want any dinner. The food would have choked me. I can't eat."

"It's precisely the same with my pig," said his lordship. "Young Belford tells me —"

Into Angela's queenly disdain there flashed a sudden animation.

"Have you seen Jimmy? What did he say?"

"That's just what I can't remember. It began with the word 'Pig' —"

"But after he had finished talking about you, I mean. Didn't he say anything about coming down here?"

"Not that I remember."

"I expect you weren't listening. You've got a very annoying habit, Uncle Clarence," said Angela maternally, "of switching your mind off and just going blah when people are talking to you. It gets you very much disliked on all sides. Didn't Jimmy say anything about me?"

"I fancy so. Yes, I am nearly sure he did."

"Well, what?"

"I cannot remember."

There was a sharp clicking noise in the darkness. It was caused by Angela's upper front teeth meeting her lower front teeth, and was followed by a sort of wordless exclamation. It seemed only too plain that the love and respect which a niece should have for an uncle were in the present instance at a very low ebb.

"I wish you wouldn't do that," said Lord Emsworth plaintively.

"Do what?"

"Make clicking noises at me."

"I will make clicking noises at you. You know perfectly well, Uncle Clarence, that you are behaving like a bohunkus."

"A what?"

"A bohunkus," explained his niece coldly, "is a very inferior sort of worm. Not the kind of worm that you see on lawns, which you can respect, but a really degraded species."

"I wish you would go in, my dear," said Lord Emsworth. "The night air may give you a chill."

"I won't go in. I came out here to look at the moon and think of Jimmy. What are you doing out here, if it comes to that?"

"I came here to think. I am greatly exercised about my pig, Empress of Blandings. For two days she has refused her food, and young Belford says she will not eat until she hears the proper call or cry. He very kindly taught it to me, but unfortunately I have forgotten it."

"I wonder you had the nerve to ask Jimmy to teach you pig-calls, considering the way you're treating him."

"But —"

"Like a leper, or something. And all I can say is that if you remember this call of his and it makes the Empress eat, you ought to be ashamed of yourself if you still refuse to let me marry him."

"My dear," said Lord Emsworth earnestly, "if through young Belford's instrumentality Empress of Blandings is induced to take nourishment once more, there is nothing I will refuse him — nothing."

"Honor bright?"

"I give you my solemn word."

"You won't let Aunt Constance bully you out of it?"

Lord Emsworth drew himself up.

"Certainly not," he said proudly. "I am always ready to listen to your Aunt Constance's views, but there are certain matters where I claim the right to act according to my own judgment." He paused and stood musing. "It began with the word 'Pig —"

From somewhere near at hand music made itself heard. The servants' hall, its day's labors ended, was refreshing itself with the housekeeper's gramophone. To Lord Emsworth the strains were merely an additional annoyance. He was not fond of music. It reminded him of his younger son, Frederick, a flat but perservering songster both in and out of the bath.

"Yes, I can distinctly recall as much as that. Pig — Pig —"

"WHO —"

Lord Emsworth leaped in the air. It was as if an electric shock had been applied to his person.

"WHO stole my heart away?" howled the gramophone. "WHO —"

The peace of the summer night was shattered by a triumphant shout.

"Pig-HOO-o-o-o-ey!"

A window opened. A large, bald head appeared. A dignified voice spoke.

"Who is there? Who is making that noise?"

"Beach!" cried Lord Emsworth. "Come out here at once."

"Very good, your lordship."

And presently the beautiful night was made still more lovely by the added attraction of the butler's presence.

"Beach, listen to this."

"Very good, your lordship."

"Pig-hoo-o-o-o-ey!"

"Very good, your lordship."

"Now you do it."

"I, your lordship?"

"Yes. It's a way you call pigs."

"I do not call pigs, your lordship," said the butler coldly.

"What do you want Beach to do it for?" asked Angela.

"Two heads are better than one. If we both learn it, it will not matter should I forget it again."

"By Jove, yes! Come on, Beach. Push it over the thorax," urged the girl eagerly. "You don't know it, but this is a matter of life and death. At-a-boy, Beach! Inflate the lungs and go to it."

It had been the butler's intention, prefacing his remarks with the statement that he had been in service at the castle for eighteen years, to explain frigidly to Lord Emsworth that it was not his place to stand in the moonlight practicing pig-calls. If, he would have gone on to add, his lordship saw the matter from a different angle, then it was his, Beach's, painful duty to tender his resignation, to become effective one month from that day.

But the intervention of Angela made this impossible to a man of chivalry and heart. A paternal fondness for the girl, dating from the days when he had stooped to enacting — and very convincingly, too, for his was a figure that lent itself to the impersonation — the *rôle* of a hippopotamus for her childish amusement, checked the words he would have uttered. She was looking at him with bright eyes, and even the rendering of pig noises seemed a small sacrifice to make for her sake.

"Very good, your lordship," he said in a low voice, his face pale and set in the moonlight. "I shall endeavor to give satisfaction. I would merely advance the suggestion, your lordship, that we move a few steps farther away from the vicinity of the servants' hall. If I were to be overheard by any of the lower domestics, it would weaken my position as a disciplinary force."

"What chumps we are!" cried Angela, inspired. "The place to do it is outside the Empress's sty. Then, if it works, we'll see it working."

Lord Emsworth found this a little abstruse, but after a moment he got it.

"Angela," he said, "you are a very intelligent girl. Where you get your brains from, I don't know. Not from my side of the family."

The bijou residence of the Empress of Blandings looked very snug and attractive in the moonlight. But beneath even the beautiful things of life there is always an underlying sadness. This was supplied in the present instance by a long, low trough, only too plainly full to the brim of succulent mash and acorns. The fast, obviously, was still in progress.

The sty stood some considerable distance from the castle walls, so that there had been ample opportunity for Lord Emsworth to rehearse his little company during the journey.

By the time they had ranged themselves against the rails, his two assistants were letter-perfect.

"Now," said his lordship.

There floated out upon the summer night a strange composite sound that sent the birds roosting in the trees above shooting off their perches like rockets. Angela's clear soprano rang out like the voice of the village blacksmith's daughter. Lord Emsworth contributed a reedy tenor. And the bass notes of Beach probably did more to startle the birds than any other one item in the program.

They paused and listened. Inside the Empress's boudoir there sounded the movement of a heavy body. There was an inquiring grunt. The next moment the sacking that covered the doorway was pushed aside, and the noble animal emerged.

"Now!" said Lord Emsworth again.

Once more that musical cry shattered the silence of the night. But it brought no responsive movement from Empress of Blandings. She stood there motionless, her nose elevated, her ears hanging down, her eyes everywhere but on the trough, where, by rights, she should now have been digging in and getting hers. A chill disappointment crept over Lord Emsworth, to be succeeded by a gust of petulant anger.

"I might have known it," he said bitterly. "That young scoundrel was deceiving me. He was playing a joke on me."

"He wasn't," cried Angela indignantly. "Was he, Beach?"

"Not knowing the circumstances, miss, I cannot venture an opinion."

"Well, why has it no effect, then?" demanded Lord Emsworth.

"You can't expect it to work right away. We've got her stirred up, haven't we? She's thinking it over, isn't she? Once more will do the trick. Ready, Beach?"

"Quite ready, miss."

"Then when I say three. And this time, Uncle Clarence, do please for goodness' sake not yowl like you did before. It was enough to put any pig off. Let it come out quite easily and gracefully. Now, then. One, two — three!"

The echoes died away. And as they did so a voice spoke.

"Community singing?"

"Jimmy!" cried Angela, whisking round.

"Hullo, Angela. Hullo, Lord Emsworth. Hullo, Beach."

"Good evening, sir. Happy to see you once more."

"Thanks. I'm spending a few days at the Vicarage with my father. I got down here by the five-five."

Lord Emsworth cut peevishly in upon these civilities.

"Young man," he said, "what do you mean by telling me that my pig would respond to that cry? It does nothing of the kind."

"You can't have done it right."

"I did it precisely as you instructed me. I have had, moreover, the assistance of Beach here and my niece Angela —"

"Let's hear a sample."

Lord Emsworth cleared his throat.

"Pig-hoo-o-o-o-ey!"

James Belford shook his head.

"Nothing like it," he said. "You want to begin the 'Hoo' in a low minor of two quarter-notes in four-four time. From this build gradually to a higher note, until at last the voice is soaring in full crescendo, reaching F sharp on the natural scale and dwelling for two retarded half-notes, then breaking into a shower of accidental grace notes."

"God bless my soul!" said Lord Emsworth, appalled. "I shall never be able to do it."

"Jimmy will do it for you," said Angela. "Now that he's engaged to me, he'll be one of the family and always popping about here. He can do it every day till the show is over."

James Belford nodded.

"I think that would be the wisest plan. It is doubtful if an amateur could ever produce real results. You need a voice that has been trained on the open prairie and that has gathered richness and strength from competing with tornadoes. You need a manly, sunburned, wind-scorched voice with a suggestion in it of the crackling of cornhusks and the whisper of evening breezes in the fodder. Like this!"

Resting his hands on the rail before him, James Belford swelled before their eyes like a young balloon. The muscles on his cheekbones stood out, his forehead became corrugated, his ears seemed to shimmer. Then, at the very height of the tension, he let it go like, as the poet beautifully puts it, the sound of a great Amen.

"Pig-HOOOOO-OOO-OOO-O-O-ey!"

They looked at him, awed. Slowly, fading off across hill and dale, the vast bellow died away. And suddenly, as it died, another, softer sound succeeded it. A sort of gulpy, gurgly, plobby, squishy, wofflesome sound, like a thousand eager men drinking soup in a foreign restaurant. And as he heard it, Lord Emsworth uttered a cry of rapture.

The Empress was feeding.

Comrade Bingo

THE THING really started in the Park — at the Marble Arch end, where blighters of every description collect on Sunday afternoons and stand on soap boxes and make speeches. It isn't often you'll find me there, but it so happened that on this particular Sabbath, having a call to pay in Manchester Square, I had taken a short cut through and found myself right in the middle of it. On the prompt side a gang of top-hatted birds were starting an open-air missionary service; on the O.P. side an atheist was hauling up his slacks with a good deal of vim, though handicapped a bit by having no roof to his mouth; a chappie who wanted a hundred million quid to finance him in a scheme for solving the problem of perpetual motion was playing to a thin house up left center; while in front of me there stood a little group of serious thinkers with a banner labeled "Heralds Of the Red Dawn"; and as I came up, one of the Heralds, a bearded egg in a slouch hat and a tweed suit, was slipping it into the Idle Rich with such breadth and vigor that I paused for a moment to get an earful. While I was standing there somebody spoke to me.

"Mr. Wooster, surely?"

Stout chappie. Couldn't place him for a second. Then I got him. Bingo Little's uncle, the one I had lunch with at the time when young Bingo was in love with that waitress at the Piccadilly bun-shop. No wonder I hadn't recognized him at first. When I had seen him last he had been a rather sloppy old gentleman — coming down to lunch, I remember, in carpet slippers and a velvet smoking-jacket; whereas now dapper simply wasn't the word. He absolutely gleamed in the sunlight in a silk hat, morning coat, lavender spats, and sponge-bag trousers, as now worn. Dressy to a degree.

"Oh, hallo!" I said. "Going strong?"

"I am in excellent health, I thank you. And you?"

"In the pink. Just been over in France for a change of air. Got back the day before yesterday. Seen anything of Bingo lately?"

"Bingo?"

"Your nephew."

"Oh, Richard? No, not very recently. Since my marriage a little coolness seems to have sprung up."

"Sorry to hear that. So you've married since I saw you, what? Mrs. Little all right?"

"My wife is happily robust. But — er — *not* Mrs. Little. Since we last met, a gracious Sovereign has been pleased to bestow on me a signal mark of his favor in the shape of — ah — a peerage. On the publication of the last Honours List I became Lord Bittlesham."

"By Jove! Really? I say, heartiest congratulations. Lord Bittlesham?" I said. "Why, you're the owner of Ocean Breeze."

"Yes. Marriage has enlarged my horizon in many directions. My wife is interested in horse-racing, and I now maintain a small stable. I understand that Ocean Breeze is fancied, as I am told the expression is, for a race which will take place at the end of the month at Goodwood, the Duke of Richmond's seat in Sussex."

"The Goodwood Cup. Rather! I've got my chemise on it for one."

"Indeed? Well, I trust the animal will justify your confidence. I know little of these matters myself, but my wife tells me that it is regarded in knowledgeable circles as what I believe is termed a snip."

At this moment I suddenly noticed that the audience was gazing in our direction with a good deal of interest, and I saw that the bearded chappie was pointing at us.

"Yes, look at them! Drink them in!" he was yelling, his voice rising above the perpetual-motion fellow's and beating the missionary service all to nothing. "There you see two typical members of the class which has down-trodden the poor for centuries. Idlers! Non-producers! Look at the tall, thin one with the face like a motor-mascot. Has he ever done an honest day's work in his life? No! A prowler, a trifler, and a blood-sucker! And I bet he still owes his tailor for those trousers!"

He seemed to me to be verging on the personal, and I didn't think a lot of it. Old Bittlesham, on the other hand, was pleased and amused.

"A great gift of expression these fellows have," he chuckled. "Very trenchant."

"And the fat one!" proceeded the chappie. "Don't miss him. Do you know who that is? That's Lord Bittlesham. One of the worst. What has he ever done except eat four square meals a day? His god is his belly, and he sacrifices burnt offerings to it till his eyes bubble. If you opened that man now you would find enough lunch to support ten working-class families for a week."

"You know, that's rather well put," I said, but the old boy didn't seem to see it. He had turned a brightish magenta and was bubbling like a kettle on the boil.

"Come away, Mr. Wooster," he said. "I am the last man to oppose the right of free speech, but I refuse to listen to this vulgar abuse any longer."

We legged it with quiet dignity, the chappie pursuing us with his foul innuendoes to the last. Dashed embarrassing.

Next day I looked in at the club, and found young Bingo in the smoking-room.

"Hallo, Bingo," I said, toddling over to his corner full of bonhomie, for I was glad to see the chump. "How's the boy?"

"Jogging along."

"I saw your uncle yesterday."

Young Bingo unleashed a grin that split his face in half.

"I know you did, you trifler. Well, sit down, old thing, and suck a bit of blood. How's the prowling these days?"

"Good Lord! You weren't there!"

"Yes, I was."

"I didn't see you."

"Yes, you did. But perhaps you didn't recognize me in the shrubbery."

"The shrubbery?"

"The beard, my boy. Worth every penny I paid for it. Defies detection."

I goggled at him.

"I don't understand."

"It's a long story. Have a martini or a small gore and soda, and I'll tell you all about it. Before we start, give me your honest opinion. Isn't she the most wonderful girl you ever saw in your puff?"

He had produced a photograph from somewhere, like a

conjuror taking a rabbit out of a hat, and was waving it in front of me. It appeared to be a female of sorts, all eyes and teeth.

"Oh, great Scott!" I said. "Don't tell me you're in love again."

He seemed aggrieved.

"What do you mean — again?"

"Well, to my certain knowledge you've been in love with at least half-a-dozen girls since the spring, and it's only July now. There was that waitress and Honoria Glossop and —"

"Oh, tush! Not to say pish! Those girls? Mere passing fancies. This is the real thing."

"Where did you meet her?"

"On top of a bus. Her name is Charlotte Corday Rowbotham."

"My God!"

"It's not her fault, poor child. Her father had her christened that because he's all for the Revolution, and it seems that the original Charlotte Corday used to go about stabbing oppressors in their baths, which entitles her to consideration and respect. You must meet old Rowbotham, Bertie. A delightful chap. Wants to massacre the bourgeoisie, sack Park Lane, and disembowel the hereditary aristocracy. Well, nothing could be fairer than that, what? But about Charlotte. We were on top of the bus and it started to rain. I offered her my umbrella, and we chatted of this and that. I fell in love and got her address, and a couple of days later I bought the beard and toddled round and met the family."

"But why the beard?"

"Well, she had told me all about her father on the bus, and I saw that to get any footing at all in the home I should have to join these Red Dawn blighters; and naturally, if I was to make speeches in the Park, where at any moment I might run into a dozen people I knew, something in the nature of a disguise was indicated. So I bought the beard, and, by Jove, old boy, I've become dashed attached to the thing. When I take it off to come in here, for instance, I feel absolutely nude. It's done me a lot of good with old Rowbotham. He thinks I'm a Bolshevist of sorts who has to go about disguised because of the police. You really must meet old Rowbotham, Bertie. I tell you what, are you doing anything tomorrow afternoon?"

"Nothing special. Why?"

"Good! Then you can have us all to tea at your flat. I had promised to take the crowd to Lyon's Popular Café after a meeting we're holding down in Lambeth, but I can save money this way; and believe me, laddie, nowadays, as far as I'm concerned, a penny saved is a penny earned. My uncle told you he'd got married?"

"Yes. And he said there was a coolness between you."

"Coolness? I'm down to zero. Ever since he married he's been launching out in every direction and economizing on *me*. I suppose that peerage cost the old devil the deuce of a sum. Even baronetcies have gone up frightfully nowadays, I'm told. And he's started a racing stable. By the way, put your last collar stud on Ocean Breeze for the Goodwood Cup. It's a cert."

"I'm going to."

"It can't lose. I mean to win enough on it to marry Charlotte with. You're going to Goodwood of course?"

"Rather!"

"So are we. We're holding a meeting on Cup day just outside the paddock."

"But I say, aren't you taking frightful risks? Your uncle's sure to be at Goodwood. Suppose he spots you? He'll be fed to the gills if he finds out that you're the fellow who ragged him in the Park."

"How the deuce is he to find out? Use your intelligence,

you prowling inhaler of red corpuscles. If he didn't spot me yesterday, why should he spot me at Goodwood? Well, thanks for your cordial invitation for tomorrow, old thing. We shall be delighted to accept. Do us well, laddie, and blessings shall reward you. By the way, I may have misled you by using the word 'tea.' None of your wafer slices of bread-and-butter. We're good trenchermen, we of the Revolution. What we shall require will be something in the order of scrambled eggs, muffins, jam, ham, cake, and sardines. Expect us at five sharp."

"But, I say, I'm not quite sure —"

"Yes, you are. Silly ass, don't you see that this is going to do you a bit of good when the Revolution breaks lose? When you see old Rowbotham sprinting up Piccadilly with a dripping knife in each hand, you'll be jolly thankful to be able to remind him that he once ate your tea and shrimps. There will be four of us — Charlotte, self, the old man, and Comrade Butt. I suppose he will insist on coming along."

"Who the devil's Comrade Butt?"

"Did you notice a fellow standing on my left in our little troupe yesterday? Small, shriveled chap. Looks like a haddock with lung-trouble. That's Butt. My rival, dash him. He's sort of semi-engaged to Charlotte at the moment. Till I came along he was the blue-eyed boy. He's got a voice like a fog-horn, and old Rowbotham thinks a lot of him. But, hang it, if I can't thoroughly encompass this Butt and cut him out and put him where he belongs among the discards — well, I'm not the man I was, that's all. He may have a big voice, but he hasn't my gift of expression. Thank heaven I was once cox of my college boat. Well, I must be pushing now. I say, you don't know how I could raise fifty quid somehow, do you?"

"Why don't you work?"

"Work?" said Bingo, surprised. "What, me? No, I shall have to think of some way. I must put at least fifty on Ocean Breeze.

Well, see you tomorrow. God bless you, old sort, and don't forget the muffins."

I don't know why, ever since I first knew him at school, I should have felt a rummy feeling of responsibility for young Bingo. I mean to say, he's not my son (thank goodness) or my brother or anything like that. He's got absolutely no claim on me at all, and yet a large-sized chunk of my existence seems to be spent in fussing over him like a bally old hen and hauling him out of the soup. I suppose it must be some rare beauty in my nature or something. At any rate, this latest affair of his worried me. He seemed to be doing his best to marry into a family of pronounced loonies, and how the deuce he thought he was going to support even a mentally afflicted wife on nothing a year beat me. Old Bittlesham was bound to knock off his allowance if he did anything of the sort; and, with a fellow like young Bingo, if you knocked off his allowance, you might just as well hit him on the head with an axe and make a clean job of it.

"Jeeves," I said, when I got home, "I'm worried."

"Sir?"

"About Mr. Little. I won't tell you about it now, because he's bringing some friends of his to tea tomorrow, and then you will be able to judge for yourself. I want you to observe closely, Jeeves, and form your decision."

"Very good, sir."

"And about the tea. Get in muffins."

"Yes, sir."

"And some jam, ham, cake, scrambled eggs, and five or six wagonloads of sardines."

"Sardines, sir?" said Jeeves, with a shudder.

"Sardines."

There was an awkward pause.

"Don't blame me, Jeeves," I said. "It isn't my fault."

"No, sir."

"Well, that's that."

"Yes, sir."

I could see the man was brooding tensely.

I've found, as a general rule in life, that the things you think are going to be the scaliest nearly always turn out not so bad after all, but it wasn't that way with Bingo's tea-party. From the moment he invited himself I felt that the thing was going to be blue round the edges, and it was. And I think the most gruesome part of the whole affair was the fact that, for the first time since I'd known him, I saw Jeeves come very near to being rattled. I suppose there's a chink in everyone's armor, and young Bingo found Jeeves's right at the drop of the flag when he breezed in with six inches or so of brown beard hanging on to his chin. I had forgotten to warn Jeeves about the beard, and it came on him absolutely out of a blue sky. I saw the man's jaw drop, and he clutched at the table for support. I don't blame him, mind you. Few people have ever looked fouler than young Bingo in the fungus. Jeeves paled a little; then the weakness passed and he was himself again. But I could see that he had been shaken.

Young Bingo was too busy introducing the mob to take much notice. They were a very C3 collection. Comrade Butt looked like one of the things that come out of dead trees after the rain; moth-eaten was the word I should have used to describe old Rowbotham; and as for Charlotte, she seemed to take me straight into another and a dreadful world. It wasn't that she was exactly bad-looking. In fact, if she had knocked off starchy foods and done Swedish exercises for a bit, she might have been quite tolerable. But there was too much of her. Billowy curves. Well-nourished perhaps expresses it best.

And, while she may have had a heart of gold, the thing you noticed about her first was that she had a tooth of gold. I knew that young Bingo, when in form, could fall in love with practically anything of the other sex, but this time I couldn't see any excuse for him at all.

"My friend Mr. Wooster," said Bingo, completing the ceremonial.

Old Rowbotham looked at me and then he looked round the room, and I could see he wasn't particularly braced. There's nothing of absolutely Oriental luxury about the old flat, but I have managed to make myself fairly comfortable, and I suppose the surroundings jarred him a bit.

"Mr. Wooster?" said old Rowbotham. "May I say Comrade Wooster?"

"I beg your pardon?"

"Are you of the movement?"

"Well — er —"

"Do you yearn for the Revolution?"

"Well, I don't know that I exactly yearn. I mean to say, as far as I can make out, the whole nub of the scheme seems to be to massacre coves like me, and I don't mind owning I'm not frightfully keen on the idea."

"But I'm talking him round," said Bingo. "I'm wrestling with him. A few more treatments ought to do the trick."

Old Rowbotham looked at me a bit doubtfully.

"Comrade Little has great eloquence," he admitted.

"I think he talks something wonderful," said the girl, and young Bingo shot a glance of such succulent devotion at her that I reeled in my tracks. It seemed to depress Comrade Butt a good deal too. He scowled at the carpet and said something about dancing on volcanoes.

"Tea is served, sir," said Jeeves.

"Tea, pa!" said Charlotte, starting at the word like the old war-horse who hears the bugle, and we got down to it.

Funny how one changes as the years roll on. At school, I remember, I would cheerfully have sold my soul for scrambled eggs and sardines at five in the afternoon; but somehow, since reaching man's estate, I had rather dropped out of the habit, and I'm bound to admit I was appalled to a goodish extent at the way the sons and daughter of the Revolution shoved their heads down and went for the foodstuffs. Even Comrade Butt cast off his gloom for a space and immersed his whole being in scrambled eggs, only coming to the surface at intervals to grab another cup of tea. Presently the hot water gave out, and I turned to Jeeves.

"More hot water."

"Very good, sir."

"Hey! what's this? What's this?" Old Rowbotham had lowered his cup and was eyeing us sternly. He tapped Jeeves on the shoulder. "No servility, my lad; no servility!"

"I beg your pardon, sir?"

"Don't call me 'sir.' Call me Comrade. Do you know what you are, my lad? You're an obsolete relic of an exploded feudal system."

"Very good, sir."

"If there's one thing that makes the blood boil in my veins —"

"Have another sardine," chipped in young Bingo — the first sensible thing he'd done since I had known him. Old Rowbotham took three and dropped the subject, and Jeeves drifted away. I could see by the look of his back what he felt.

At last, just as I was beginning to feel that it was going on forever, the thing finished. I woke up to find the party getting ready to leave.

Sardines and about three quarts of tea had mellowed old Rowbotham. There was quite a genial look in his eye as he shook my hand.

"I must thank you for your hospitality, Comrade Wooster," he said.

"Oh, not at all! Only too glad —"

"Hospitality!" snorted the man Butt, going off in my ear like a depth charge. He was scowling in a morose sort of manner at young Bingo and the girl, who were giggling together by the window. "I wonder the food didn't turn to ashes in our mouths! Eggs! Muffins! Sardines! All wrung from the bleeding lips of the starving poor!"

"Oh, I say! What a beastly idea!"

"I will send you some literature on the subject of the Cause," said old Rowbotham. "And soon, I hope, we shall see you at one of our little meetings."

Jeeves came in to clear away, and found me sitting among the ruins. It was all very well for Comrade Butt to knock the food, but he had pretty well finished the ham, and if you had shoved the remainder of the jam into the bleeding lips of the starving poor it would hardly have made them sticky.

"Well, Jeeves," I said, "how about it?"

"I would prefer to express no opinion, sir."

"Jeeves, Mr. Little is in love with that female."

"So I gathered, sir. She was slapping him in the passage."

I clutched the brow.

"Slapping him?"

"Yes, sir. Roguishly."

"Great Scott! I didn't know it had got as far as that. How did Comrade Butt seem to be taking it? Or perhaps he didn't see?"

"Yes, sir, he observed the entire proceedings. He struck me as extremely jealous."

"I don't blame him. Jeeves, what are we to do?"

"I could not say, sir."

"It's a bit thick."

"Very much so, sir."

And that was all the consolation I got from Jeeves.

I had promised to meet young Bingo next day, to tell him what I thought of his infernal Charlotte, and I was mooching slowly up St. James's Street, trying to think how the dickens I could explain to him, without hurting his feelings, that I considered her one of the world's foulest when who should come toddling out of the Devonshire Club but old Bittlesham and Bingo himself. I hurried on and overtook them.

"What-ho!" I said.

The result of this simple greeting was a bit of a shock. Old Bittlesham quivered from head to foot like a pole-axed blancmange. His eyes were popping and his face had gone sort of greenish.

"Mr. Wooster!" He seemed to recover somewhat, as if I wasn't the worst thing that could have happened to him. "You gave me a severe start."

"Oh, sorry!"

"My uncle," said young Bingo in a hushed, bedside sort of voice, "isn't feeling quite himself this morning. He's had a threatening letter."

"I go in fear of my life," said old Bittlesham.

"Threatening letter?"

"Written," said old Bittlesham, "in an uneducated hand and couched in terms of uncompromising menace. Mr. Wooster, do you recall a sinister, bearded man who assailed me in no measured terms in Hyde Park last Sunday?"

I jumped, and shot a look at young Bingo. The only expression on his face was one of grave, kindly concern.

"Why — ah — yes," I said. "Bearded man. Chap with a beard."

"Could you identify him, if necessary?"

"Well, I — er — how do you mean?"

"The fact is, Bertie," said Bingo, "we think this man with the beard is at the bottom of all this business. I happened to be walking late last night through Pounceby Gardens, where Uncle Mortimer lives, and as I was passing his house a fellow came hurrying down the steps in a furtive sort of way. Probably he had just been shoving the letter in at the front door. I noticed that he had a beard. I didn't think any more of it, however, until this morning, when Uncle Mortimer showed me the letter he had received and told me about the chap in the Park. I'm going to make inquiries."

"The police should be informed," said Lord Bittlesham.

"No," said young Bingo, firmly, "not at this stage of the proceedings. It would hamper me. Don't you worry, Uncle; I think I can track this fellow down. You leave it all to me. I'll pop you into a taxi now, and go and talk it over with Bertie."

"You're a good boy, Richard," said old Bittlesham, and we put him in a passing cab and pushed off. I turned and looked young Bingo squarely in the eye ball.

"Did you send that letter?" I said.

"Rather! You ought to have seen it, Bertie! One of the best gent's ordinary threatening letters I ever wrote."

"But where's the sense of it?"

"Bertie, my lad," said Bingo, taking me earnestly by the coat-sleeve, "I had an excellent reason. Posterity may say of me what it will, but one thing it can never say — that I have not a good solid business head. Look here!" He waved a bit of paper in front of my eyes.

"Great Scott!" It was a check — an absolute, dashed check

for fifty of the best, signed Bittlesham and made out to the order of R. Little. "What's that for?"

"Expenses," said Bingo, pouching it. "You don't suppose an investigation like this can be carried on for nothing, do you? I now proceed to the bank and startle them into a fit with it. Later I edge round to my bookie and put the entire sum on Ocean Breeze. What you want in situations of this kind, Bertie, is tact. If I had gone to my uncle and asked him for fifty quid, would I have got it? No! But by exercising tact — Oh! by the way, what do you think of Charlotte?"

"Well — er —"

Young Bingo massaged my sleeve affectionately.

"I know, old man, I know. Don't try to find words. She bowled you over, eh? Left you speechless, what? I know! That's the effect she has on everybody. Well, I leave you here, laddie. Oh, before we part — Butt! What of Butt? Nature's worst blunder, don't you think?"

"I must say I've seen cheerier souls."

"I think I've got him licked, Bertie. Charlotte is coming to the Zoo with me this afternoon. Alone. And later on to the pictures. That looks like the beginning of the end, what? Well, toodle-oo, friend of my youth. If you've nothing better to do this morning, you might take a stroll along Bond Street and be picking out a wedding present."

I lost sight of Bingo after that. I left messages a couple of times at the club, asking him to ring me up, but they didn't have any effect. I took it that he was too busy to respond. The Heralds of the Red Dawn also passed out of my life, though Jeeves told me he had met Comrade Butt one evening and had a brief chat with him. He reported Butt as gloomier than ever. In the competition for the bulging Charlotte, Butt had apparently gone right back in the betting.

"Mr. Little would appear to have eclipsed him entirely, sir," said Jeeves.

"Bad news, Jeeves; bad news!"

"Yes, sir."

"I suppose what it amounts to, Jeeves, is that, when young Bingo really takes his coat off and starts in, there is no power of God or man that can prevent him making a chump of himself."

"It would seem so, sir," said Jeeves.

Then Goodwood came along, and I dug out the best suit and popped down.

I never know, when I'm telling a story, whether to cut the thing down to plain facts or whether to drool on and shove in a lot of atmosphere and all that. I mean, many a cove would no doubt edge into the final spasm of this narrative with a long description of Goodwood, featuring the blue sky, the rolling prospect, the joyous crowds of pickpockets, and the parties of the second part who were having their pockets picked, and — in a word — what-not. But better give it a miss, I think. Even if I wanted to go into details about the bally meeting I don't think I'd have the heart to. The thing's too recent. The anguish hasn't had time to pass. You see, what happened was that Ocean Breeze (curse him!) finished absolutely nowhere for the Cup. Believe me, nowhere.

These are the times that try men's souls. It's never pleasant to be caught in the machinery when a favorite comes un-stitched, and in the case of this particular dashed animal, one had come to look on the running of the race as a pure for-mality, a sort of quaint, old-world ceremony to be gone through before one sauntered up to the bookie and collected. I had wandered out of the paddock to try and forget, when I bumped into old Bittlesham, and he looked so rattled and pur-ple, and his eyes were standing out of his head at such an angle, that I simply pushed my hand out and shook his in silence.

"Me, too," I said. "Me, too. How much did you drop?"

"Drop?"

"On Ocean Breeze."

"I did not bet on Ocean Breeze."

"What! You owned the favorite for the Cup and didn't back it!"

"I never bet on horse-racing. It is against my principles. I am told that the animal failed to win the contest."

"Failed to win! Why, he was so far behind that he nearly came in first in the next race."

"Tut!" said old Bittlesham.

"Tut is right," I agreed. Then the rumminess of the thing struck me. "But if you haven't dropped a parcel over the race," I said, "why are you looking so rattled?"

"That fellow is here!"

"What fellow?"

"That bearded man."

It will show you to what an extent the iron had entered into my soul when I say that this was the first time I had given a thought to young Bingo. I suddenly remembered now that he had told me he would be at Goodwood.

"He is making an inflammatory speech at this very moment, specifically directed at me. Come! Where that crowd is." He lugged me along and, by using his weight scientifically, got us into the front rank. "Look! Listen!"

Young Bingo was certainly tearing off some ripe stuff. Inspired by the agony of having put his little all on a stumer that hadn't finished in the first six, he was fairly letting himself go on the subject of the blackness of the hearts of plutocratic owners who allowed a trusting public to imagine a horse was the real goods when it couldn't trot the length of its stable without getting its legs crossed and sitting down to rest. He then went on to draw what I'm bound to say was a most moving picture of the ruin of a working-man's home, due to this dishonesty. He showed us the working-man, all optimism and simple trust, believing every word he read in the papers about Ocean Breeze's form; depriving his wife and children of food in order to back the brute; going without beer so as to be able to cram an extra bob on; robbing the baby's money-box with a hatpin on the eve of the race; and finally getting let down with a thud. Dashed impressive it was. I could see old Rowbotham nodding his head gently, while poor old Butt glowered at the speaker with ill-concealed jealousy. The audience ate it.

"But what does Lord Bittlesham care," shouted Bingo, "if the poor working-man loses his hard-earned savings? I tell you, friends and comrades, you may talk, and you may argue, and you may cheer, and you may pass resolutions, but what you need is Action! Action! The world won't be a fit place for honest men to live in till the blood of Lord Bittlesham and his kind flows in rivers down the gutters of Park Lane!"

Roars of approval from the populace, most of whom, I suppose, had had their little bit on blighted Ocean Breeze, and were feeling it deeply. Old Bittlesham bounded over to a large, sad policeman who was watching the proceedings, and appeared to be urging him to rally round. The policeman pulled at his mustache, and smiled gently, but that was as far as he seemed inclined to go; and old Bittlesham came back to me, puffing not a little.

"It's monstrous! The man definitely threatens my personal safety, and that policeman declines to interfere. Said it was just talk. Talk! It's monstrous!"

"Absolutely," I said, but I can't say it seemed to cheer him up much.

Comrade Butt had taken the center of the stage now. He had a voice like the Last Trump, and you could hear every word he said, but somehow he didn't seem to be clicking. I suppose the fact was he was too impersonal, if that's the word I want. After Bingo's speech the audience was in the mood for something a good deal snappier than just general remarks about the Cause. They had started to heckle the poor blighter pretty freely when he stopped in the middle of a sentence, and I saw that he was staring at old Bittlesham.

The crowd thought he had dried up.

"Suck a lozenge," shouted someone.

Comrade Butt pulled himself together with a jerk, and even from where I stood I could see the nasty gleam in his eye.

"Ah," he yelled, "you may mock, comrades; you may jeer and sneer; and you may scoff; but let me tell you that the movement is spreading every day and every hour. Yes, even amongst the so-called upper classes it's spreading. Perhaps you'll believe me when I tell you that here today on this very spot we have in our little band one of our most earnest workers, the nephew of that very Lord Bittlesham whose name you were hooting but a moment ago."

And before poor old Bingo had a notion of what was up, he had reached out a hand and grabbed the beard. It came off all in one piece, and, well as Bingo's speech had gone, it was simply nothing compared with the hit made by this bit of business. I heard old Bittlesham give one short, sharp snort of amazement at my side, and then any remarks he may have made were drowned in thunders of applause.

I'm bound to say that in this crisis young Bingo acted with a good deal of decision and character. To grab Comrade Butt by the neck and try to twist his head off was with him the work of a moment. But before he could get any results the sad policeman, brightening up like magic, had charged in, and the next minute he was shoving his way back through the crowd, with Bingo in his right hand and Comrade Butt in his left.

"Let me pass, sir, please," he said, civilly, as he came up against old Bittlesham, who was blocking the gangway.

"Eh?" said old Bittlesham, still dazed.

At the sound of his voice young Bingo looked up quickly from under the shadow of the policeman's right hand, and as he did so all the stuffing seemed to go out of him with a rush. For an instant he drooped like a bally lily, and then shuffled brokenly on. His air was the air of a man who has got it in the neck properly.

Sometimes when Jeeves has brought in my morning tea and shoved it on the table beside my bed, he drifts silently from the room and leaves me to go to it; at other times he sort of shimmies respectfully in the middle of the carpet, and then I know that he wants a word or two. On the day after I had got back from Goodwood I was lying on my back, staring at the ceiling, when I noticed that he was still in my midst.

"Oh, hallo," I said. "Yes?"

"Mr. Little called earlier in the morning, sir."

"Oh, by Jove, what? Did he tell you about what happened?"

"Yes, sir. It was in connection with that that he wished to see you. He proposes to retire to the country and remain there for some little while."

"Dashed sensible."

"That was my opinion also, sir. There was, however, a slight financial difficulty to be overcome. I took the liberty of advancing him ten pounds on your behalf to meet current expenses. I trust that meets with your approval, sir?"

"Oh, of course. Take a tenner off the dressing-table."

"Very good, sir."

"Jeeves," I said.

"Sir?"

"What beats me is how the dickens the thing happened. I mean, how did the chappie Butt ever get to know who he was?"

Jeeves coughed.

"There, sir, I fear I may have been somewhat to blame."

"You? How?"

"I fear I may carelessly have disclosed Mr. Little's identity to Mr. Butt on the occasion when I had that conversation with him."

I sat up.

"What!"

"Indeed, now that I recall the incident, sir, I distinctly remember saying that Mr. Little's work for the Cause really seemed to me to deserve something in the nature of public recognition. I greatly regret having been the means of bringing about a temporary estrangement between Mr. Little and his lordship. And I am afraid there is another aspect to the matter. I am also responsible for the breaking-off of relations between Mr. Little and the young lady who came to tea here."

I sat up again. It's a rummy thing, but the silver lining had absolutely escaped my notice till then.

"Do you mean to say it's off?"

"Completely, sir. I gathered from Mr. Little's remarks that his hopes in the direction may now be looked on as definitely quenched. If there were no other obstacle, the young lady's father, I am informed by Mr. Little, now regards him as a spy and a deceiver."

"Well, I'm dashed!"

"I appear inadvertently to have caused much trouble, sir."

"Jeeves!" I said.

"Sir?"

"How much money is there on the dressing-table?"

"In addition to the ten-pound note which you instructed me to take, sir, there are two five-pound notes, three one-pounds, a ten-shillings, two half-crowns, a florin, four shillings, a sixpence, and a halfpenny, sir."

"Collar it all," I said. "You've earned it."

Monkey Business

❧ A TANKARD OF STOUT had just squashed a wasp as it crawled on the arm of Miss Postlethwaite, our popular barmaid, and the conversation in the bar-parlor of the Anglers' Rest had turned to the subject of physical courage.

The Tankard himself was inclined to make light of the whole affair, urging modestly that his profession, that of a fruit farmer, gave him perhaps a certain advantage over his fellow men when it came to dealing with wasps.

"Why, sometimes in the picking season," said the Tankard, "I've had as many as six standing on each individual plum, rolling their eyes at me and daring me to come on."

Mr. Mulliner looked up from his hot Scotch and lemon.

"Suppose they had been gorillas?" he said.

The Tankard considered this.

"There wouldn't be room," he argued, "not on an ordinary-sized plum."

"Gorillas?" said a Small Bass, puzzled.

"And I'm sure if it had been a gorilla Mr. Bunyan would

have squashed it just the same," said Miss Postlethwaite, and she gazed at the Tankard with wholehearted admiration in her eyes.

Mr. Mulliner smiled gently.

"Strange," he said, "how even in these orderly, civilized days women still worship heroism in the male. Offer them wealth, brains, looks, amiability, skill at card tricks or at playing the ukulele . . . unless these are accompanied by physical courage they will turn away in scorn."

"Why gorillas?" asked the Small Bass, who liked to get these things settled.

"I was thinking of a distant cousin of mine whose life became for a time considerably complicated owing to one of these animals. Indeed, it was the fact that this gorilla's path crossed his that nearly lost Montrose Mulliner the hand of Rosalie Beamish."

The Small Bass still appeared mystified.

"I shouldn't have thought anybody's path *would* have crossed a gorilla's. I'm forty-five next birthday, and I've never so much as seen a gorilla."

"Possibly Mr. Mulliner's cousin was a big-game hunter," said a Gin Fizz.

"No," said Mr. Mulliner. "He was an assistant-director in the employment of the Perfecto-Zizzbaum Motion Picture Corporation of Hollywood, and the gorilla of which I speak was one of the cast of the super-film, *Black Africa,* a celluloid epic of the clashing of elemental passions in a land where might is right and the strong man comes into his own. Its capture in its native jungle was said to have cost the lives of seven half-dozen members of the expedition, and at the time when this story begins it was lodged in a stout cage on the Perfecto-Zizzbaum lot at a salary of seven hundred and fifty dollars a week, with billing guaranteed in letters not smaller than those of Edmund Wigham and Luella Benstead, the stars."

In ordinary circumstances (said Mr. Mulliner) this gorilla would have been to my distant cousin Montrose merely one of a thousand fellow-workers on the lot. If you had asked him, he would have said that he wished the animal every kind of success in its chosen profession but that, for all the chance there was of them ever, as it were, getting together, they were just ships that pass in the night. It is doubtful, indeed, if he would even have bothered to go down to its cage and look at it, had not Rosalie Beamish asked him to do so. As he put it to himself, if a man's duties brought him into constant personal contact with Mr. Schnellenhamer, the President of the Corporation, where was the sense of wasting time looking at gorillas? *Blasé* about sums up his attitude.

But Rosalie was one of the extra girls in *Black Africa* and so had a natural interest in a brother artist. And as she and Montrose were engaged to be married, her word, of course, was law. Montrose had been planning to play draughts that afternoon with his friend, George Pybus, of the Press department, but he good-naturedly canceled the fixture and accompanied Rosalie to the animal's headquarters.

He was more than ordinarily anxious to oblige her today, because they had recently been having a little tiff. Rosalie had been urging him to go to Mr. Schnellenhamer and ask for a rise of salary: and this Montrose, who was excessively timid by nature, was reluctant to do. There was something about being asked to pay out money that always aroused the head of the firm's worst passions.

When he met his betrothed outside the commissary, he was relieved to find her in a more amiable mood than she had been of late. She prattled merrily of this and that as they walked along, and Montrose was congratulating himself that there was not a cloud on the sky when, arriving at the cage, he found Captain Jack Fosdyke there, prodding at the gorilla with a natty cane.

This Captain Jack Fosdyke was a famous explorer who had been engaged to superintend the production of *Black Africa*. And the fact that Rosalie's professional duties necessitated a rather close association with him had caused Montrose a good deal of uneasiness. It was not that he did not trust her, but love makes a man jealous and he knew the fascination of these lean, brown, hard-bitten adventurers of the wilds.

As they came up, the explorer turned, and Montrose did not like the chummy look in the eye which he cocked at the girl. Nor, for the matter of that, did he like the other's bold smile. And he wished that in addressing Rosalie Captain Fosdyke would not preface his remarks with the words "Ah, there, girlie."

"Ah, there, girlie," said the Captain. "Come to see the monk?"

Rosalie was staring open-mouthed through the bars.

"Doesn't he look fierce!" she cried.

Captain Jack Fosdyke laughed carelessly.

"Tchah!" he said, once more directing the ferrule of his cane at the animal's ribs. "If you had led the rough, tough, slam-bang, every-man-for-himself life I have, you wouldn't be frightened of gorillas. Bless my soul, I remember once in Equatorial Africa I was strolling along with my elephant gun and my trusty native bearer, 'Mlongi, and a couple of the brutes dropped out of a tree and started throwing their weight about and behaving as if the place belonged to them. I soon put a stop to that, I can tell you. Bang, bang, left and right, and two more skins for my collection. You have to be firm with gorillas. Dining anywhere tonight, girlie?"

"I am dining with Mr. Mulliner at the Brown Derby."

"Mr. who?"

"This is Mr. Mulliner."

"Oh, that?" said Captain Fosdyke, scrutinizing Montrose in a supercilious sort of way, as if he had just dropped out of a tree before him. "Well, some other time, eh?"

And, giving the gorilla a final prod, he sauntered away.

Rosalie was silent for a considerable part of the return journey. When at length she spoke, it was in a vein that occasioned Montrose the gravest concern.

"Isn't he wonderful!" she breathed. "Captain Fosdyke, I mean."

"Yes?" said Montrose coldly.

"I think he's splendid. So strong, so intrepid. Have you asked Mr. Schnellenhamer for that raise yet?"

"Er — no," said Montrose. "I am — how shall I put it? — biding my time."

There was another silence.

"Captain Fosdyke isn't afraid of Mr. Schnellenhamer," said Rosalie pensively. "He slaps him on the back."

"Nor am I afraid of Mr. Schnellenhamer," replied Montrose, stung. "I would slap him on the back myself if I considered that it would serve any useful end. My delay in asking for that raise is simply due to the fact that in these matters of finance a certain tact and delicacy have to be observed. Mr. Schnellenhamer is a busy man, and I have enough consideration not to intrude my personal affairs on him at a time when he is occupied with other matters."

"I see," said Rosalie, and there the matter rested. But Montrose remained uneasy. There had been a gleam in her eyes and a rapt expression on her face as she spoke of Captain Fosdyke which he had viewed with concern. Could it be, he asked himself, that she was falling a victim to the man's undeniable magnetism? He decided to consult his friend, George Pybus, of the Press department, on the matter. George was a knowledgeable young fellow and would doubtless have something constructive to suggest.

George Pybus listened to his tale with interest and said it reminded him of a girl he had loved and lost in Des Moines, Iowa.

"She ditched me for a prize-fighter," said George. "There's no getting away from it, girls do get fascinated by the strong, tough male."

Montrose's heart sank.

"You don't really think —?"

"It is difficult to say. One does not know how far this thing has gone. But I certainly feel that we must lose no time in drafting out some scheme whereby you shall acquire a glamour which will counteract the spell of this Fosdyke. I will devote a good deal of thought to the matter."

And it was on the very next afternoon, as he sat with Rosalie in the commissary sharing with her a Steak Pudding Marlene Dietrich, that Montrose noticed that the girl was in the grip of some strong excitement.

"Monty," she exclaimed, almost before she had dug out the first kidney, "do you know what Captain Fosdyke said this morning?"

Montrose choked.

"If that fellow has been insulting you," he cried, "I'll . . . Well, I shall be extremely annoyed," he concluded with a good deal of heat.

"Don't be silly. He wasn't talking to me. He was speaking to Luella Benstead. You know she's getting married again soon . . ."

"Odd how these habits persist."

". . . and Captain Fosdyke said why didn't she get married in the gorilla's cage. For the publicity."

"He did?"

Montrose laughed heartily. A quaint idea, he felt. Bizarre, even.

"She said she wouldn't dream of it. And then Mr. Pybus, who happened to be standing by, suddenly got the most wonderful idea. He came up to me and said why shouldn't you and I get married in the gorilla's cage."

Montrose's laughter died away.

"You and I?"

"Yes."

"George Pybus suggested that?"

"Yes."

Montrose groaned in spirit. He was telling himself that he might have known that something like this would have been the result of urging a member of the Press department to exercise his intellect. The brains of members of the Press departments of motion-picture studios resemble soup at a cheap restaurant. It is wiser not to stir them.

"Think what a sensation it would make! No more extra work for me after that. I'd get parts, and good ones. A girl can't get anywhere in this business without publicity."

Montrose licked his lips. They had become very dry. He was thinking harshly of George Pybus. It was just loose talking like George Pybus's, he felt, that made half the trouble in this world.

"But don't you feel," he said, "that there is something a little undignified about publicity? In my opinion, a true artist ought to be above it. And I think you should not overlook another, extremely vital aspect of the matter. I refer to the deleterious effect which such an exhibition as Pybus suggests would have upon those who read about it in the papers. Speaking for my-self," said Montrose, "there is nothing I should enjoy more than a quiet wedding in a gorilla's cage. But has one the right to pander to the morbid tastes of a sensation-avid public? I am not a man who often speaks of these deeper things — on the surface, no doubt, I seem careless and happy-go-lucky — but I do hold very serious views on a citizen's duties in this fevered modern age. I consider that each one of us should do all that lies in his power to fight the ever-growing trend of the public mind towards the morbid and the hectic. I have a very real feeling that the body politic can never become healthy while this appetite for sensation persists. If America is not to go the way of Babylon and Rome, we must come back to normalcy and the sane outlook. It is not much that a man in my humble position can do to stem the tide, but at least I can refrain from adding fuel to its flames by getting married in gorillas' cages."

Rosalie was gazing at him incredulously.

"You don't mean you won't do it?"

"It would not be right."

"I believe you're scared."

"Nothing of the kind. It is purely a question of civic conscience."

"You *are* scared. To think," said Rosalie vehemently, "that I should have linked my lot with a man who's afraid of a teentsy-weentsy gorilla."

Montrose could not let this pass.

"It is not a teentsy-weentsy gorilla. I should describe the animal's muscular development as well above the average."

"And the keeper would be outside the cage with a spiked stick."

"*Outside* the cage!" said Montrose thoughtfully.

Rosalie sprang to her feet in sudden passion.

"Good-bye!"

"But you haven't finished your steak-pudding."

"Good-bye," she repeated. "I see now what your so-called love is worth. If you are going to start denying me every little thing before we're married, what would you be like after? I'm glad I have discovered your true character in time. Our engagement is at an end."

Montrose was pale to the lips, but he tried to reason with her.

"But Rosalie," he urged, "surely a girl's wedding-day ought to be something for her to think of all her life — to recall with dreamily smiling lips as she knits the tiny garments or cooks the evening meal for the husband she adores. She ought to be able to look back and live again through the solemn hush in the church, savor once more the sweet scent of the lilies-of-the-valley, hear the rolling swell of the organ and the grave voice of the clergyman reading the service. What memories would you have if you carried out this plan that you suggest? One only — that of a smelly monkey. Have you reflected upon this, Rosalie?"

But she was obdurate.

"Either you marry me in the gorilla's cage, or you don't marry me at all. Mr. Pybus says it is certain to make the front page, with photographs and possibly even a short editorial on the right stuff being in the modern girl despite her surface irresponsibility."

"You will feel differently tonight, dear, when we meet for dinner."

"We shall not meet for dinner. If you are interested, I may inform you that Captain Fosdyke invited me to dine with him and I intend to do so."

"Rosalie!"

"There is a man who really is a man. When he meets a gorilla, he laughs in its face."

"Very rude."

"A million gorillas couldn't frighten him. Good-bye, Mr. Mulliner. I must go and tell him that when I said this morning that I had a previous engagement, I was mistaken."

She swept out, and Montrose went on with his steak-pudding like one in a dream.

It is possible (said Mr. Mulliner, taking a grave sip of his hot Scotch and lemon and surveying the company with a thoughtful eye) that what I have told you may have caused you to form a dubious opinion of my distant cousin Montrose. If so, I am not surprised. In the scene which I have just related, no one is better aware than myself that he has not shown up well. Reviewing his shallow arguments, we see through them, as Rosalie did; and, like Rosalie, we realize that he had feet of clay — and cold ones, to boot.

But I would urge in extenuation of his attitude that Montrose Mulliner, possibly through some constitutional defect such as an insufficiency of hormones, had been from childhood timorous in the extreme. And his work as an assistant-director had served very noticeably to increase this innate pusillanimity.

It is one of the drawbacks to being an assistant-director that virtually everything that happens to him is of a nature to create an inferiority-complex — or, if one already exists, to deepen it. He is habitually addressed as "Hey, you" and alluded to in the third person as "that fathead." If anything goes wrong on the set, he gets the blame and is ticked off not only by the producer but also by the director and all the principals involved. Finally, he has to be obsequious to so many people that it is little wonder that he comes in time to resemble one of the more shrinking and respectful breeds of rabbit. Five years of assistant-directing had so sapped Montrose's morale that nowadays he frequently found himself starting up and apologizing in his sleep.

It is proof, then, of the great love which he had for Rosalie Beamish that, encountering Captain Jack Fosdyke a few days later, he should have assailed him with bitter reproaches. Only love could have impelled him to act in a manner so foreign to his temperament.

The fact was, he blamed the Captain for all that had occurred. He considered that he had deliberately unsettled Rosalie and influenced her mind with the set purpose of making her dissatisfied with the man to whom she had plighted her troth.

"If it wasn't for you," he concluded warmly, "I feel sure I could have reasoned her out of what is nothing but a passing girlish whim. But you have infatuated her, and now where do I get off?"

The Captain twirled his mustache airily.

"Don't blame me, my boy. All my life I have been cursed by this fatal attraction of mine for the sex. Poor little moths, they will beat their wings against the bright light of my personality. Remind me to tell you some time of an interesting episode which occurred in the harem of the King of the 'Mbongos. There is something about me which is — what shall I say? — hypnotic. It is not my fault that this girl has compared us. It was inevitable that she should compare us. And having compared us what does she see? On the one hand, a man with a soul of chilled steel who can look his gorilla in the eye and make it play ball. On the other — I use the term in the kindliest possible sense — a crawling worm. Well, good-bye, my boy, glad to have seen you and had this little chat," said Captain Fosdyke. "I like you young fellows to bring your troubles to me."

For some moments after he had gone, Montrose remained

standing motionless, while all the repartees which he might have made surged through his mind in a glittering procession. Then his thoughts turned once more to the topic of gorillas.

It is possible that it was the innuendoes uttered by Captain Fosdyke that now awoke in Montrose something which bore a shadowy resemblance to fortitude. Certainly, until this conversation, he had not intended to revisit the gorilla's cage, one sight of its occupant having been ample for him. Now, stung by the other's slurs, he decided to go and have another look at the brute. It might be that further inspection would make it seem less formidable. He had known this to happen before. The first time he had seen Mr. Schnellenhamer, for example, he had had something not unlike a fit of what our grandparents used to call the "vapors." Now, he could bear him with at least an assumption of nonchalance.

He made his way to the cage, and was presently exchanging glances with the creature through the bars.

Alas, any hope he may have had that familiarity would breed contempt died as their eyes met. Those well-gnashed teeth, that hideous shagginess (a little reminiscent of a stockbroker motoring to Brighton in a fur coat), filled him with all the old familiar qualms. He tottered back and, with some dim idea of pulling himself together, took a banana from the bag which he had bought at the commissary to see him through the long afternoon. And, as he did so, there suddenly flashed upon him the recollection of an old saw which he had heard in his infancy — The Gorilla Never Forgets. In other words, Do the square thing by gorillas, and they will do the square thing by you.

His heart leaped within him. He pushed the banana through the bars with a cordial smile, and was rejoiced to find it readily accepted. In rapid succession he passed over the others. A banana a day keeps the gorilla away, he felt jubilantly.

By standing treat to this animal regardless of cost, he reasoned, he would so ingratiate himself with it as to render the process of getting married in its cage both harmless and agreeable. And it was only when his guest had finished the last of the fruit that he realized with a sickening sense of despair that he had got his facts wrong and that his whole argument, based on a false premise, fell to the ground and became null and void.

It was the elephant who never forgot — not the gorilla. It all came back to him now. He was practically sure that gorillas had never been mentioned in connection with the subject of mnemonics. Indeed, for all he knew, these creatures might be famous for the shortness of their memory — with the result that if later on he were to put on pin-striped trousers and a top hat and enter this animal's cage with Rosalie on his arm and the studio band playing the Wedding March, all recollection of those bananas would probably have passed completely through its fat head, and it would totally fail to recognize its benefactor.

Moodily crumpling the bag, Montrose turned away. This, he felt, was the end.

I have a tender heart (said Mr. Mulliner), and I dislike to dwell on the spectacle of a human being groaning under the iron heel of Fate. Such morbid gloating, I consider, is better left to the Russians. I will spare you, therefore, a detailed analysis of my distant cousin Montrose's emotions as the long day wore on. Suffice it to say that by a few minutes to five o'clock he had become a mere toad beneath the harrow. He wandered aimlessly to and fro about the lot in the growing dusk, and it seemed to him that the falling shades of evening resembled the cloud that had settled upon his life.

He was roused from these meditations by a collision with

some solid body and, coming to himself, discovered that he had been trying to walk through his old friend, George Pybus of the Press department. George was standing beside his car, apparently on the point of leaving for the day.

It is one more proof of Montrose Mulliner's gentle nature that he did not reproach George Pybus for the part he had taken in darkening his outlook. All he did was to gape and say:

"Hullo! You off?"

George Pybus climbed into the car and started the engine.

"Yes," he said, "and I'll tell you why. You know that gorilla?"

With a shudder which he could not repress, Montrose said he knew the gorilla.

"Well, I'll tell you something," said George Pybus. "Its agent has been complaining that we've been throwing all the publicity to Luella Benstead and Edmund Wigham. So the boss sent out a hurry call for quick thinking. I told him that you and Rosalie Beamish were planning to get married in its cage, but I've seen Rosalie and she tells me you've backed out. Scarcely the spirit I should have expected in you, Montrose."

Montrose did his best to assume a dignity which he was far from feeling.

"One has one's code," he said. "One dislikes to pander to the morbidity of a sensation-avid . . ."

"Well, it doesn't matter, anyway," said George Pybus, "because I got another idea, and a better one. This one is a pippin. At five sharp this evening, Pacific Standard Time, that gorilla's going to be let out of its cage and will menace hundreds. If that doesn't land him on the front page . . ."

Montrose was appalled.

"But you can't do that!" he gasped. "Once let that awful brute out of its cage and it may tear people to shreds."

George Pybus reassured him.

"Nobody of any consequence. The stars have all been notified and are off the lot. So are the directors. Also the executives, all except Mr. Schnellenhamer, who is cleaning up some work in his office. He will be quite safe there, of course. Nobody ever got into Mr. Schnellenhamer's office without waiting four hours in the ante-room. Well, I must be off," said George Pybus. "I've got to dress and get out to Malibu for dinner."

And, so speaking, he trod on the accelerator and was speedily lost to view in the gathering darkness.

It was a few moments later that Montrose, standing rooted to the spot, became aware of a sudden distant uproar: and, looking at his watch, he found that it was precisely five o'clock.

The spot to which Montrose had been standing rooted was in that distant part of the lot where the outdoor sets are kept permanently erected, so that a director with — let us suppose — a London street scene to shoot is able instantly to lay his hands on a back alley in Algiers, a medieval castle, or a Parisian boulevard — none of which is any good to him but which makes him feel that the studio is trying to be helpful.

As far as Montrose's eye could reach, Spanish patios, thatched cottages, tenement buildings, estaminets, Oriental bazaars, Kaffir kraals and the residences of licentious New York clubmen stood out against the evening sky: and the fact that he selected as his haven of refuge one of the tenement buildings was due to its being both tallest and nearest.

Like all outdoor sets, it consisted of a front just like the real thing and a back composed of steps and platforms. Up these steps he raced, and on the topmost of the platforms he halted and sat down. He was still unable to think very coherently, but in a dim sort of way he was rather proud of his agility and resource. He felt that he had met a grave crisis well. He did not know what the record was for climbing a flight of steps with a gorilla loose in the neighborhood, but he would have felt surprise if informed that he had not lowered it.

The uproar which had had such a stimulating effect upon him was now increasing in volume: and, oddly, it appeared to have become stationary. He glanced down through the window of his tenement building, and was astonished to observe below him a dense crowd. And what perplexed him most about this crowd was that it was standing still and looking up.

Scarcely, felt Montrose, intelligent behavior on the part of a crowd with a savage gorilla after it.

There was a good deal of shouting going on, but he found himself unable to distinguish any words. A woman who stood in the forefront of the throng appeared particularly animated. She was waving an umbrella in a rather neurotic manner.

The whole thing, as I say, perplexed Montrose. What these people thought they were doing, he was unable to say. He was still speculating on the matter when a noise came to his ears.

It was the crying of a baby.

Now, with all these mother-love pictures so popular, the presence of a baby on the lot was not in itself a thing to occasion surprise. It is a very unambitious mother in Hollywood who, the moment she finds herself and child doing well, does not dump the little stranger into a perambulator and wheel it round to the casting-office in the hope of cashing in. Ever since he had been with the Perfecto-Zizzbaum, Montrose had seen a constant stream of offspring riding up and trying to break into the game. It was not, accordingly, the fact of a baby being among those present that surprised him. What puzzled him about this particular baby was that it seemed to be so close at hand. Unless the acoustics were playing odd tricks, the infant, he was convinced, was sharing this eyrie of his. And

how a mere baby, handicapped probably by swaddling-clothes
and a bottle, could have shinned up all those steps bewildered
him to such an extent that he moved along the planks to
investigate.

And he had not gone three paces when he paused, aghast.
With his hairy back towards him, the gorilla was crouching
over something that lay on the ground. And another bellow
told him that this was the baby in person: and instantly Montrose saw what must have occurred. His reading of magazine
stories had taught him that, once a gorilla gets loose, the first
thing it does is to snatch a baby from a perambulator and
climb to the nearest high place. It is pure routine.

This, then, was the position in which my distant cousin
Montrose found himself at eight minutes past five on this
misty evening. A position calculated to test the fortitude of
the sternest.

Now, it has been well said that with nervous, highly-strung
men like Montrose Mulliner, a sudden call upon their man-
hood is often enough to revolutionize their whole character.
Psychologists have frequently commented on this. We are too
ready, they say, to dismiss as cowards those who merely require the stimulus of the desperate emergency to bring out all
their latent heroism. The crisis comes, and the craven turns
magically into the paladin.

With Montrose, however, this was not the case. Ninety-nine
out of a hundred of those who knew him would have scoffed
at the idea of him interfering with an escaped gorilla to save
the life of a child, and they would have been right. To tiptoe
backwards, holding his breath, was with Montrose Mulliner
the work of a moment. And it was the fact that he did it so
quickly that wrecked his plans. Stubbing a heel on a loose

board in his haste, he fell backwards with a crash. And when the stars had ceased to obscure his vision, he found himself gazing up into the hideous face of the gorilla.

On the last occasion when the two had met, there had been iron bars between them: and even with this safeguard Montrose, as I have said, had shrunk from the creature's evil stare. Now, meeting the brute as it were socially, he experienced a thrill of horror such as had never come to him even in nightmares. Closing his eyes, he began to speculate as to which limb, when it started to tear him limb from limb, the animal would start with.

The one thing of which he was sure was that it would begin operations by uttering a fearful snarl: and when the next sound that came to his ears was a deprecating cough he was so astonished that he could keep his eyes closed no longer. Opening them, he found the gorilla looking at him with an odd, apologetic expression on its face.

"Excuse me, sir," said the gorilla, "but are you by any chance a family man?"

For an instant, on hearing the question, Montrose's astonishment deepened. Then he realized what must have happened. He must have been torn limb from limb without knowing it, and now he was in heaven. Though even this did not altogether satisfy him as an explanation, for he had never expected to find gorillas in heaven.

The animal now gave a sudden start.

"Why, it's you! I didn't recognize you at first. Before going any further, I should like to thank you for those bananas. They were delicious. A little something round about the middle of the afternoon picks one up quite a bit, doesn't it."

Montrose blinked. He could still hear the noise of the crowd below. His bewilderment increased.

"You speak very good English for a gorilla" was all he could find to say. And, indeed, the animal's diction had been remarkable for its purity.

The gorilla waved the compliment aside modestly.

"Oh, well, Balliol, you know. Dear old Balliol. One never quite forgets the lessons one learned at Alma Mater, don't you think? You are not an Oxford man, by any chance?"

"No."

"I came down in '26. Since then I have been knocking around a good deal, and a friend of mine in the circus business suggested to me that the gorilla field was not overcrowded. Plenty of room at the top was his expression. And I must say," said the gorilla, "I've done pretty well at it. The initial expenditure comes high, of course — you don't get a skin like this for nothing — but there's virtually no overhead. Of course, to become a co-star in a big feature film, as I have done, you need a good agent. Mine, I am glad to say, is a capital man of business. Stands no nonsense from these motion-picture magnates."

Montrose was not a quick thinker, but he was gradually adjusting his mind to the facts.

"Then you're not a real gorilla?"

"No, no. Synthetic, merely."

"You wouldn't tear anyone limb from limb?"

"My dear chap! My idea of a nice time is to curl up with a good book. I am happiest among my books."

Montrose's last doubts were resolved. He extended his hand cordially.

"Pleased to meet you, Mr. . . . ."

"Waddesley-Davenport. Cyril Waddesley-Davenport. And I am extremely happy to meet you, Mr. . . . ."

"Mulliner. Montrose Mulliner."

They shook hands warmly. From down below came the hoarse uproar of the crowd. The gorilla started.

"The reason I asked you if you were a family man," it said, "was that I hoped you might be able to tell me what is the best method of procedure to adopt with a crying baby. I don't seem able to stop the child. And all my own silly fault, too. I see now I should never have snatched it from its perambulator. If you want to know what is the matter with me, I am too much the artist. I simply had to snatch that baby. It was how I saw the scene. I *felt* it . . . felt it *here*," said the gorilla, thumping the left side of its chest. "And now what?"

Montrose reflected.

"Why don't you take it back?"

"To its mother?"

"Certainly."

"But . . ." The gorilla pulled doubtfully at its lower lip. "You have seen that crowd. Did you happen to observe a woman standing in the front row waving an umbrella?"

"The mother?"

"Precisely. Well, you know as well as I do, Mulliner, what an angry woman can do with an umbrella."

Montrose thought again.

"It's all right," he said. "I have it. Why don't you sneak down the back steps? Nobody will see you. The crowd's in front, and it's almost dark."

The gorilla's eyes lit up. It slapped Montrose gratefully on the shoulder.

"My dear chap! The very thing. But as regards the baby . . ."

"I will restore it."

"Capital! I don't know how to thank you, dear fellow," said the gorilla. "By Jove, this is going to be a lesson to me in future not to give way to the artist in me. You don't know how I've been feeling about that umbrella. Well, then, in case we don't meet again, always remember that the Lotos Club finds me when I am in New York. Drop in any time you happen to be in that neighborhood, and we'll have a bite to eat and a good talk."

And what of Rosalie, meanwhile? Rosalie was standing beside the bereaved mother, using all her powers of cajolery to try to persuade Captain Jack Fosdyke to go to the rescue: and the Captain was pleading technical difficulties that stood in the way.

"Dash my buttons," he said, "if only I had my elephant gun and my trusty native bearer, 'Mlongi, here, I'd pretty soon know what to do about it. As it is, I'm handicapped."

"But you told me yesterday that you had often strangled gorillas with your bare hands."

"Not *gor*-illas, dear lady — *por*-illas. A species of South American wombat, and very good eating they make, too."

"You're afraid!"

"Afraid? Jack Fosdyke afraid? How they would laugh on the Lower Zambesi if they could hear you say that."

"You are! You, who advised me to have nothing to do with the man I love because he was of a mild and diffident nature."

Captain Jack Fosdyke twirled his mustache.

"Well, I don't notice," he sneered, "that he . . ." He broke off, and his jaw slowly fell. Round the corner of the building was walking Montrose Mulliner. His bearing was erect, even jaunty, and he carried the baby in his arms. Pausing for an instant to allow the busily-clicking cameras to focus on him, he advanced towards the stupefied mother and thrust the child into her arms.

"That's that," he said carelessly, dusting his fingers. "No, no, please," he went on. "A mere nothing."

For the mother was kneeling before him, endeavoring to

kiss his hand. It was not only maternal love that prompted the action. That morning she had signed up her child at seventy-five dollars a week for the forthcoming picture *Tiny Fingers,* and all through these long, anxious minutes it had seemed as though the contract must be a total loss.

Rosalie was in Montrose's arms, sobbing.

"Oh, Monty!"

"There, there!"

"How I misjudged you!"

"We all make mistakes."

"I made a bad one when I listened to that man there," said Rosalie, darting a scornful look at Captain Jack Fosdyke. "Do you realize that, for all his boasting, he would not move a step to save that poor child?"

"Not a step?"

"Not a single step."

"Bad, Fosdyke," said Montrose. "Rather bad. Not quite the straight bat, eh?"

"Tchah!" said the baffled man, and he turned on his heel and strode away. He was still twirling his mustache, but a lot that got him.

Rosalie was clinging to Montrose.

"You aren't hurt? Was it a fearful struggle?"

"Struggle?" Montrose laughed. "Oh, dear no. There was no struggle. I very soon showed the animal that I was going to stand no nonsense. I generally find with gorillas that all one needs is the power of the human eye. By the way, I've been thinking it over and I realize that I may have been a little un-reasonable about that idea of yours. I still would prefer to get married in some nice, quiet church, but if you feel you want the ceremony to take place in that animal's cage, I shall be delighted."

She shivered.

"I couldn't do it. I'd be scared."

Montrose smiled understandingly.

"Ah, well," he said, "it is perhaps not unnatural that a delicately nurtured woman should be of less tough stuff than the more rugged male. Shall we be strolling along? I want to look in on Mr. Schnellenhamer and arrange about that raise of mine. You won't mind waiting while I pop in at his office?"

"My hero!" whispered Rosalie.

Jeeves and the Impending Doom

IT WAS the morning of the day on which I was slated to pop down to my Aunt Agatha's place at Woollam Chersey in the county of Herts for a visit of three solid weeks; and, as I seated myself at the breakfast table, I don't mind confessing that the heart was singularly heavy. We Woosters are men of iron, but beneath my intrepid exterior at that moment there lurked a nameless dread.

"Jeeves," I said, "I am not the old merry self this morning."

"Indeed, sir?"

"No, Jeeves. Far from it. Far from the old merry self."

"I am sorry to hear that, sir."

He uncovered the fragrant eggs and b., and I pronged a moody forkful.

"Why — this is what I keep asking myself, Jeeves — why has my Aunt Agatha invited me to her country seat?"

"I could not say, sir."

"Not because she is fond of me."

"No, sir."

"It is a well-established fact that I give her a pain in the neck. How it happens I cannot say, but every time our paths cross, so to speak, it seems to be a mere matter of time before I perpetrate some ghastly floater and have her hopping after me with her hatchet. The result being that she regards me as a worm and an outcast. Am I right or wrong, Jeeves?"

"Perfectly correct, sir."

"And yet now she has absolutely insisted on my scratching all previous engagements and buzzing down to Woollam Chersey. She must have some sinister reason of which we know nothing. Can you blame me, Jeeves, if the heart is heavy?"

"No, sir. Excuse me, sir; I fancy I heard the front-door bell."

He shimmered out, and I took another listless stab at the e. and bacon.

"A telegram, sir," said Jeeves, re-entering the presence.

"Open it, Jeeves, and read contents. Who is it from?"

"It is unsigned, sir."

"You mean there's no name at the end of it?"

"That is precisely what I was endeavoring to convey, sir."

"Let's have a look."

I scanned the thing. It was a rummy communication. Rummy. No other word.

As follows:

REMEMBER WHEN YOU COME HERE ABSOLUTELY VITAL MEET
PERFECT STRANGERS.

We Woosters are not very strong in the head, particularly at breakfast-time; and I was conscious of a dull ache between the eyebrows.

"What does it mean, Jeeves?"

"I could not say, sir."

"It says 'come here.' Where's here?"

"You will notice that the message was handed in at Woollam Chersey, sir."

"You're absolutely right. At Woollam, as you very cleverly spotted, Chersey. This tells us something, Jeeves."

"What, sir?"

"I don't know. It couldn't be from my Aunt Agatha, do you think?"

"Hardly, sir."

"No, you're right again. Then all we can say is that some person unknown, resident at Woollam Chersey, considers it absolutely vital for me to meet perfect strangers. But why should I meet perfect strangers, Jeeves?"

"I could not say, sir."

"And yet, looking at it from another angle, why shouldn't I?"

"Precisely, sir."

"Then what it comes to is that the thing is a mystery, which time alone can solve. We must wait and see, Jeeves."

"The very expression I was about to employ, sir."

I hit Woollam Chersey at about four o'clock, and found Aunt Agatha in her lair, writing letters. And, from what I know of her, probably offensive letters, with nasty postscripts. She regarded me with not a fearful lot of joy.

"Oh, there you are, Bertie."

"Yes, here I am."

"There's a smut on your nose."

I plied the handkerchief.

"I am glad you have arrived so early. I want to have a word with you before you meet Mr. Filmer."

"Who?"

"Mr. Filmer, the Cabinet Minister. He is staying in the house. Surely even you must have heard of Mr. Filmer?"

"Oh, rather," I said, though as a matter of fact the bird was completely unknown to me. What with one thing and another, I'm not frightfully up in the *personnel* of the political world.

"I particularly wish you to make a good impression on Mr. Filmer."

"Right-ho."

"Don't speak in that casual way, as if you supposed that it was perfectly natural that you would make a good impression upon him. Mr. Filmer is a serious-minded man of high character and purpose, and you are just the type of vapid and frivolous wastrel against which he is most likely to be prejudiced."

Hard words, of course, from one's own flesh and blood, but well in keeping with past form.

"You will endeavor, therefore, while you are here not to display yourself in the *rôle* of a vapid and frivolous wastrel. In the first place, you will give up smoking during your visit."

"Oh, I say!"

"Mr. Filmer is president of the Anti-Tobacco League. Nor will you drink alcoholic stimulants."

"Oh, dash it!"

"And you will kindly exclude from your conversation all that is suggestive of the bar, the billiard-room, and the stage-door. Mr. Filmer will judge you largely by your conversation."

I rose to a point of order.

"Yes, but why have I got to make an impression on this — on Mr. Filmer?"

"Because," said the old relative, giving me the eye, "I particularly wish it."

Not, perhaps, a notably snappy come-back as come-backs go; but it was enough to show me that that was more or less that; and I beetled out with an aching heart.

I headed for the garden, and I'm dashed if the first person I saw wasn't young Bingo Little.

Bingo Little and I have been pals practically from birth. Born in the same village within a couple of days of one another, we went through kindergarten, Eton, and Oxford together; and, grown to riper years, we have enjoyed in the old metrop. full many a first-class binge in each other's society. If there was one fellow in the world, I felt, who could alleviate the horrors of this blighted visit of mine, that bloke was young Bingo Little.

But how he came to be there was more than I could understand. Some time before, you see, he had married the celebrated authoress Rosie M. Banks; and the last I had seen of him he had been on the point of accompanying her to America on a lecture tour. I distinctly remembered him cursing rather freely because the trip would mean his missing Ascot.

Still, rummy as it might seem, here he was. And aching for the sight of a friendly face, I gave tongue like a bloodhound.

"Bingo!"

He spun round; and, by Jove, his face wasn't friendly after all. It was what they call contorted. He waved his arms at me like a semaphore.

"Ssh!" he hissed. "Would you ruin me?"

"Eh?"

"Didn't you get my telegram?"

"Was that *your* telegram?"

"Of course it was my telegram."

"Then why didn't you sign it?"

"I did sign it."

"No, you didn't. I couldn't make out what it was all about."

"Well, you got my letter."

"What letter?"

"My letter."

"I didn't get any letter."

"Then I must have forgotten to post it. It was to tell you that I was down here tutoring your cousin Thomas, and that it was essential that, when we met, you should treat me as a perfect stranger."

"But why?"

"Because if your aunt supposed that I was a pal of yours, she would naturally sack me on the spot."

"Why?"

Bingo raised his eyebrows.

"Why? Be reasonable, Bertie. If you were your aunt, and you knew the sort of chap you were, would you let a fellow you knew to be your best pal tutor your son?"

This made the old head swim a bit, but I got his meaning after a while, and I had to admit that there was much rugged good sense in what he said. Still, he hadn't explained what you might call the nub or gist of the mystery.

"I thought you were in America," I said.

"Well, I'm not."

"Why not?"

"Never mind why not. I'm not."

"But why have you taken a tutoring job?"

"Never mind why. I have my reasons. And I want you to get it into your head, Bertie — to get it right through the concrete — that you and I must not be seen hobnobbing. Your foul cousin was caught smoking in the shrubbery the day before yesterday, and that has made my position pretty tottery, because your aunt said that if I had exercised an adequate surveillance over him, it couldn't have happened. If, after that, she finds out I'm a friend of yours, nothing can save me from being shot out. And it is vital that I am not shot out."

"Why?"

"Never mind why."

At this point he seemed to think he heard somebody coming, for he suddenly leaped with incredible agility into a laurel bush. And I toddled along to consult Jeeves about these rummy happenings.

"Jeeves," I said, repairing to the bedroom, where he was unpacking my things, "you remember that telegram?"

"Yes, sir."

"It was from Mr. Little. He's here, tutoring my young Cousin Thomas."

"Indeed, sir?"

"I can't understand it. He appears to be a free agent, if you know what I mean; and yet would any man who was a free agent wantonly come to a house which contained my Aunt Agatha?"

"It seems peculiar, sir."

"Moreover, would anybody of his own free will and as a mere pleasure-seeker tutor my Cousin Thomas, who is notoriously a tough egg and a fiend in human shape?"

"Most improbable, sir."

"These are deep waters, Jeeves."

"Precisely, sir."

"And the ghastly part of it all is that he seems to consider it necessary, in order to keep his job, to treat me like a long-lost leper. Thus killing my only chance of having anything approaching a decent time in this abode of desolation. For do you realize, Jeeves, that my aunt says I mustn't smoke while I'm here?"

"Indeed, sir?"

"Nor drink."

"Why is this, sir?"

"Because she wants me — for some dark and furtive reason which she will not explain — to impress a fellow named Filmer."

"Too bad, sir. However, many doctors, I understand, advocate such abstinence as the secret of health. They say it promotes a freer circulation of the blood and insures the arteries against premature hardening."

"Oh, do they? Well, you can tell them next time you see them that they are silly asses."

"Very good, sir."

And so began what, looking back along a fairly eventful career, I think I can confidently say was the scaliest visit I have ever experienced in the course of my life. What with the agony of missing the life-giving cocktail before dinner; the painful necessity of being obliged, every time I wanted a quiet cigarette, to lie on the floor in my bedroom and puff the smoke up the chimney; the constant discomfort of meeting Aunt Agatha round unexpected corners, and the fearful strain on the morale of having to chum with the Right Hon. A. B. Filmer, it was not long before Bertram was up against it to an extent hitherto undreamed of.

I played golf with the Right Hon. every day, and it was only by biting the Wooster lip and clenching the fists till the knuckles stood out white under the strain that I managed to pull through. The Right Hon. punctuated some of the ghastliest golf I have ever seen with a flow of conversation which, as far as I was concerned, went completely over the top; and, all in all, I was beginning to feel pretty sorry for myself when, one night as I was in my room listlessly donning the soup-and-fish in preparation for the evening meal, in trickled young Bingo and took my mind off my own troubles.

For when it is a question of a pal being in the soup, we

Woosters no longer think of self; and that poor old Bingo was knee-deep in the bisque was made plain by his mere appearance — which was that of a cat which has just been struck by a half-brick and is expecting another shortly.

"Bertie," said Bingo, having sat down on the bed and diffused silent gloom for a moment, "how is Jeeves's brain these days?"

"Fairly strong on the wing, I fancy. How is the gray matter, Jeeves? Surging about pretty freely?"

"Yes, sir."

"Thank Heaven for that," said young Bingo, "for I require your soundest counsel. Unless right-thinking people take strong steps through the proper channels, my name will be mud."

"What's wrong, old thing?" I asked, sympathetically.

Bingo plucked at the coverlet.

"I will tell you," he said. "I will also now reveal why I am staying in this pest-house, tutoring a kid who requires not education in the Greek and Latin languages but a swift slosh on the base of the skull with a black-jack. I came here, Bertie, because it was the only thing I could do. At the last moment before she sailed to America, Rosie decided that I had better stay behind and look after the Peke. She left me a couple of hundred quid to see me through till her return. This sum, judiciously expended over the period of her absence, would have been enough to keep Peke and self in moderate affluence. But you know how it is."

"How what is?"

"When someone comes slinking up to you in the club and tells you that some cripple of a horse can't help winning even if it develops lumbago and the botts ten yards from the starting-post. I tell you, I regarded the thing as a cautious and conservative investment."

"You mean you planked the entire capital on a horse?"

Bingo laughed bitterly.

"If you could call the thing a horse. If it hadn't shown a flash of speed in the straight, it would have got mixed up with the next race. It came in last, putting me in a dashed delicate position. Somehow or other I had to find the funds to keep me going, so that I could win through till Rosie's return without her knowing what had occurred. Rosie is the dearest girl in the world; but if you were a married man, Bertie, you would be aware that the best of wives is apt to cut up rough if she finds that her husband has dropped six weeks' housekeeping money on a single race. Isn't that so, Jeeves?"

"Yes, sir. Women are odd in that respect."

"It was a moment for swift thinking. There was enough left from the wreck to board the Peke out at a comfortable home. I signed him up for six weeks at the Kosy Komfort Kennels at Kingsbridge, Kent, and tottered out, a broken man, to get a tutoring job. I landed the kid Thomas. And here I am."

It was a sad story, of course, but it seemed to me that, awful as it might be to be in constant association with my Aunt Agatha and young Thos, he had got rather well out of a tight place.

"All you have to do," I said, "is to carry on here for a few weeks more, and everything will be oojah-cum-spiff."

Bingo barked bleakly.

"A few weeks more! I shall be lucky if I stay two days. You remember I told you that your aunt's faith in me as a guardian of her blighted son was shaken a few days ago by the fact that he was caught smoking. I now find that the person who caught him smoking was the man Filmer. And ten minutes ago young Thomas told me that he was proposing to inflict some hideous revenge on Filmer for having reported him to your aunt. I don't know what he is going to do, but if he does it, out I inevitably go on my left ear. Your aunt thinks the world of Filmer and would sack me on the spot. And three weeks before Rosie gets back!"

I saw all.

"Jeeves," I said.

"Sir?"

"I see all. Do you see all?"

"Yes, sir."

"Then flock round."

"I fear, sir —"

Bingo gave a low moan.

"Don't tell me, Jeeves," he said, brokenly, "that nothing suggests itself."

"Nothing at the moment, I regret,to say, sir."

Bingo uttered a stricken woofle like a bull-dog that has been refused cake.

"Well, then, the only thing I can do, I suppose," he said somberly, "is not to let the pie-faced little thug out of my sight for a second."

"Absolutely," I said. "Ceaseless vigilance, eh, Jeeves?"

"Precisely, sir."

"But meanwhile, Jeeves," said Bingo in a low, earnest voice, "you will be devoting your best thought to the matter, won't you?"

"Most certainly, sir."

"Thank you, Jeeves."

"Not at all, sir."

I will say for young Bingo that, once the need for action arrived, he behaved with an energy and determination which compelled respect. I suppose there was not a minute during the next two days when the kid Thos was able to say to himself: "Alone at last!" But on the evening of the second day

Aunt Agatha announced that some people were coming over on the morrow for a spot of tennis, and I feared that the worst must now befall.

Young Bingo, you see, is one of those fellows who, once their fingers close over the handle of a tennis racquet, fall into a sort of trance in which nothing outside the radius of the lawn exists for them. If you came up to Bingo in the middle of a set and told him that panthers were devouring his best friend in the kitchen garden, he would look at you and say: "Oh, ah?" or words to that effect. I knew that he would not give a thought to young Thomas and the Right Hon. till the last ball had bounced, and, as I dressed for dinner that night, I was conscious of an impending doom.

"Jeeves," I said, "have you ever pondered on Life?"

"From time to time, sir, in my leisure moments."

"Grim, isn't it, what?"

"Grim, sir?"

"I mean to say, the difference between things as they look and things as they are."

"The trousers perhaps a half-inch higher, sir. A very slight adjustment of the braces will effect the necessary alteration. You were saying, sir?"

"I mean, here at Woollam Chersey we have apparently a happy, care-free country-house party. But beneath the glittering surface, Jeeves, dark currents are running. One gazes at the Right Hon. wrapping himself round the salmon mayonnaise at lunch, and he seems a man without a care in the world. Yet all the while a dreadful fate is hanging over him, creeping nearer and nearer. What exact steps do you think the kid Thomas intends to take?"

"In the course of an informal conversation which I had with the young gentleman this afternoon, sir, he informed me that he had been reading a romance entitled *Treasure Island*, and had been much struck by the character and actions of a certain Captain Flint. I gathered that he was weighing the advisability of modeling his own conduct on that of the Captain."

"But, good heavens, Jeeves! If I remember *Treasure Island,* Flint was the bird who went about hitting people with a cutlass. You don't think young Thomas would bean Mr. Filmer with a cutlass?"

"Possibly he does not possess a cutlass, sir."

"Well, with anything."

"We can but wait and see, sir. The tie, if I might suggest it, sir, a shade more tightly knotted. One aims at the perfect butterfly effect. If you will permit me —"

"What do ties matter, Jeeves, at a time like this? Do you realize that Mr. Little's domestic happiness is hanging in the scale?"

"There is no time, sir, at which ties do not matter."

I could see the man was pained, but I did not try to heal the wound. What's the word I want? Preoccupied. I was too preoccupied, don't you know. And distrait. Not to say careworn.

I was still careworn when, next day at half-past two, the revels commenced on the tennis lawn. It was one of those close, baking days, with thunder rumbling just round the corner, and it seemed to me that there was a brooding menace in the air.

"Bingo," I said, as we pushed forth to do our bit in the first doubles, "I wonder what young Thos will be up to this afternoon, with the eye of authority no longer on him?"

"Eh?" said Bingo, absently. Already the tennis look had come into his face, and his eye was glazed. He swung his racquet and snorted a little.

"I don't see him anywhere," I said.

"You don't what?"

"See him."

"Who?"

"Young Thos."

"What about him?"

I let it go.

The only consolation I had in the black period of the open-ing of the tourney was the fact that the Right Hon. had taken a seat among the spectators and was wedged in between a couple of females with parasols. Reason told me that even a kid so steeped in sin as young Thomas would hardly perpe-trate any outrage on a man in such a strong strategic position. Considerably relieved, I gave myself up to the game; and was in the act of putting it across the local curate with a good deal of vim when there was a roll of thunder and the rain started to come down in buckets.

We all stampeded for the house, and had gathered in the drawing-room for tea, when suddenly Aunt Agatha, looking up from a cucumber-sandwich, said:

"Has anybody seen Mr. Filmer?"

It was one of the nastiest jars I have ever experienced.

What with my fast serve zipping sweetly over the net and the man of God utterly unable to cope with my slow-bending return down the center-line, I had for some little time been living, as it were, in another world. I now came down to earth with a bang, and my slice of cake, slipping from my nerveless fingers, fell to the ground and was wolfed by Aunt Agatha's spaniel, Robert. Once more I seemed to become conscious of an impending doom.

For this man Filmer, you must understand, was not one of those men who are lightly kept from the tea-table. A hearty trencherman, and particularly fond of his five o'clock couple of cups and bite of muffin, he had until this afternoon always been well up among the leaders in the race for the food-trough. If one thing was certain, it was that only the machinations of some enemy could be keeping him from being in the drawing-room now, complete with nose-bag.

"He must have got caught in the rain and be sheltering somewhere in the grounds," said Aunt Agatha. "Bertie, go out and find him. Take a raincoat to him."

"Right-ho!" I said. My only desire in life now was to find the Right Hon. And I hoped it wouldn't be merely his body.

I put on a raincoat and tucked another under my arm, and was sallying forth, when in the hall I ran into Jeeves.

"Jeeves," I said, "I fear the worst. Mr. Filmer is missing."

"Yes, sir."

"I am about to scour the grounds in search of him."

"I can save you the trouble, sir. Mr. Filmer is on the island in the middle of the lake."

"In this rain? Why doesn't the chump row back?"

"He has no boat, sir."

"Then how can he be on the island?"

"He rowed there, sir. But Master Thomas rowed after him and set his boat adrift. He was informing me of the circumstances a moment ago, sir. It appears that Captain Flint was in the habit of marooning people on islands, and Master Thomas felt that he could pursue no more judicious course than to follow his example."

"But, good Lord, Jeeves! The man must be getting soaked."

"Yes, sir. Master Thomas commented upon that aspect of the matter."

It was a time for action.

"Come with me, Jeeves!"

"Very good, sir."

I buzzed for the boathouse.

My Aunt Agatha's husband, Spenser Gregson, who is on

the Stock Exchange, had recently cleaned up to an amazing extent in Sumatra Rubber, and Aunt Agatha, in selecting a country estate, had lashed out on an impressive scale. There were miles of what they call rolling parkland, trees in considerable profusion well provided with doves and what-not cooing in no uncertain voice, gardens full of roses, and also stables, outhouses, and messuages, the whole forming a rather fruity *tout ensemble*. But the feature of the place was the lake.

It stood to the east of the house, beyond the rose garden, and covered several acres. In the middle of it was an island. In the middle of the island was a building known as the Octagon. And in the middle of the Octagon, seated on the roof and spouting water like a public fountain, was the Right Hon. A. B. Filmer. As we drew nearer, striking a fast clip with self at the oars and Jeeves handling the tiller-ropes, we heard cries of gradually increasing volume, if that's the expression I want; and presently, up aloft, looking from a distance as if he were perched on top of the bushes, I located the Right Hon. It seemed to me that even a Cabinet Minister ought to have had more sense than to stay right out in the open like that when there were trees to shelter under.

"A little more to the right, Jeeves."

"Very good, sir."

I made a neat landing.

"Wait here, Jeeves."

"Very good, sir. The head gardener was informing me this morning, sir, that one of the swans had recently nested on this island."

"This is no time for natural-history gossip, Jeeves," I said, a little severely, for the rain was coming down harder than ever and the Wooster trouser-legs were already considerably moistened.

"Very good, sir."

I pushed my way through the bushes. The going was sticky and took about eight and elevenpence off the value of my Sure-Grip tennis shoes in the first two yards: but I persevered, and presently came out in the open and found myself in a sort of clearing facing the Octagon.

This building was run up somewhere in the last century, I have been told, to enable the grandfather of the late owner to have some quiet place out of earshot of the house where he could practice the fiddle. From what I know of fiddlers, I should imagine that he had produced some fairly frightful sounds there in his time: but they can have been nothing to the ones that were coming from the roof of the place now. The Right Hon., not having spotted the arrival of the rescue-party, was apparently trying to make his voice carry across the waste of waters to the house; and I'm not saying it was not a good sporting effort. He had one of those highish tenors, and his yowls seemed to screech over my head like shells.

I thought it about time to slip him the glad news that assistance had arrived, before he strained a vocal cord.

"Hi!" I shouted, waiting for a lull.

He poked his head over the edge.

"Hi!" he bellowed, looking in every direction but the right one, of course.

"Hi!"

"Hi!"

"Hi!"

"Hi!"

"Oh!" he said, spotting me at last.

"What-ho!" I replied, sort of clinching the thing.

I suppose the conversation can't be said to have touched a frightfully high level up to this moment; but probably we should have got a good deal brainier very shortly — only just then, at the very instant when I was getting ready to say something good, there was a hissing noise like a tire bursting in a nest of cobras, and out of the bushes to my left there popped something so large and white and active that, thinking quicker than I have ever done in my puff, I rose like a rocketing pheasant, and, before I knew what I was doing, had begun the climb for life. Something slapped against the wall about an inch below my right ankle, and any doubts I may have had about remaining below vanished. The lad who bore 'mid snow and ice the banner with the strange device "Excelsior!" was the model for Bertram.

"Be careful!" yipped the Right Hon.

I was.

Whoever built the Octagon might have constructed it especially for this sort of crisis. Its walls had grooves at regular intervals which were just right for the hands and feet, and it wasn't very long before I was parked up on the roof beside the Right Hon., gazing down at one of the largest and shortest-tempered swans I had ever seen. It was standing below, stretching up a neck like a hosepipe, just where a bit of brick, judiciously bunged, would catch it amidships.

I bunged the brick and scored a bull's-eye.

The Right Hon. didn't seem any too well pleased.

"Don't tease it!" he said.

"It teased me," I said.

The swan extended another eight feet of neck and gave an imitation of steam escaping from a leaky pipe. The rain continued to lash down with what you might call indescribable fury, and I was sorry that in the agitation inseparable from shinning up a stone wall at practically a second's notice I had dropped the raincoat which I had been bringing with me for my fellow-rooster. For a moment I thought of offering him mine, but wiser counsels prevailed.

"How near did it come to getting you?" I asked.

"Within an ace," replied my companion, gazing down with a look of marked dislike. "I had to make a very rapid spring."

The Right Hon. was a tubby little chap who looked as if he had been poured into his clothes and had forgotten to say "When!" and the picture he conjured up, if you know what I mean, was rather pleasing.

"It is no laughing matter," he said, shifting the look of dislike to me.

"Sorry."

"I might have been seriously injured."

"Would you consider bunging another brick at the bird?"

"Do nothing of the sort. It will only annoy him."

"Well, why not annoy him? He hasn't shown such a dashed lot of consideration for our feelings."

The Right Hon. now turned to another aspect of the matter.

"I cannot understand how my boat, which I fastened securely to the stump of a willow-tree, can have drifted away."

"Dashed mysterious."

"I begin to suspect that it was deliberately set loose by some mischievous person."

"Oh, I say, no, hardly likely, that. You'd have seen them doing it."

"No, Mr. Wooster. For the bushes form an effective screen. Moreover, rendered drowsy by the unusual warmth of the afternoon, I dozed off for some little time almost immediately I reached the island."

This wasn't the sort of thing I wanted his mind dwelling on, so I changed the subject.

"Wet, isn't it, what?" I said.

"I had already observed it," said the Right Hon. in one of those nasty, bitter voices. "I thank you, however, for drawing the matter to my attention."

Chitchat about the weather hadn't gone with much of a bang, I perceived. I had a shot at Bird Life in the Home Counties.

"Have you ever noticed," I said, "how a swan's eyebrows sort of meet in the middle?"

"I have had every opportunity of observing all that there is to observe about swans."

"Gives them a sort of peevish look, what?"

"The look to which you allude has not escaped me."

"Rummy," I said, rather warming to my subject, "how bad an effect family life has on a swan's disposition."

"I wish you would select some other topic of conversation than swans."

"No, but really, it's rather interesting. I mean to say, our old pal down there is probably a perfect ray of sunshine in normal circumstances. Quite the domestic pet, don't you know. But purely and simply because the little woman happens to be nesting —"

I paused. You will scarcely believe me, but until this moment, what with all the recent bustle and activity, I had clean forgotten that, while we were treed up on the roof like this, there lurked all the time in the background one whose giant brain, if notified of the emergency and requested to flock round, would probably be able to think up half-a-dozen schemes for solving our little difficulties in a couple of minutes.

"Jeeves!" I shouted.

"Sir?" came a faint respectful voice from the great open spaces.

"My man," I explained to the Right Hon. "A fellow of infinite resource and sagacity. He'll have us out of this in a minute. Jeeves!"

"Sir?"

"I'm sitting on the roof."

"Very good, sir."

"Don't say 'Very good.' Come and help us. Mr. Filmer and I are treed, Jeeves."

"Very good, sir."

"Don't keep saying 'Very good.' It's nothing of the kind. The place is alive with swans."

"I will attend to the matter immediately, sir."

I turned to the Right Hon. I even went so far as to pat him on the back. It was like slapping a wet sponge.

"All is well," I said. "Jeeves is coming."

"What can he do?"

I frowned a trifle. The man's tone had been peevish, and I didn't like it.

"That," I replied with a touch of stiffness, "we cannot say until we see him in action. He may pursue one course, or he may pursue another. But on one thing you can rely with the utmost confidence — Jeeves will find a way. See, here he comes stealing through the undergrowth, his face shining with the light of pure intelligence. There are no limits to Jeeves's brain-power. He virtually lives on fish."

I bent over the edge and peered into the abyss.

"Look out for the swan, Jeeves."

"I have the bird under close observation, sir."

The swan had been uncoiling a further supply of neck in our direction; but now he whipped round. The sound of a voice speaking in his rear seemed to affect him powerfully. He subjected Jeeves to a short, keen scrutiny; and then, taking in some breath for hissing purposes, gave a sort of jump and charged ahead.

"Look out, Jeeves!"

"Very good, sir."

Well, I could have told that swan it was no use. As swans

go, he may have been well up in the ranks of the intelligentsia; but, when it came to pitting his brains against Jeeves, he was simply wasting his time. He might just as well have gone home at once.

Every young man starting life ought to know how to cope with an angry swan, so I will briefly relate the proper procedure. You begin by picking up the raincoat which somebody has dropped; and then, judging the distance to a nicety, you simply shove the raincoat over the bird's head; and, taking the boat-hook which you have prudently brought with you, you insert it underneath the swan and heave. The swan goes into a bush and starts trying to unscramble itself; and you saunter back to your boat, taking with you any friends who may happen at the moment to be sitting on roofs in the vicinity. That was Jeeves's method, and I cannot see how it could have been improved upon.

The Right Hon. showing a turn of speed of which I would not have believed him capable, we were in the boat in considerably under two ticks.

"You behaved very intelligently, my man," said the Right Hon. as we pushed away from the shore.

"I endeavor to give satisfaction, sir."

The Right Hon. appeared to have said his say for the time being. From that moment he seemed to sort of huddle up and meditate. Dashed absorbed he was. Even when I caught a crab and shot about a pint of water down his neck he didn't seem to notice it.

It was only when we were landing that he came to life again.

"Mr. Wooster."

"Oh, ah?"

"I have been thinking of that matter of which I spoke to you some time back — the problem of how my boat can have got adrift."

I didn't like this.

"The dickens of a problem," I said. "Better not bother about it any more. You'll never solve it."

"On the contrary, I have arrived at a solution, and one which I think is the only feasible solution. I am convinced that my boat was set adrift by the boy Thomas, my hostess's son."

"Oh, I say, no! Why?"

"He had a grudge against me. And it is the sort of thing only a boy, or one who is practically an imbecile, would have thought of doing."

He legged it for the house, and I turned to Jeeves, aghast. Yes, you might say aghast.

"You heard, Jeeves?"

"Yes, sir."

"What's to be done?"

"Perhaps Mr. Filmer, on thinking the matter over, will decide that his suspicions are unjust."

"But they aren't unjust."

"No, sir."

"Then what's to be done?"

"I could not say, sir."

I pushed off rather smartly to the house and reported to Aunt Agatha that the Right Hon. had been salved, and then I toddled upstairs to have a hot bath, being considerably soaked from stem to stern as the result of my rambles. While I was enjoying the grateful warmth, a knock came at the door.

It was Benson, Aunt Agatha's butler.

"Mrs. Gregson desires me to say, sir, that she would be glad to see you as soon as you are ready."

"But she has seen me."

"I gather that she wishes to see you again, sir."

"Oh, right-ho."

I lay beneath the surface for another few minutes; then, having dried the frame, went along the corridor to my room. Jeeves was there, fiddling about with underclothing.

"Oh, Jeeves," I said, "I've just been thinking. Oughtn't somebody to go and give Mr. Filmer a spot of quinine or something? Errand of mercy, what?"

"I have already done so, sir."

"Good. I wouldn't say I like the man frightfully, but I don't want him to get a cold in the head." I shoved on a sock. "Jeeves," I said, "I suppose you know that we've got to think of something pretty quick? I mean to say, you realize the position? Mr. Filmer suspects young Thomas of doing exactly what he did do, and if he brings home the charge Aunt Agatha will undoubtedly fire Mr. Little, and then Mrs. Little will find out what Mr. Little has been up to, and what will be the upshot and outcome, Jeeves? I will tell you. It will mean that Mrs. Little will get the goods on Mr. Little to an extent to which, though only a bachelor myself, I should say that no wife ought to get the goods on her husband if the proper give-and-take of married life — what you might call the essential balance, as it were — is to be preserved. Women bring these things up, Jeeves. They do not forget and forgive."

"Very true, sir."

"Then how about it?"

"I have already attended to the matter, sir."

"You have?"

"Yes, sir. I had scarcely left you when the solution of the affair presented itself to me. It was a remark of Mr. Filmer's that gave me the idea."

"Jeeves, you're a marvel!"

"Thank you very much, sir."

"What was the solution?"

"I conceived the notion of going to Mr. Filmer and saying that it was you who had stolen his boat, sir."

The man flickered before me. I clutched a sock in a feverish grip.

"Saying — what?"

"At first Mr. Filmer was reluctant to credit my statement. But I pointed out to him that you had certainly known that he was on the island — a fact which he agreed was highly significant. I pointed out, furthermore, that you were a light-hearted young gentleman, sir, who might well do such a thing as a practical joke. I left him quite convinced, and there is now no danger of his attributing the action to Master Thomas."

I gazed at the blighter spellbound.

"And that's what you consider a neat solution?" I said.

"Yes, sir. Mr. Little will now retain his position as desired."

"And what about me?"

"You are also benefited, sir."

"Oh, I am, am I?"

"Yes, sir. I have ascertained that Mrs. Gregson's motive in inviting you to this house was that she might present you to Mr. Filmer with a view to your becoming his private secretary."

"What!"

"Yes, sir. Benson, the butler, chanced to overhear Mrs. Gregson in conversation with Mr. Filmer on the matter."

"Secretary to that superfatted bore! Jeeves, I could never have survived it."

"No, sir. I fancy you would not have found it agreeable. Mr. Filmer is scarcely a congenial companion for you. Yet, had Mrs. Gregson secured the position for you, you might have found it embarrassing to decline to accept it."

"Embarrassing is right!"

"Yes, sir."

"But I say, Jeeves, there's just one point which you seem to have overlooked. Where exactly do I get off."

"Sir?"

"I mean to say, Aunt Agatha sent word by Purvis just now that she wanted to see me. Probably she's polishing up her hatchet at this very moment."

"It might be the most judicious plan not to meet her, sir."

"But how can I help it?"

"There is a good, stout water-pipe running down the wall immediately outside this window, sir. And I could have the two-seater waiting outside the park gates in twenty minutes."

I eyed him with reverence.

"Jeeves," I said, "you are always right. You couldn't make it five, could you?"

"Let us say ten, sir."

"Ten it is. Lay out some raiment suitable for travel, and leave the rest to me. Where is this water-pipe of which you speak so highly?"

Open House

❧ Mr. Mulliner put away the letter he had been reading, and beamed contentedly on the little group in the bar-parlor of the Anglers' Rest.

"Most gratifying," he murmured.

"Good news?" we asked.

"Excellent," said Mr. Mulliner. "The letter was from my nephew Eustace, who is attached to our Embassy in Switzerland. He had fully justified the family's hopes."

"Doing well, is he?"

"Capitally," said Mr. Mulliner.

He chuckled reflectively.

"Odd," he said, "now that the young fellow has made so signal a success, to think what a business we had getting him to undertake the job. At one time it seemed as if it would be hopeless to try to persuade him. Indeed, if Fate had not taken a hand . . ."

"Didn't he want to become attached to the Embassy?"

"The idea revolted him. Here was this splendid opening,

dangled before his eyes through the influence of his godfather, Lord Knubble of Knopp, and he stoutly refused to avail himself of it. He wanted to stay in London, he said. He liked London, he insisted, and he jolly well wasn't going to stir from the good old place.

To the rest of his relations (said Mr. Mulliner) this obduracy seemed mere capriciousness. But I, possessing the young fellow's confidence, knew that there were solid reasons behind his decision. In the first place, he knew himself to be the favorite nephew of his Aunt Georgiana, relict of the late Sir Cuthbert Beazley-Beazley, Bart., a woman of advanced years and more than ample means. And, secondly, he had recently fallen in love with a girl of the name of Marcella Tyrrwhitt.

" 'A nice sort of chump I should be, buzzing off to Switzerland,' " he said to me one day when I had been endeavoring to break down his resistance. " 'I've got to stay on the spot, haven't I, to give Aunt Georgiana the old oil from time to time? And if you suppose a fellow can woo a girl like Marcella Tyrrwhitt through the medium of the post, you are vastly mistaken. Something occurred this morning which makes me think she's weakening, and that's just the moment when the personal touch is so essential. Come one, come all, this rock shall fly from its firm base as soon as I,' " said Eustace, who, like so many of the Mulliners, had a strong vein of the poetic in him.

What had occurred that morning, I learned later, was that Marcella Tyrrwhitt had rung my nephew up on the telephone.

"Hullo!" she said. "Is that Eustace?"

"Yes," said Eustace, for it was.

"I say, Eustace," proceeded the girl, "I'm leaving for Paris tomorrow."

"You aren't!" said Eustace.

"Yes, I am, you silly ass," said the girl, "and I've got the tickets to prove it. Listen, Eustace. There's something I want you to do for me. You know my canary?"

"William?"

"William is right. And you know my Peke?"

"Reginald?"

"Reginald is correct. Well, I can't take them with me, because William hates traveling and Reginald would have to go into quarantine for six months when I got back, which would make him froth with fury. So will you give them a couple of beds at your flat while I'm away?"

"Absolutely," said Eustace. "We keep open house, we Mulliners."

"You won't find them any trouble. There's nothing of the athlete about Reginald. A brisk walk of twenty minutes in the park sets him up for the day, as regards exercise. And as for food, give him whatever you're having yourself — raw meat, puppy biscuits, and so on. Don't let him have cocktails. They unsettle him."

"Right-ho," said Eustace. "The scenario seems pretty smooth so far. How about William?"

"*In re* William, he's a bit of an eccentric in the food line. Heaven knows why, but he likes bird-seed and groundsel. Couldn't touch the stuff myself. You get bird-seed at a bird-seed shop."

"And groundsel, no doubt, at the groundseller's?"

"Exactly. And you have to let William out of his cage once or twice a day, so that he can keep his waist-line down by fluttering about the room. He comes back all right as soon as he's had his bath. Do you follow all that?"

"Like a leopard," said Eustace.

"I bet you don't."

"Yes, I do. Brisk walk Reginald. Brisk flutter William."

"You've got it. All right, then. And remember that I set a high value on those two, so guard them with your very life."

"Absolutely," said Eustace. "Rather! You bet. I should say so. Positively."

Ironical, of course, it seems now, in the light of what occurred subsequently, but my nephew told me that that was the happiest moment of his life.

He loved this girl with every fiber of his being, and it seemed to him that, if she selected him out of all her circle for this intensely important trust, it must mean that she regarded him as a man of solid worth and one she could lean on.

"These others," she must have said to herself, running over the roster of her friends. "What are they, after all? Mere butterflies. But Eustace Mulliner — ah, that's different. Good stuff there. A young fellow of character."

He was delighted, also, for another reason. Much as he would miss Marcella Tyrrwhitt, he was glad that she was leaving London for a while, because his love-life at the moment had got into something of a tangle, and her absence would just give him nice time to do a little adjusting and unscrambling.

Until a week or so before he had been deeply in love with another girl — a certain Beatrice Watterson. And then, one night at a studio party, he had met Marcella and had instantly discerned in her an infinitely superior object for his passion.

It is this sort of thing that so complicates life for the young man about town. He is too apt to make his choice before walking the whole length of the counter. He bestows a strong man's love on Girl A and is just congratulating himself when along comes Girl B, whose very existence he had not suspected, and he finds that he has picked the wrong one and has to work like a beaver to make the switch.

What Eustace wanted to do at this point was to taper off with Beatrice, thus clearing the stage and leaving himself free to concentrate his whole soul on Marcella. And Marcella's departure from London would afford him the necessary leisure for the process.

So, by the way of tapering off with Beatrice, he took her to tea the day Marcella left, and at tea Beatrice happened to mention, as girls will, that it would be her birthday next Sunday, and Eustace said: "Oh, I say, really? Come and have a bite of lunch at my flat," and Beatrice said that she would love it, and Eustace said that he must give her something top-hole as a present, and Beatrice said, "Oh, no, really, you mustn't," and Eustace said Yes, dash it, he was resolved. Which started the tapering process nicely, for Eustace knew that on the Sunday he was due down at his Aunt Georgiana's at Wittleford-cum-Bagsley-on-Sea for the week-end, so that when the girl arrived all eager for lunch and found not only that her host was not there but that there was not a birthday present in sight of any description, she would be deeply offended and would become cold and distant and aloof.

Tact, my nephew tells me, is what you need on these occasions. You want to gain the desired end without hurting anybody's feelings. And, no doubt, he is right.

After tea he came back to his flat and took Reginald for a brisk walk and gave William a flutter, and went to bed that night, feeling that God was in His heaven and all right with the world.

The next day was warm and sunny, and it struck Eustace that William would appreciate it if he put his cage out on the window-sill so that he could get the actinic rays into his system. He did this, accordingly, and, having taken Reginald for his saunter, returned to the flat, feeling that he had earned the morning bracer. He instructed Blenkinsop, his man, to bring the materials, and soon peace was reigning in the home to a noticeable extent. William was trilling lustily on the window-sill, Reginald was resting from his exertions under the sofa, and Eustace had begun to sip his whisky-and-soda without a care in the world, when the door opened and Blenkinsop announced a visitor.

"Mr. Orlando Wotherspoon," said Blenkinsop, and withdrew, to go on with the motion-picture magazine which he had been reading in the pantry.

Eustace placed his glass on the table and rose to extend the courtesies in a somewhat puzzled, not to say befogged, state of mind. The name Wotherspoon had struck no chord, and he could not recollect ever having seen the man before in his life.

And Orlando Wotherspoon was not the sort of person who, once seen, is easily forgotten. He was built on large lines, and seemed to fill the room to overflowing. In physique, indeed, he was not unlike what Primo Carnera would have been, if Carnera had not stunted his growth by smoking cigarettes when a boy. He was preceded by a flowing mustache of the outsize soup-strainer kind, and his eyes were of the piercing type which one associates with owls, sergeant-majors, and Scotland Yard inspectors.

Eustace found himself not a little perturbed.

"Oh, hullo!" he said.

Orlando Wotherspoon scrutinized him keenly and, it appeared to Eustace, with hostility. If Eustace had been a rather more than ordinarily unpleasant black beetle this man would have looked at him in much the same fashion. The expression in his eyes was that which comes into the eyes of suburban householders when they survey slugs among their lettuces.

"Mr. Mulliner?" he said.

"I shouldn't wonder," said Eustace, feeling that this might well be so.

"My name is Wotherspoon."

"Yes," said Eustace. "So Blenkinsop was saying, and he's a fellow I've found I can usually rely on."

"I live in the block of flats across the gardens."

"Yes?" said Eustace, still at a loss. "Have a pretty good time?"

"In answer to your question, my life is uniformly tranquil. This morning, however, I saw a sight which shattered my peace of mind and sent the blood racing hotly through my veins."

"Too bad when it's like that," said Eustace. "What made your blood carry on in the manner described?"

"I will tell you, Mr. Mulliner. I was seated in my window a few minutes ago, drafting out some notes for my forthcoming speech at the annual dinner of Our Dumb Chums' League, of which I am perpetual vice-president, when, to my horror, I observed a fiend torturing a helpless bird. For a while I gazed in appalled stupefaction, while my blood ran cold."

"Hot, you said."

"First hot, then cold. I seethed with indignation at this fiend."

"I don't blame you," said Eustace. "If there's one type of chap I bar, it's a fiend. Who was the fellow?"

"Mulliner," said Orlando Wotherspoon, pointing a finger that looked like a plantain or some unusually enlarged banana, "thou art the man!"

"What!"

"Yes," repeated the other, "you! Mulliner, the Bird-Bullier! Mulliner, the Scourge of Our Feathered Friends! What do you mean, you Torquemada, by placing that canary on the window-sill in the full force of the burning sun? How would you feel if some pop-eyed assassin left *you* out in the sun without a hat, to fry where you stood?" He went to the window and hauled the cage in. "It is men like you, Mulliner, who block the wheels of the world's progress and render societies like Our Dumb Chums' League necessary."

"I thought the bally bird enjoyed it," said Eustace feebly.

"Mulliner, you lie!" said Orlando Wotherspoon.

And he looked at Eustace in a way that convinced the latter, who had suspected it from the first, that he had not made a new friend.

"By the way," he said, hoping to ease the strain, "have a spot?"

"I will not have a spot!"

"Right-ho," said Eustace. "No spot. But, coming back to the agenda, you wrong me, Wotherspoon. Foolish, mistaken, I may have been, but, as God is my witness, I meant well. Honestly, I thought William would be tickled pink if I put his cage out in the sun."

"Tchah!" said Orlando Wotherspoon.

And, as he spoke, the dog Reginald, hearing voices, crawled out from under the sofa in the hope that something was going on which might possibly culminate in coffee-sugar.

At the sight of Reginald's honest face, Eustace brightened. A cordial friendship had sprung up between these two based on mutual respect. He extended a hand and chirruped.

Unfortunately, Reginald, suddenly getting a close-up of that mustache and being convinced by the sight of it that plots against his person were toward, uttered a piercing scream and dived back under the sofa, where he remained, calling urgently for assistance.

Orlando Wotherspoon put the worst construction on the incident.

"Ha, Mulliner!" he said. "This is vastly well! Not content

with inflicting fiendish torments on canaries, it would seem that you also slake your inhuman fury on this innocent dog, so that he runs, howling, at the mere sight of you."

Eustace tried to put the thing right.

"I don't think it's the mere sight of me he objects to," he said. "In fact, I've frequently seen him take quite a long, steady look at me without wincing."

"Then to what, pray, do you attribute the animal's visible emotion?"

"Well, the fact is," said Eustace, "I fancy the root of the trouble is that he doesn't much care for that mustache of yours."

His visitor began to roll up his left coat-sleeve in a meditative way.

"Are you venturing, Mulliner, to criticize my mustache?"

"No, no," said Eustace. "I admire it."

"I would be sorry," said Orlando Wotherspoon, "to think that you were aspersing my mustache, Mulliner. My grandmother has often described it as the handsomest in the West End of London. 'Leonine' is the adjective she applies to it. But perhaps you regard my grandmother as prejudiced? Possibly you consider her a foolish old woman whose judgments may be lightly set aside?"

"Absolutely not," said Eustace.

"I am glad," said Wotherspoon. "You would have been the third man I have thrashed within an inch of his life for insulting my grandmother. Or is it," he mused, "the fourth? I could consult my books and let you know."

"Don't bother," said Eustace.

There was a lull in the conversation.

"Well, Mulliner," said Orlando Wotherspoon at length, "I will leave you. But let me tell you this. You have not heard the last of me. You see this?" He produced a note-book. "I keep here a black list of fiends who must be closely watched. Your Christian name, if you please?"

"Eustace."

"Age?"

"Twenty-four."

"Height?"

"Five foot ten."

"Weight?"

"Well," said Eustace, "I was around ten stone eleven when you came in. I think I'm a bit lighter now."

"Let us say ten stone seven. Thank you, Mr. Mulliner. Everything is now in order. You have been entered on the list of suspects on whom I make a practice of paying surprise visits. From now on, you will never know when I may or may not knock upon your door."

"Any time you're passing," said Eustace.

"Our Dumb Chums' League," said Orlando Wotherspoon, putting away his note-book, "is not unreasonable in these matters. We of the organization have instructions to proceed in the matter of fiends with restraint and deliberation. For the first offense, we are content to warn. After that . . . I must remember, when I return home, to post you a copy of our latest booklet. It sets forth in detail what happened to J. B. Stokes, of 9, Manglesbury Mansions, West Kensington, on his ignoring our warning to him to refrain from throwing vegetables at his cat. Good morning, Mr. Mulliner. Do not trouble to see me to the door."

Young men of my nephew Eustace's type are essentially resilient. This interview had taken place on the Thursday. By Friday, at about one o'clock, he had practically forgotten the entire episode. And by noon on Saturday he was his own merry self once more.

It was on this Saturday, as you may remember, that Eustace

was to go down to Wittleford-cum-Bagsley-on-Sea to spend the week-end with his aunt Georgiana.

Wittleford-cum-Bagsley-on-Sea, so I am informed by those who have visited it, is not a Paris or a pre-War Vienna. In fact, once the visitor has strolled along the pier and put pennies in the slot machines, he has shot his bolt as far as the hectic whirl of pleasure, for which the younger generation is so avid, is concerned.

Nevertheless, Eustace found himself quite looking forward to the trip. Apart from the fact that he would be getting himself in solid with a woman who combined the possession of a hundred thousand pounds in Home Rails with a hereditary tendency to rheumatic trouble of the heart, it was pleasant to reflect that in about twenty-four hours from the time he started, the girl Beatrice would have called at the empty flat and gone away in a piqued and raised-eyebrow condition, leaving him free to express his individuality in the matter of the girl Marcella.

He whistled gaily as he watched Blenkinsop pack.

"You have thoroughly grasped the program outlined for the period of my absence, Blenkinsop?" he said.

"Yes, sir."

"Take Master Reginald for the daily stroll."

"Yes, sir."

"See that Master William does his fluttering."

"Yes, sir."

"And don't get them mixed. I mean, don't let Reginald flutter and take William for a walk."

"No, sir."

"Right!" said Eustace. "And on Sunday, Blenkinsop — tomorrow, that is to say — a young lady will be turning up for lunch. Explain to her that I'm not here, and give her anything she wants."

"Very good, sir."

Eustace set out upon his journey with a light heart. Arrived at Wittleford-cum-Bagsley-on-Sea, he passed a restful week-end playing double patience with his aunt, tickling her cat under the left ear from time to time, and walking along the esplanade. On the Monday he caught the one-forty train back to London, his aunt cordial to the last.

"I shall be passing through London on my way to Harrogate next Friday," she said, as he was leaving. "Perhaps you will give me tea?"

"I shall be more than delighted, Aunt Georgiana," said Eustace. "It has often been a great grief to me that you allow me so few opportunities of entertaining you in my little home. At four-thirty next Friday. Right!"

Everything seemed to him to be shaping so satisfactorily that his spirits were at their highest. He sang in the train to quite a considerable extent.

"What-ho, Blenkinsop!" he said, entering the flat in a very nearly rollicking manner. "Everything all right?"

"Yes, sir," said Blenkinsop. "I trust that you have enjoyed an agreeable week-end, sir?"

"Topping," said Eustace. "How are the dumb chums?"

"Master William is in robust health, sir."

"Splendid! And Reginald?"

"Of Master Reginald I cannot speak with the authority of first-hand knowledge, sir, as the young lady removed him yesterday."

Eustace clutched at a chair.

"Removed him?"

"Yes, sir. Took him away. If you recall your parting instructions, sir, you enjoined upon me that I should give the young lady anything she wanted. She selected Master Reginald. She desired me to inform you that she was sorry to have missed you but quite understood that you could not disappoint your aunt, and that, as you insisted on giving her a birthday present, she had taken Master Reginald."

Eustace pulled himself together with a strong effort. He saw that nothing was to be gained by upbraiding the man. Blenkinsop, he realized, had acted according to his lights. He told himself that he should have remembered that his valet was of a literal turn of mind and always carried out instructions to the letter.

"Get her on the 'phone, quick," he said.

"Impossible, I fear, sir. The young lady informed me that she was leaving for Paris by the two o'clock train this afternoon."

"Then, Blenkinsop," said Eustace, "give me a quick one."

"Very good, sir."

The restorative seemed to clear the young man's head.

"Blenkinsop," he said, "give me your attention. Don't let your mind wander. We've got to do some close thinking — some very close thinking."

"Yes, sir."

In simple words Eustace explained the position of affairs. Blenkinsop clicked his tongue. Eustace held up a restraining hand.

"Don't do that, Blenkinsop."

"No, sir."

"At any other moment I should be delighted to listen to you giving your imitation of a man drawing corks out of champagne bottles. But not now. Reserve it for the next party you attend."

"Very good, sir."

Eustace returned to the matter in hand.

"You see the position I am in? We must put our heads together, Blenkinsop. How can I account satisfactorily to Miss Tyrrwhitt for the loss of her dog?"

"Would it not be feasible to inform the young lady that you took the animal for a walk in the park and that it slipped its collar and ran away?"

"Very nearly right, Blenkinsop," said Eustace, "but not quite. What actually happened was that *you* took it for a walk and, like a perfect chump, went and lost it."

"Well, really, sir —"

"Blenkinsop," said Eustace, "if there is one drop of the old feudal spirit in your system, now is the time to show it. Stand by me in this crisis, and you will not be the loser."

"Very good, sir."

"You realize, of course, that when Miss Tyrrwhitt returns it will be necessary for me to curse you pretty freely in her presence, but you must read between the lines and take it all in a spirit of pure badinage."

"Very good, sir."

"Right-ho, then, Blenkinsop. Oh, by the way, my aunt will be coming to tea on Friday."

"Very good, sir."

These preliminaries settled, Eustace proceeded to pave the way. He wrote a long and well-phrased letter to Marcella, telling her that, as he was unfortunately confined to the house with one of his bronchial colds, he had been compelled to depute the walk-in-the-park-taking of Reginald to his man Blenkinsop, in whom he had every confidence. He went on to say that Reginald, thanks to his assiduous love and care, was in the enjoyment of excellent health and that he would always look back with wistful pleasure to the memory of their long, cozy evenings together. He drew a picture of Reginald and himself sitting side by side in silent communion — he deep in

some good book, Reginald meditating on this and that —
which almost brought the tears to his eyes.

Nevertheless, he was far from feeling easy in his mind.
Women, he knew, in moments of mental stress are always apt
to spray the blame a good deal. And, while Blenkinsop would
presumably get the main stream, there might well be a few
drops left over which would come in his direction.

For, if this girl Marcella Tyrrwhitt had a defect, it was that
the generous warmth of her womanly nature led her now and
then to go off the deep end somewhat heartily. She was one
of those tall, dark girls with flashing eyes who tend to a certain
extent, in times of stress, to draw themselves to their full
height and let their male *vis-à-vis* have it squarely in the neck.
Time had done much to heal the wound, but he could still
recall some of the things she had said to him the night when
they had arrived late at the theater, to discover that he had left
the tickets on his sitting-room mantelpiece. In two minutes
any competent biographer would have been able to gather ma-
terial for a complete character-sketch. He had found out more
about himself in that one brief interview than in all the rest of
his life.

Naturally, therefore, he brooded a good deal during the
next few days. His friends were annoyed at this period by his
absent-mindedness. He developed a habit of saying "What?"
with a glazed look in his eyes and then sinking back and drain-
ing his glass, all of which made him something of a dead
weight in general conversation.

You would see him sitting hunched up in a corner with his
jaw drooping, and a very unpleasant spectacle it was. His fellow members began to complain about it. They said the taxi-
dermist had no right to leave him lying about the club after
removing his insides, but ought to buckle to and finish stuffing
him and make a job of it.

He was sitting like this one afternoon when suddenly, as he raised his eyes to see if there was a waiter handy, he caught sight of the card on the wall which bore upon it the date and the day of the week. And the next moment a couple of fellow-members who had thought he was dead and were just going to ring to have him swept away were stunned to observe him leap to his feet and run swiftly from the room.

He had just discovered that it was Friday, the day his Aunt Georgiana was coming to tea at his flat. And he only had about three and a half minutes before the kick-off.

A speedy cab took him quickly home, and he was relieved, on entering the flat, to find that his aunt was not there. The tea-table had been set out, but the room was empty except for William, who was trying over a song in his cage. Greatly relieved, Eustace went to the cage and unhooked the door, and William, after jumping up and down for a few moments in the eccentric way canaries do, hopped out and started to flutter to and fro.

It was at this moment that Blenkinsop came in with a well-laden plate.

"Cucumber sandwiches, sir," said Blenkinsop. "Ladies are usually strongly addicted to them."

Eustace nodded. The man's instinct had not led him astray. His aunt was passionately addicted to cucumber sandwiches. Many a time he had seen her fling herself on them like a starving wolf.

"Her ladyship not arrived?" he said.

"Yes, sir. She stepped down the street to dispatch a telegram. Would you desire me to serve cream, sir, or will the ordinary milk suffice?"

"Cream? Milk?"

"I have laid out an extra saucer."

"Blenkinsop," said Eustace, passing a rather feverish hand

across his brow, for he had much to disturb him these days. "You appear to be talking of something, but it does not penetrate. What is all this babble of milk and cream? Why do you speak in riddles of extra saucers?"

"For the cat, sir."

"What cat?"

"Her ladyship was accompanied by her cat, Francis."

The strained look passed from Eustace's face.

"Oh? Her cat?"

"Yes, sir."

"Well, in regard to nourishment, it gets milk — the same as the rest of us — and likes it. But serve it in the kitchen, because of the canary."

"Master Francis is not in the kitchen, sir."

"Well, in the pantry or my bedroom or wherever he is."

"When last I saw Master Francis, sir, he was enjoying a cooling stroll on the windowsill."

And at this juncture there silhouetted itself against the evening sky a lissome form.

"Here! Hi! My gosh! I say! Dash it!" exclaimed Eustace, eyeing it with unconcealed apprehension.

"Yes, sir," said Blenkinsop. "Excuse me, sir. I fancy I heard the front-door bell."

And he withdrew, leaving Eustace a prey to the liveliest agitation.

Eustace, you see, was still hoping, in spite of having been so remiss in the matter of the dog, to save his stake, if I may use the expression, on the canary. In other words, when Marcella Tyrrwhitt returned and began to be incisive on the subject of the vanished Reginald, he wished to be in a position to say "True! True! In the matter of Reginald, I grant that I have failed you. But pause before you speak and take a look at that canary — fit as a fiddle and bursting with health. Any why? Because of my unremitting care."

A most unpleasant position he would be in if, in addition to having to admit that he was one Peke down on the general score, he also had to reveal that William, his sheet-anchor, was inextricably mixed up with the gastric juices of a cat which the girl did not even know by sight.

And that this tragedy was imminent he was sickeningly aware from the expression on the animal's face. It was a sort of devout, ecstatic look. He had observed much the same kind of look on the face of his Aunt Georgiana when about to sail into the cucumber sandwiches. Francis was inside the room now, and was gazing up at the canary with a steady, purposeful eye. His tail was twitching at the tip.

The next moment, to the accompaniment of a moan of horror from Eustace, he had launched himself into the air in the bird's direction.

Well, William was no fool. Where many a canary would have blenched, he retained his *sang-froid* unimpaired. He moved a little to the left, causing the cat to miss by a foot. And his beak, as he did so, was curved in a derisive smile. In fact, thinking it over later, Eustace realized that right from the beginning William had the situation absolutely under control and wanted nothing but to be left alone to enjoy a good laugh.

At the moment, however, this did not occur to Eustace. Shaken to the core, he supposed the bird to be in the gravest peril. He imagined it to stand in need of all the aid and comfort he could supply. And springing quickly to the tea-table, he rummaged among its contents for something that would serve him as ammunition in the fray.

The first thing he put his hand on was the plate of cucumber sandwiches. These, with all the rapidity at his command, he discharged, one after the other. But, though a few found their mark, there was nothing in the way of substantial results. The very nature of a cucumber sandwich makes it poor throwing. He could have obtained direct hits on Francis all day without slowing him up. In fact, the very moment after the last sandwich had struck him in the ribs, he was up in the air again, clawing hopefully.

William side-stepped once more, and Francis returned to earth. And Eustace, emotion ruining his aim, missed him by inches with a sultana cake, three muffins, and a lump of sugar.

Then, desperate, he did what he should, of course, have done at the very outset. Grabbing the table-cloth, he edged round with extraordinary stealth till he was in the cat's immediate rear, and dropped it over him just as he was tensing his muscles for another leap. Then, flinging himself on the mixture of cat and table-cloth, he wound them up into a single convenient parcel.

Exceedingly pleased with himself Eustace felt at this point. It seemed to him that he had shown resource, intelligence, and an agility highly creditable in one who had not played Rugby football for years. A good deal of bitter criticism was filtering through the cloth, but he overlooked it. Francis, he knew when he came to think the thing over calmly, would realize that he deserved all he was getting. He had always found Francis a fair-minded cat, when the cold sobriety of his judgment was not warped by the sight of canaries.

He was about to murmur a word or two to this effect, in the hope of inducing the animal to behave less like a gyroscope, when, looking round, he perceived that he was not alone.

Standing grouped about the doorway were his Aunt Georgiana, the girl Marcella Tyrrwhitt, and the well-remembered figure of Orlando Wotherspoon.

"Lady Beazley-Beazley, Miss Tyrrwhitt, Mr. Orlando Wotherspoon," announced Blenkinsop. "Tea is served, sir."

A wordless cry broke from Eustace's lips. The table-cloth fell from his nerveless fingers. And the cat, Francis, falling on his head on the carpet, shot straight up the side of the wall and entrenched himself on top of the curtains.

There was a pause. Eustace did not know quite what to say. He felt embarrassed.

It was Orlando Wotherspoon who broke the silence.

"So!" said Orlando Wotherspoon. "At your old games, Mulliner, I perceive."

Eustace's Aunt Georgiana was pointing dramatically.

"He threw cucumber sandwiches at my cat!"

"So I observe," said Wotherspoon. He spoke in an unpleasant, quiet voice, and he was looking not unlike a high priest of one of the rougher religions who runs his eye over the human sacrifice preparatory to asking his caddy for the niblick. "Also, if I mistake not, sultana cake and muffins."

"Would you require fresh muffins, sir?" asked Blenkinsop.

"The case, in short, would appear to be on all fours," proceeded Wotherspoon, "with that of J. B. Stokes, of 9, Manglesbury Mansions, West Kensington."

"Listen!" said Eustace, backing towards the window. "I can explain everything."

"There is no need of explanations, Mulliner," said Orlando Wotherspoon. He had rolled up the left sleeve of his coat and was beginning to roll up the right. He twitched his biceps to limber it up. "The matter explains itself."

Eustace's Aunt Georgiana, who had been standing under the curtain making chirruping noises, came back to the group in no agreeable frame of mind. Overwrought by what had occurred, Francis had cut her dead, and she was feeling it a good deal.

"If I may use your telephone, Eustace," she said quietly, "I would like to ring up my lawyer and disinherit you. But first," she added to Wotherspoon, who was now inhaling and expelling the breath from his nostrils in rather a disturbing manner, "would you oblige me by thrashing him within an inch of his life?"

"I was about to do so, madam," replied Wotherspoon courteously. "If this young lady will kindly stand a little to one side —"

"Shall I prepare some more cucumber sandwiches, sir?" asked Blenkinsop.

"Wait!" cried Marcella Tyrrwhitt, who hitherto had not spoken.

Orlando Wotherspoon shook his head gently.

"If, deprecating scenes of violence, it is your intention, Miss Tyrrwhitt — Any relation of my old friend Major-General George Tyrrwhitt of the Buffs, by the way?"

"My uncle."

"Well, well! I was dining with him only last night."

"It's a small world, after all," said Lady Beazley-Beazley.

"It is, indeed," said Orlando Wotherspoon. "So small that I feel there is scarcely room in it for both Mulliner the Cat-Slosher and myself. I shall therefore do my humble best to eliminate him. And, as I was about to say, if, deprecating scenes of violence, you were about to plead for the young man, it will, I fear, be useless. I can listen to no intercession. The regulations of Our Dumb Chums' League are very strict."

Marcella Tyrrwhitt uttered a hard, rasping laugh.

"Intercession?" she said. "What do you mean? — intercession? I wasn't going to intercede for this wambling misfit. I was going to ask if I could have first whack."

"Indeed? Might I inquire why?"

Marcella's eyes flashed. Eustace became convinced, he tells me, that she had Spanish blood in her.

"Would you desire another sultana cake, sir?" asked Blenkinsop.

"I'll tell you why," cried Marcella. "Do you know what this man has done? I left my dog, Reginald, in his care, and he swore to guard and cherish him. And what occurred? My back was hardly turned when he went and gave him away as a birthday present to some foul female of the name of Beatrice Something."

Eustace uttered a strangled cry. "Let me explain!"

"I was in Paris," proceeded Marcella, "walking along the Champs-Élysées, and I saw a girl coming towards me with a Peke, and I said to myself: 'Hello, that Peke looks extraordinarily like my Reginald,' and then she came up and it was Reginald, and I said: 'Here! Hey! What are you doing with my Peke Reginald?' and this girl said: 'What do you mean, your Peke Reginald? It's my Peke Percival, and it was given to me as a birthday present by a friend of mine named Eustace Mulliner.' And I bounded on to the next aeroplane and came over here to tear him into little shreds. And what I say is, it's a shame if I'm not to be allowed a go at him after all the trouble and expense I've been put to."

And burying her lovely face in her hands, she broke into uncontrollable sobs.

Orlando Wotherspoon looked at Lady Beazley-Beazley. Lady Beazley-Beazley looked at Orlando Wotherspoon. There was pity in their eyes.

"There, there!" said Lady Beazley-Beazley. "There, there, there, my dear!"

"Believe me, Miss Tyrrwhitt," said Orlando Wotherspoon, patting her shoulder paternally, "there are few things I would not do for the niece of my old friend Major-General George Tyrrwhitt of the Buffs, but this is an occasion when, much as it may distress me, I must be firm. I shall have to make my report at the annual committee-meeting of Our Dumb Chums' League, and how would I look, explaining that I had stepped aside and allowed a delicately nurtured girl to act for me in a matter so important as the one now on the agenda? Consider, Miss Tyrrwhitt! Reflect!"

"That's all very well," sobbed Marcella, "but all the way over, all during those long, weary hours in the aeroplane, I was buoying myself up with the thought of what I was going to do to Eustace Mulliner when we met. See! I picked out my heaviest parasol."

Orlando Wotherspoon eyed the dainty weapon with an indulgent smile.

"I fear that would hardly meet such a case as this," he said. "You had far better leave the conduct of this affair to me."

"Did you say more muffins, sir?" asked Blenkinsop.

"I do not wish to boast," said Wotherspoon, "but I have had considerable experience. I have been formally thanked by my committee on several occasions."

"So you see, dear," said Lady Beazley-Beazley, soothingly, "it will be ever so much better to —"

"Any buttered toast, fancy cakes, or macaroons?" asked Blenkinsop.

"— leave the matter entirely in Mr. Wotherspoon's hands. I know just how you feel. I am feeling the same myself. But even in these modern days, my dear, it is the woman's part to efface herself and —"

"Oh, well!" said Marcella moodily.

Lady Beazley-Beazley folded her in her arms and over her shoulder nodded brightly at Orlando Wotherspoon.

"Please go on, Mr. Wotherspoon," she said.

Wotherspoon bowed, with a formal word of thanks. And, turning, was just in time to see Eustace disappearing through the window.

The fact is, as this dialogue progressed, Eustace had found himself more and more attracted by that open window. It had seemed to beckon to him. And at this juncture, dodging lightly round Blenkinsop, who had now lost his grip entirely and was suggesting things like watercress and fruit-salad, he precipitated himself into the depths and, making a good landing, raced for the open spaces at an excellent rate of speed.

That night, heavily cloaked and disguised in a false mustache, he called at my address, clamoring for tickets to Switzerland. He arrived there some few days later, and ever since has stuck to his duties with unremitting energy.

So much so that, in that letter which you saw me reading, he informs me that he had just been awarded the Order of the Crimson Edelweiss, Third Class, with crossed cuckoo-clocks, carrying with it the right to yodel in the presence of the Vice-President. A great honor for so young a man.

Ukridge's Dog College

❧ "LADDIE," said Stanley Featherstonehaugh Ukridge, that much-enduring man, helping himself to my tobacco and slipping the pouch absently into his pocket, "listen to me, you son of Belial."

"What?" I said, retrieving the pouch.

"Do you want to make an enormous fortune?"

"I do."

"Then write my biography. Bung it down on paper, and we'll split the proceeds. I've been making a pretty close study of your stuff lately, old horse, and it's all wrong. The trouble with you is that you don't plumb the wellsprings of human nature and all that. You just think up some rotten yarn about some-dam-thing-or-other and shove it down. Now if you tackled my life, you'd have something worth writing about. Pots of money in it, my boy — English serial rights and American serial rights and book rights, and dramatic rights and movie rights — well, you can take it from me that, at a conservative estimate, we should clean up at least fifty thousand pounds apiece."

"As much as that?"

"Fully that. And listen, laddie, I'll tell you what. You're a good chap and we've been pals for years, so I'll let you have my share of the English serial rights for a hundred pounds down."

"What makes you think I've got a hundred pounds?"

"Well, then, I'll make it my share of the English *and* American serial rights for fifty."

"You collar's come off its stud."

"How about my complete share of the whole dashed outfit for twenty-five?"

"Not for me, thanks."

"Then I'll tell you what, old horse," said Ukridge, inspired. "Just lend me half a crown to be going on with."

If the leading incidents of S. F. Ukridge's disreputable career are to be given to the public — and not, as some might suggest, decently hushed up — I suppose I am the man to write them. Ukridge and I have been intimate since the days of school. Together we sported on the green, and when he was expelled no one missed him more than I. An unfortunate business, this expulsion. Ukridge's generous spirit, ever ill-attuned to school rules, caused him eventually to break the solemnest of them all by sneaking out at night to try his skill at the co-conut-shies of the local village fair; and his foresight in putting on scarlet whiskers and a false nose for the expedition was completely neutralized by the fact that he absent-mindedly wore his school cap throughout the entire proceedings. He left the next morning, regretted by all.

After this there was a hiatus of some years in our friendship.

I was at Cambridge, absorbing culture, and Ukridge, as far as I could gather from his rare letters and the reports of mutual acquaintances, was flitting about the world like a snipe. Somebody met him in New York, just off a cattle ship. Somebody else saw him in Buenos Aires. Somebody, again, spoke sadly of having been pounced on by him at Monte Carlo and touched for a fiver. It was not until I settled down in London that he came back into my life. We met in Piccadilly one day, and resumed our relations where they had been broken off. Old associations are strong, and the fact that he was about my build and so could wear my socks and shirts drew us very close together.

Then he disappeared again, and it was a month or more before I got news of him.

It was George Tupper who brought the news. George was head of the school in my last year, and he has fulfilled exactly the impeccable promise of those early days. He is in the Foreign Office, doing well and much respected. He has an earnest, pulpy heart and takes other people's troubles very seriously. Often he had mourned to me like a father over Ukridge's erratic progress through life, and now, as he spoke, he seemed to be filled with a solemn joy, as over a reformed prodigal.

"Have you heard about Ukridge?" said George Tupper. "He has settled down at last. Gone to live with an aunt of his who owns one of those big houses on Wimbledon Common. A very rich woman. I am delighted. It will be the making of the old chap."

I suppose he was right in a way, but to me this tame subsidence into companionship with a rich aunt in Wimbledon seemed somehow an indecent, almost a tragic, end to a colorful career like that of S. F. Ukridge. And when I met the man a week later my heart grew heavier still.

It was in Oxford Street at the hour when women come up

from the suburbs to shop, and he was standing among the dogs and commissionaires outside Selfridge's. His arms were full of parcels, his face was set in a mask of wan discomfort, and he was so beautifully dressed that for an instant I did not recognize him. Everything which the Correct Man wears was assembled on his person, from the silk hat to the patent-leather boots, and, as he confided to me in the first minute, he was suffering the tortures of the damned. The boots pinched him, the hat hurt his forehead, and the collar was worse than the hat and boots combined.

"She makes me wear them," he said, moodily, jerking his head towards the interior of the store and uttering a sharp howl as the movement caused the collar to gouge his neck.

"Still," I said, trying to turn his mind to happier things, "you must be having a great time. George Tupper tells me that your aunt is rich. I suppose you're living off the fat of the land."

"The browsing and sluicing are good," admitted Ukridge. "But it's a wearing life, laddie. A wearing life, old horse."

"Why don't you come and see me sometimes?"

"I'm not allowed out at night."

"Well, shall I come and see you?"

A look of poignant alarm shot out from under the silk hat.

"Don't dream of it, laddie," said Ukridge, earnestly. "Don't dream of it. You're a good chap — my best pal and all that sort of thing — but the fact is, my standing in the home's none too solid even now, and one sight of you would knock my prestige into hash. Aunt Julia would think you worldly."

"I'm not worldly."

"Well, you look worldly. You wear a squash hat and a soft collar. If you don't mind my suggesting it, old horse, I think, if I were you, I'd pop off now before she comes out. Good-bye, laddie."

"Ichabod!" I murmured sadly to myself as I passed on down Oxford Street. "Ichabod!"

I should have had more faith. I should have known my Ukridge better. I should have realized that a London suburb could no more imprison that great man permanently than Elba did Napoleon.

One afternoon, as I let myself into the house in Ebury Street of which I rented at that time the bedroom and sitting-room on the first floor, I came upon Bowles, my landlord, standing in listening attitude at the foot of the stairs.

"Good afternoon, sir," said Bowles. "A gentleman is waiting to see you. I fancy I heard him calling me a moment ago."

"Who is he?"

"A Mr. Ukridge, sir. He —"

A vast voice boomed out from above.

"Bowles, old horse!"

Bowles, like all other proprietors of furnished apartments in the south-western district of London, was an ex-butler, and about him, as about all ex-butlers, there clung like a garment an aura of dignified superiority which had never failed to crush my spirit. He was a man of portly aspect, with a bald head and prominent eyes of a lightish green — eyes that seemed to weigh me dispassionately and find me wanting. "Hm!" they seemed to say. "Young — very young. And not at all what I have been accustomed to in the best places." To hear this dignitary addressed — and in a shout at that — as "old horse" affected me with much the same sense of imminent chaos as would afflict a devout young curate if he saw his bishop slapped on the back. The shock, therefore, when he responded not merely mildly but with what almost amounted to camaraderie was numbing.

"Sir?" cooed Bowles.

"Bring me six bones and a corkscrew."

"Very good, sir."

Bowles retired, and I bounded upstairs and flung open the door of my sitting-room.

"Great Scott!" I said, blankly.

The place was a sea of Pekingese dogs. Later investigation reduced their numbers to six, but in that first moment there seemed to be hundreds. Goggling eyes met mine wherever I looked. The room was a forest of waving tails. With his back against the mantelpiece, smoking placidly, stood Ukridge.

"Hallo, laddie!" he said, with a genial wave of the hand, as if to make me free of the place. "You're just in time. I've got to dash off and catch a train in a quarter of an hour. Stop it, you mutts!" he bellowed, and the six Pekingese, who had been barking steadily since my arrival, stopped in mid-yap, and were still. Ukridge's personality seemed to exercise a magnetism over the animal kingdom, from ex-butlers to Pekes, which bordered on the uncanny. "I'm off to Sheep's Cray, in Kent. Taken a cottage there."

"Are you going to live there?"

"Yes."

"But what about your aunt?"

"Oh, I've left her. Life is stern and life is earnest, and if I mean to make a fortune I've got to bustle about and not stay cooped up in a place like Wimbledon."

"Something in that."

"Besides which, she told me the very sight of me made her sick and she never wanted to see me again."

I might have guessed, directly I saw him, that some upheaval had taken place. The sumptuous raiment which had made him such a treat to the eye at our last meeting was gone, and he was back in his pre-Wimbledon costume, which was, as the advertisements say, distinctively individual. Over gray flannel trousers, a golf coat and a brown sweater he wore like a royal robe a bright yellow mackintosh. His collar had broken free from its stud and showed a couple of inches of bare neck. His hair was disordered, and his masterful nose was topped by a pair of steel-rimmed pince-nez cunningly attached to his flapping ears with ginger-beer wire. His whole appearance spelled revolt.

Bowles manifested himself with a plateful of bones.

"That's right. Chuck 'em down on the floor."

"Very good, sir."

"I like that fellow," said Ukridge, as the door closed. "We had a dashed interesting talk before you came in. Did you know he had a cousin on the music-halls?"

"He hasn't confided in me much."

"He's promised me an introduction to him later on. May be useful to be in touch with a man who knows the ropes. You see, laddie, I've hit on the most amazing scheme." He swept his arm round dramatically, overturning a plaster cast of the Infant Samuel at Prayer. "All right, all right, you can mend it with glue or something, and, anyway, you're probably better without it. Yessir, I've hit on a great scheme. The idea of a thousand years."

"What's that?"

"I'm going to train dogs."

"Train dogs?"

"For the music-hall stage. Dog acts, you know. Performing dogs. Pots of money in it. I start in a modest way with these six. When I've taught 'em a few tricks, I sell them to a fellow in the profession for a large sum and buy twelve more. I train those, sell 'em for a large sum, and with the money buy twenty-four more. I train those —"

"Here, wait a minute." My head was beginning to swim. I had a vision of England paved with Pekingese dogs, all doing tricks. "How do you know you'll be able to sell them?"

"Of course I shall. The demand's enormous. Supply can't cope with it. At a conservative estimate I should think I ought to scoop in four or five thousand pounds the first year. That, of course, is before the business really starts to expand."

"I see."

"When I get going properly, with a dozen assistants under me and an organized establishment, I shall begin to touch the big money. What I'm aiming at is a sort of Dogs' College out in the country somewhere. Big place with a lot of ground. Regular classes and a set curriculum. Large staff, each member of it with so many dogs under his care, me looking on and superintending. Why, once the thing starts moving it'll run itself, and all I shall have to do will be to sit back and endorse the checks. It isn't as if I would have to confine my operations to England. The demand for performing dogs is universal throughout the civilized world. America wants performing dogs. Australia wants performing dogs. Africa could do with a few, I've no doubt. My aim, laddie, is gradually to get a monopoly of the trade. I want everybody who needs a performing dog of any description to come automatically to me. And I'll tell you what, laddie. If you'd like to put up a bit of capital, I'll let you in on the ground floor."

"No, thanks."

"All right. Have it your own way. Only don't forget that there was a fellow who put nine hundred dollars into the Ford Car business when it was starting and he collected a cool forty million. I say, is that clock right? Great Scott! I'll be missing my train. Help me mobilize these dashed animals."

Five minutes later, accompanied by the six Pekingese and bearing about him a pound of my tobacco, three pairs of my socks, and the remains of a bottle of whisky, Ukridge departed in a taxi-cab for Charing Cross Station to begin his life-work.

Perhaps six weeks passed, six quiet Ukridgeless weeks, and

then one morning I received an agitated telegram. Indeed, it was not so much a telegram as a cry of anguish. In every word of it there breathed the tortured spirit of a great man who has battled in vain against overwhelming odds. It was the sort of telegram which Job might have sent off after a lengthy session with Bildad the Shuhite: —

COME HERE IMMEDIATELY, LADDIE. LIFE AND DEATH MAT-
TER, OLD HORSE. DESPERATE SITUATION. DON'T FAIL ME.

It stirred me like a bugle. I caught the next train.

The White Cottage, Sheep's Cray — destined, presumably, to become in future years a historic spot and a Mecca for dog-loving pilgrims — was a small and battered building standing near the main road to London at some distance from the village. I found it without difficulty, for Ukridge seemed to have achieved a certain celebrity in the neighborhood; but to effect an entry was a harder task. I rapped for a full minute without result, then shouted, and I was about to conclude that Ukridge was not at home when the door suddenly opened. As I was just giving a final bang at the moment, I entered the house in a manner reminiscent of one of the Ballet Russe practicing a new and difficult step.

"Sorry, old horse," said Ukridge. "Wouldn't have kept you waiting if I'd known who it was. Thought you were Gooch, the grocer — goods supplied to the value of six pounds three and a penny."

"I see."

"He keeps hounding me for his beastly money," said Ukridge, bitterly, as he led the way into the sitting-room. "It's a little hard. Upon my Sam, it's a little hard. I come down here to inaugurate a vast business and do the natives a bit of good by establishing a growing industry in their midst, and the first thing you know they turn round and bite the hand that was going to feed them. I've been hampered and rattled by these blood-suckers ever since I got here. A little trust, a little sympathy, a little of the good old give-and-take spirit — that was all I asked. And what happened? They wanted a bit on account! Kept bothering me for a bit on account, I'll trouble you, just when I needed all my thoughts and all my energy and every ounce of concentration at my command for my extraordinarily difficult and delicate work. *I* couldn't give them a bit on account. Later on, if they had only exercised reasonable patience, I would no doubt have been in a position to settle their infernal bills fifty times over. But the time was not ripe. I reasoned with the men. I said, 'Here am I, a busy man, trying hard to educate six Pekingese dogs for the music-hall stage, and you come distracting my attention and impairing my efficiency by babbling about a bit on account. It isn't the pull-together spirit,' I said. 'It isn't the spirit that wins to wealth. These narrow petty-cash ideas can never make for success.' But no, they couldn't see it. They started calling here at all hours and waylaying me in the public highways till life became an absolute curse. And now what do you think has happened?"

"What?"

"The dogs."

"Got distemper?"

"No. Worse. My landlord's pinched them as security for his infernal rent! Sneaked the stock. Tied up the assets. Crippled the business at the very outset. Have you ever in your life heard of anything so dastardly? I know I agreed to pay the damned rent weekly and I'm about six weeks behind, but, my gosh! surely a man with a huge enterprise on his hands isn't supposed to have to worry about these trifles when he's occupied with the most delicate — Well, I put all that to old Nickerson, but a fat lot of good it did. So then I wired to you."

"Ah!" I said, and there was a brief and pregnant pause.

"I thought," said Ukridge, meditatively, "that you might be able to suggest somebody I could touch."

He spoke in a detached and almost casual way, but his eye was gleaming at me significantly, and I avoided it with a sense of guilt. My finances at the moment were in their customary unsettled condition — rather more so, in fact, than usual, owing to unsatisfactory speculations at Kempton Park on the previous Saturday; and it seemed to me that, if ever there was a time for passing the buck, this was it. I mused tensely. It was an occasion for quick thinking.

"George Tupper!" I cried, on the crest of a brain-wave.

"George Tupper?" echoed Ukridge, radiantly, his gloom melting like fog before the sun. "The very man, by gad! It's a most amazing thing, but I never thought of him. George Tupper, of course! Bighearted George, the old school chum. He'll do it like a shot and won't miss the money. These Foreign Office blokes have always got a spare tenner or two tucked away in the old sock. They pinch it out of the public funds. Rush back to town, laddie, with all speed, get hold of Tuppy, lush him up, and bite his ear for twenty quid. Now is the time for all good men to come to the aid of the party."

I had been convinced that George Tupper would not fail us, nor did he. He parted without a murmur — even with enthusiasm. The consignment was one that might have been made to order for him. As a boy, George used to write sentimental poetry for the school magazine, and now he is the sort of man who is always starting subscription lists and getting up memorials and presentations. He listened to my story with the serious official air which these Foreign Office fellows put on

when they are deciding whether to declare war on Switzerland
or send a firm note to San Marino, and was reaching for
his check-book before I had been speaking two minutes.
Ukridge's sad case seemed to move him deeply.

"Too bad," said George. "So he is training dogs, is he? Well,
it seems very unfair that if he has at last settled down to real
work, he should be hampered by financial difficulties at the
outset. We ought to do something practical for him. After
all, a loan of twenty pounds cannot relieve the situation
permanently."

"I think you're a bit optimistic if you're looking on it as a
loan."

"What Ukridge needs is capital."

"He thinks that, too. So does Gooch, the grocer."

"Capital," repeated George Tupper, firmly, as if he were reasoning with the plenipotentiary of some Great Power. "Every
venture requires capital at first." He frowned thoughtfully.
"Where can we obtain capital for Ukridge?"

"Rob a bank."

George Tupper's face cleared.

"I have it!" he said. "I will go straight over to Wimbledon
tonight and approach his aunt."

"Aren't you forgetting that Ukridge is about as popular
with her as a cold Welsh rabbit?"

"There may be a temporary estrangement, but if I tell her
the facts and impress upon her that Ukridge is really making
a genuine effort to earn a living —"

"Well, try it if you like. But she will probably set the parrot
on to you."

"It will have to be done diplomatically, of course. It might
be as well if you did not tell Ukridge what I propose to do. I
do not wish to arouse hopes which may not be fulfilled."

A blaze of yellow on the platform of Sheep's Cray Station

next morning informed me that Ukridge had come to meet my train. The sun poured down from a cloudless sky, but it took more than sunshine to make Stanley Featherstonehaugh Ukridge discard his mackintosh. He looked like an animated blob of mustard.

When the train rolled in, he was standing in solitary grandeur trying to light his pipe, but as I got out I perceived that he had been joined by a sad-looking man, who, from the rapid and earnest manner in which he talked and the vehemence of his gesticulations, appeared to be ventilating some theme on which he felt deeply. Ukridge was looking warm and harassed, and as I approached, I could hear his voice booming in reply.

"My dear sir, my dear old horse, do be reasonable, do try to cultivate the big, broad flexible outlook —"

He saw me and broke away — not unwillingly — and, gripping my arm, drew me off along the platform. The sad-looking man followed irresolutely.

"Have you got the stuff, laddie?" inquired Ukridge, in a tense whisper. "Have you got it?"

"Yes, here it is."

"Put it back, put it back!" moaned Ukridge in agony, as I felt in my pocket. "Do you know who that was I was talking to? Gooch, the grocer!"

"Goods supplied to the value of six pounds three and a penny?"

"Absolutely!"

"Well, now's your chance. Fling him a purse of gold. That'll make him look silly."

"My dear old horse, I can't afford to go about the place squandering my cash simply in order to make grocers look silly. That money is earmarked for Nickerson, my landlord."

"Oh! I say, I think the six-pounds-three-and-a-penny bird is following us."

"Then for goodness' sake, laddie, let's get a move on! If that man knew we had twenty quid on us, our lives wouldn't be safe. He'd make one spring."

He hurried me out of the station and led the way up a shady lane that wound off through the fields, slinking furtively "like one that on a lonesome road doth walk in fear and dread, and having once looked back walks on and turns no more his head, because he knows a frightful fiend doth close behind him tread." As a matter of fact, the frightful fiend had given up the pursuit after the first few steps, and a moment later I drew this fact to Ukridge's attention, for it was not the sort of day on which to break walking records unnecessarily.

He halted, relieved, and mopped his spacious brow with a handkerchief which I recognized as having once been my property.

"Thank goodness we've shaken him off," he said. "Not a bad chap in his way, I believe — a good husband and father, I'm told, and sings in the church choir. But no vision. That's what he lacks, old horse — vision. He can't understand that all vast industrial enterprises have been built up on a system of liberal and cheerful credit. Won't realize that credit is the life-blood of commerce. Without credit commerce has no elasticity. And if commerce has no elasticity, what dam' good is it?"

"I don't know."

"Nor does anybody else. Well, now that he's gone, you can give me that money. Did old Tuppy cough up cheerfully?"

"Blithely."

"I knew it," said Ukridge, deeply moved, "I knew it. A good fellow. One of the best. I've always liked Tuppy. A man you can rely on. Some day, when I get going on a big scale, he shall have this back a thousandfold. I'm glad you brought small notes."

"Why?"

"I want to scatter 'em about on the table in front of this Nickerson blighter."

"Is this where he lives?"

We had come to a red-roofed house, set back from the road amidst trees. Ukridge wielded the knocker forcefully.

"Tell Mr. Nickerson," he said to the maid, "that Mr. Ukridge has called and would like a word."

About the demeanor of the man who presently entered the room into which we had been shown there was that subtle but well-marked something which stamps your creditor all the world over. Mr. Nickerson was a man of medium height, almost completely surrounded by whiskers, and through the shrubbery he gazed at Ukridge with frozen eyes, shooting out waves of deleterious animal magnetism. You could see at a glance that he was not fond of Ukridge. Take him for all in all, Mr. Nickerson looked like one of the less amiable prophets of the Old Testament about to interview the captive monarch of the Amalekites.

"Well?" he said, and I have never heard the word spoken in a more forbidding manner.

"I've come about the rent."

"Ah!" said Mr. Nickerson, guardedly.

"To pay it," said Ukridge.

"To pay it!" ejaculated Mr. Nickerson, incredulously.

"Here!" said Ukridge, and with a superb gesture flung money on the table.

I understand now why the massive-minded man had wanted small notes. They made a brave display. There was a light breeze blowing in through the open window, and so musical a rustling did it set up as it played about the heaped-up wealth that Mr. Nickerson's austerity seemed to vanish like breath off a razor-blade. For a moment a dazed look came into his eyes and he swayed slightly; then, as he started to gather up the money, he took on the benevolent air of a bishop blessing pilgrims. As far as Mr. Nickerson was concerned, the sun was up.

"Why, thank you, Mr. Ukridge, I'm sure," he said. "Thank you very much. No hard feelings, I trust?"

"Not on my side, old horse," responded Ukridge, affably. "Business is business."

"Exactly."

"Well, I may as well take those dogs now," said Ukridge, helping himself to a cigar from a box which he had just discovered on the mantelpiece and putting a couple more in his pocket in the friendliest way. "The sooner they're back with me, the better. They've lost a day's education as it is."

"Why, certainly, Mr. Ukridge, certainly. They are in the shed at the bottom of the garden. I will get them for you at once."

He retreated through the door, babbling ingratiatingly.

"Amazing how fond these blokes are of money," sighed Ukridge. "It's a thing I don't like to see. Sordid, I call it. That blighter's eyes were gleaming, positively gleaming, laddie, as he scooped up the stuff. Good cigars these," he added, pocketing three more.

There was a faltering footstep outside, and Mr. Nickerson re-entered the room. The man appeared to have something on his mind. A glassy look was in his whisker-bordered eyes, and his mouth, though it was not easy to see it through the jungle, seemed to me to be sagging mournfully. He resembled a minor prophet who has been hit behind the ear with a stuffed eel-skin.

"Mr. Ukridge!"

"Hallo?"

"The — the little dogs!"

"Well?"

"The little dogs!"

"What about them?"

"They have gone!"

"Gone?"

"Run away!"

"Run away? How the devil could they run away?"

"There seems to have been a loose board at the back of the shed. The little dogs must have wriggled through. There is no trace of them to be found."

Ukridge flung up his arms despairingly. He swelled like a captive balloon. His pince-nez rocked on his nose, his mackintosh flapped menacingly, and his collar sprang off its stud. He brought his fist down with a crash on the table.

"Upon my Sam!"

"I am extremely sorry —"

"Upon my Sam!" cried Ukridge. "It's hard. It's pretty hard. I come down here to inaugurate a great business, which would eventually have brought trade and prosperity to the whole neighborhood, and I have hardly had time to turn round and attend to the preliminary details of the enterprise when this man comes and sneaks my dogs. And now he tells me with a light laugh —"

"Mr. Ukridge, I assure you —"

"Tells me with a light laugh that they've gone. Gone! Gone where? Why, dash it, they may be all over the county. A fat chance I've got of ever seeing them again. Six valuable Pekingese, already educated practically to the stage where they could have been sold at an enormous profit —"

Mr. Nickerson was fumbling guiltily, and now he produced from his pocket a crumpled wad of notes, which he thrust agitatedly upon Ukridge, who waved them away with loathing.

"This gentleman," boomed Ukridge, indicating me with a

sweeping gesture, "happens to be a lawyer. It is extremely lucky that he chanced to come down today to pay me a visit. Have you followed the proceedings closely?"

I said I had followed them very closely.

"Is it your opinion that an action will lie?"

I said it seemed highly probable, and this expert ruling appeared to put the final touch on Mr. Nickerson's collapse. Almost tearfully he urged the notes on Ukridge.

"What's this?" said Ukridge, loftily.

"I — I thought, Mr. Ukridge, that, if it were agreeable to you, you might consent to take your money back, and — and consider the episode closed."

Ukridge turned to me with raised eyebrows.

"Ha!" he cried. "Ha, ha!"

"Ha, ha!" I chorused, dutifully.

"He thinks that he can close the episode by giving me my money back. Isn't that rich?"

"Fruity," I agreed.

"Those dogs were worth hundreds of pounds, and he thinks he can square me with a rotten twenty. Would you have believed it if you hadn't heard it with your own ears, old horse?"

"Never!"

"I'll tell you what I'll do," said Ukridge, after thought. "I'll take this money." Mr. Nickerson thanked him. "And there are one or two trifling accounts which want settling with some of the local tradesmen. You will square those —"

"Certainly, Mr. Ukridge, certainly."

"And after that — well, I'll have to think it over. If I decide to institute proceedings, my lawyer will communicate with you in due course."

And we left the wretched man, cowering despicably behind his whiskers.

It seemed to me, as we passed down the tree-shaded lane

and out into the white glare of the road, that Ukridge was bearing himself in his hour of disaster with a rather admirable fortitude. His stock-in-trade, the life-blood of his enterprise, was scattered all over Kent, probably never to return, and all that he had to show on the other side of the balance-sheet was the canceling of a few weeks' back rent and the paying-off of Gooch, the grocer, and his friends. It was a situation which might well have crushed the spirit of an ordinary man, but Ukridge seemed by no means dejected. Jaunty, rather. His eyes shone behind their pince-nez and he whistled a rollicking air. When presently he began to sing, I felt that it was time to create a diversion.

"What are you going to do?" I asked.

"Who, me?" said Ukridge, buoyantly. "Oh, I'm coming back to town on the next train. You don't mind hoofing it to the next station, do you? It's only five miles. It might be a trifle risky to start from Sheep's Cray."

"Why risky?"

"Because of the dogs, of course."

"Dogs?"

Ukridge hummed a gay strain.

"Oh, yes. I forgot to tell you about that. I've got 'em."

"What?"

"Yes. I went out late last night and pinched them out of the shed." He chuckled amusedly. "Perfectly simple. Only needed a clear, level head. I borrowed a dead cat and tied a string to it, legged it to old Nickerson's garden after dark, dug a board out of the back of the shed, and shoved my head down and chirruped. The dogs came trickling out, and I hared off, towing old Colonel Cat on his string. Great run while it lasted, laddie. Hounds picked up the scent right away and started off in a bunch at fifty miles an hour. Cat and I doing a steady fifty-five. Thought every minute old Nickerson would hear and start blazing away with a gun, but nothing happened. I led the pack across country for a run of twenty minutes without a check, parked the dogs in my sitting-room, and so to bed. Took it out of me, by gosh! Not so young as I was."

I was silent for a moment, conscious of a feeling almost of reverence. This man was undoubtedly specious. There had always been something about Ukridge that dulled the moral sense.

"Well," I said at length, "you've certainly got vision."

"Yes?" said Ukridge, gratified.

"*And* the big, broad, flexible outlook."

"Got to, laddie, nowadays. The foundation of a successful business career."

"And what's the next move?"

We were drawing near to the White Cottage. It stood and broiled in the sunlight, and I hoped that there might be something cool to drink inside it. The window of the sitting-room was open, and through it came the yapping of Pekingese.

"Oh, I shall find another cottage somewhere else," said Ukridge, eyeing his little home with a certain sentimentality. "That won't be hard. Lots of cottages all over the place. And then I shall buckle down to serious work. You'll be astounded at the progress I've made already. In a minute I'll show you what those dogs can do."

"They can bark, all right."

"Yes. They seem excited about something. You know, laddie, I've had a great idea. When I saw you at your rooms my scheme was to specialize in performing dogs for the music-halls — what you might call professional dogs. But I've been thinking it over, and now I don't see why I shouldn't go in for developing amateur talent as well. Say you have a dog — Fido, the household pet — and you think it would brighten the home if he could do a few tricks from time to time. Well, you're a busy man, you haven't the time to give up to teaching him. So you just tie a label to his collar and ship him off for a month to the Ukridge Dog College, and back he comes, thoroughly educated. No trouble, no worry, easy terms. Upon my Sam, I'm not sure there isn't more money in the amateur branch than in the professional. I don't see why eventually dog-owners shouldn't send their dogs to me as a regular thing, just as they send their sons to Eton and Winchester. My golly! this idea's beginning to develop. I'll tell you what — how would it be to issue special collars to all dogs which have graduated from my college? Something distinctive which everybody would recognize. See what I mean? Sort of badge of honor. Fellow with a dog entitled to wear the Ukridge collar would be in a position to look down on the bloke whose dog hadn't got one. Gradually it would get so that anybody in a decent social position would be ashamed to be seen out with a non-Ukridge dog. The thing would become a landslide. Dogs would pour in from all corners of the country. More work than I could handle. Have to start branches. The scheme's colossal. Millions in it, my boy! Millions!" He paused with his fingers on the handle of the front door. "Of course," he went on, "just at present it's no good blinking the fact that I'm hampered and handicapped by lack of funds and can only approach the thing on a small scale. What it amounts to, laddie, is that somehow or other I've got to get capital."

It seemed the moment to spring the glad news.

"I promised him I wouldn't mention it," I said, "for fear it might lead to disappointment, but as a matter of fact George Tupper is trying to raise some capital for you. I left him last night starting out to get it."

"George Tupper!" — Ukridge's eyes dimmed with a not unmanly emotion — "George Tupper! By Gad, that fellow is the salt of the earth. Good, loyal fellow! A true friend. A man you can rely on. Upon my Sam, if there were more fellows about like old Tuppy, there wouldn't be all this modern pessimism and unrest. Did he seem to have any idea where he could raise a bit of capital for me?"

"Yes. He went round to tell your aunt about your coming down here to train those Pekes, and — What's the matter?"

A fearful change had come over Ukridge's jubilant front. His eyes bulged, his jaw sagged. With the addition of a few feet of gray whiskers, he would have looked exactly like the recent Mr. Nickerson.

"My aunt?" he mumbled, swaying on the door-handle.

"Yes. What's the matter? He thought, if he told her all about it, she might relent and rally round."

The sigh of a gallant fighter at the end of his strength forced its way up from Ukridge's mackintosh-covered bosom.

"Of all the dashed, infernal, officious, meddling, muddling, fat-headed, interfering asses," he said, wanly, "George Tupper is the worst."

"What do you mean?"

"The man oughtn't to be at large. He's a public menace."

"But —"

"Those dogs *belong* to my aunt. I pinched them when she chucked me out!"

Inside the cottage the Pekingese were still yapping industriously.

"Upon my Sam," said Ukridge, "it's a little hard."

I think he would have said more, but at this point a voice spoke with a sudden and awful abruptness from the interior of the cottage. It was a woman's voice, a quiet, steely voice, a voice, it seemed to me, that suggested cold eyes, a beaky nose; and hair like gun metal.

"Stanley!"

That was all it said, but it was enough. Ukridge's eye met

mine in a wild surmise. He seemed to shrink into his mackintosh like a snail surprised while eating lettuce.

"Stanley!"

"Yes, Aunt Julia?" quavered Ukridge.

"Come here. I wish to speak to you."

"Yes, Aunt Julia."

I sidled out into the road. Inside the cottage the yapping of
the Pekingese had become quite hysterical. I found myself
trotting, and then — though it was a warm day — running
quite rapidly. I could have stayed if I had wanted to, but somehow I did not want to. Something seemed to tell me that on
this holy domestic scene I should be an intruder.

What it was that gave me that impression I do not know —
probably vision or the big, broad, flexible outlook.

The Story of Webster

❧ "CATS are not dogs!"

There is only one place where you can hear good things like that thrown off quite casually in the general run of conversation, and that is the bar-parlor of the Anglers' Rest. It was there, as we sat grouped about the fire, that a thoughtful Pint of Bitter made the statement just recorded.

Although the talk up to this point had been dealing with Einstein's Theory of Relativity, we readily adjusted our minds to cope with the new topic. Regular attendance at the nightly sessions over which Mr. Mulliner presides with such unfailing dignity and geniality tends to produce mental nimbleness. In our little circle I have known an argument on the Final Destination of the Soul to change inside forty seconds into one concerning the best method of preserving the juiciness of bacon fat.

"Cats," proceeded the Pint of Bitter, "are selfish. A man waits on a cat hand and foot for weeks, humoring its lightest whim, and then it goes and leaves him flat because it has found a place down the road where the fish is more frequent."

"What I've got against cats," said a Lemon Sour, speaking feelingly, as one brooding on a private grievance, "is their unreliability. They lack candor and are not square shooters. You get your cat and you call him Thomas or George, as the case may be. So far, so good. Then one morning you wake up and find six kittens in the hat-box and you have to reopen the whole matter, approaching it from an entirely different angle."

"If you want to know what's the trouble with cats," said a red-faced man with glassy eyes, who had been rapping on the table for his fourth whisky, "they've got no tact. That's what's the trouble with them. I remember a friend of mine had a cat. Made quite a pet of that cat, he did. And what occurred? What was the outcome? One night he came home rather late and was feeling for the keyhole with his corkscrew; and, believe me or not, his cat selected that precise moment to jump on the back of his neck out of a tree. No tact."

Mr. Mulliner shook his head.

"I grant you all this," he said, "but still, in my opinion, you have not got quite to the root of the matter. The real objection to the great majority of cats is their insufferable air of superiority. Cats, as a class, have never completely got over the snootiness caused by the fact that in Ancient Egypt they were worshiped as gods. This makes them too prone to set themselves up as critics and censors of the frail and erring human beings whose lot they share. They stare rebukingly. They view with concern. And on a sensitive man this often has the worst effects, inducing an inferiority complex of the gravest kind. It is odd that the conversation should have taken this turn," said Mr. Mulliner, sipping his hot Scotch and lemon, "for I was thinking only this afternoon of the rather strange case of my cousin Edward's son, Lancelot."

"I knew a cat —" began a Small Bass.

My cousin Edward's son, Lancelot (said Mr. Mulliner), was, at the time of which I speak, a comely youth of some twenty-five summers. Orphaned at an early age, he had been brought up in the home of his Uncle Theodore, the saintly Dean of Bolsover; and it was a great shock to that good man when Lancelot, on attaining his majority, wrote from London to inform him that he had taken a studio in Bott Street, Chelsea, and proposed to remain in the metropolis and become an artist.

The Dean's opinion of artists was low. As a prominent member of the Bolsover Watch Committee, it had recently been his distasteful duty to be present at a private showing of the super-super-film *Palettes of Passion,* and he replied to his nephew's communication with a vibrant letter, in which he emphasized the grievous pain it gave him to think that one of his flesh and blood should deliberately be embarking on a career which must inevitably lead sooner or later to the painting of Russian princesses lying on divans in the seminude with their arms round tame jaguars. He urged Lancelot to return and become a curate while there was yet time.

But Lancelot was firm. He deplored the rift between himself and a relative whom he had always respected; but he was dashed if he meant to go back to an environment where his individuality had been stifled and his soul confined in chains. And for four years there was silence between uncle and nephew.

During these years Lancelot had made progress in his chosen profession. At the time at which this story opens, his prospects seemed bright. He was painting the portrait of Brenda, only daughter of Mr. and Mrs. B. B. Carberry-Pirbright, of

11, Maxton Square, South Kensington, which meant thirty pounds in his sock on delivery. He had learned to cook eggs and bacon. He had practically mastered the ukulele. And, in addition, he was engaged to be married to a fearless young *vers libre* poetess of the name of Gladys Bingley, better known as The Sweet Singer of Garbidge Mews, Fulham — a charming girl who looked like a pen-wiper.

It seemed to Lancelot that life was very full and beautiful. He lived joyously in the present, giving no thought to the past.

But how true it is that the past is inextricably mixed up with the present and that we can never tell when it may not spring some delayed bomb beneath our feet. One afternoon, as he sat making a few small alterations in the portrait of Brenda Carberry-Pirbright, his fiancée entered.

He had been expecting her to call, for today she was going off for a three weeks' holiday to the South of France, and she had promised to look in on her way to the station. He laid down his brush and gazed at her with a yearning affection, thinking for the thousandth time how he worshiped every spot of ink on her nose. Standing there in the doorway with her bobbed hair sticking out in every direction like a golliwog's, she made a picture that seemed to speak to his very depths.

"Hullo, Reptile!" he said lovingly.

"What-ho, Worm!" said Gladys, maidenly devotion shining through the monocle which she wore in her left eye. "I can stay just half an hour."

"Oh, well, half an hour soon passes," said Lancelot. "What's that you've got there?"

"A letter, ass. What did you think it was?"

"Where did you get it?"

"I found the postman outside."

Lancelot took the envelope from her and examined it.

"Gosh!" he said.

"What's the matter?"

"It's from my Uncle Theodore."

"I didn't know you had an Uncle Theodore."

"Of course I have. I've had him for years."

"What's he writing to you about?"

"If you'll kindly keep quiet for two seconds, if you know how," said Lancelot, "I'll tell you."

And in a clear voice which, like that of all the Mulliners, however distant from the main branch, was beautifully modulated, he read as follows:

> The Deanery
> Bolsover
> Wilts

My dear Lancelot,

As you have, no doubt, already learned from your *Church Times,* I have been offered and have accepted the vacant Bishopric of Bongo-Bongo in West Africa. I sail immediately to take up my new duties, which I trust will be blessed.

In these circumstances, it becomes necessary for me to find a good home for my cat Webster. It is, alas, out of the question that he should accompany me, as the rigors of the climate and the lack of essential comforts might well sap a constitution which has never been robust.

I am dispatching him, therefore, to your address, my dear boy, in a straw-lined hamper, in the full confidence that you will prove a kindly and conscientious host.

> With cordial good wishes
> Your affectionate uncle,
> Theodore Bongo-Bongo

For some moments after he had finished reading this communication, a thoughtful silence prevailed in the studio. Finally Gladys spoke.

"Of all the nerve!" she said. "I wouldn't do it."

"Why not?"

"What do you want with a cat?"

Lancelot reflected.

"It is true," he said, "that, given a free hand, I would prefer not to have my studio turned into a cattery or cat-bin. But consider the special circumstances. Relations between Uncle Theodore and self have for the last few years been a bit strained. In fact, you might say we had definitely parted brass rags. It looks to me as if he were coming round. I should describe this letter as more or less what you might call an olive branch. If I lush this cat up satisfactorily, shall I not be in a position later on to make a swift touch?"

"He is rich, this bean?" said Gladys, interested.

"Extremely."

"Then," said Gladys, "consider my objections withdrawn. A good stout check from a grateful cat-fancier would undoubtedly come in very handy. We might be able to get married this year."

"Exactly," said Lancelot. "A pretty loathsome prospect, of course, but still, as we've arranged to do it, the sooner we get it over, the better, what?"

"Absolutely."

"Then that's settled. I accept custody of cat."

"It's the only thing to do," said Gladys. "Meanwhile, can you lend me a comb? Have you such a thing in your bedroom?"

"What do you want with a comb?"

"I got some soup in my hair at lunch. I won't be a minute."

She hurried out, and Lancelot, taking up the letter again,

found that he had omitted to read a continuation of it on the back page.

It was to the following effect:

P.S. In establishing Webster in your home, I am actuated by another motive than the simple desire to see to it that my faithful friend and companion is adequately provided for.

From both a moral and an educative standpoint, I am convinced that Webster's society will prove of inestimable value to you. His advent, indeed, I venture to hope, will be a turning-point in your life. Thrown, as you must be, incessantly among loose and immoral Bohemians, you will find in this cat an example of upright conduct which cannot but act as an antidote to the poison cup of temptation which is, no doubt, hourly pressed to your lips.

P.P.S. Cream only at midday, and fish not more than three times a week.

He was reading these words for the second time, when the front-door bell rang and he found a man on the steps with a hamper. A discreet mew from within revealed its contents, and Lancelot, carrying it into the studio, cut the strings.

"Hi!" he bellowed, going to the door.

"What's up?" shrieked his betrothed from above.

"The cat's come."

"All right. I'll be down in a jiffy."

Lancelot returned to the studio.

"What-ho, Webster!" he said cheerily. "How's the boy?"

The cat did not reply. It was sitting with bent head, performing that wash and brush-up which a journey by rail renders so necessary.

In order to facilitate these toilet operations, it had raised its left leg and was holding it rigidly in the air. And there flashed into Lancelot's mind an old superstition handed on to him, for what it was worth, by one of the nurses of his infancy. If, this woman had said, you creep up to a cat when its leg is in the air and give it a pull, then you make a wish and your wish comes true in thirty days.

It was a pretty fancy, and it seemed to Lancelot that the theory might as well be put to the test. He advanced warily, therefore, and was in the act of extending his fingers for the pull when Webster, lowering the leg, turned and raised his eyes.

He looked at Lancelot. And suddenly with sickening force, there came to Lancelot the realization of the unpardonable liberty he had been about to take.

Until this moment, though the postscript to his uncle's letter should have warned him, Lancelot Mulliner had had no suspicion of what manner of cat this was that he had taken into his home. Now, for the first time, he saw him steadily and saw him whole.

Webster was very large and very black and very composed. He conveyed the impression of being a cat of deep reserves. Descendant of a long line of ecclesiastical ancestors who had conducted their decorous courtships beneath the shadow of cathedrals and on the back walls of bishops' palaces, he had that exquisite poise which one sees in high dignitaries of the church. His eyes were clear and steady, and seemed to pierce to the very roots of the young man's soul, filling him with a sense of guilt.

Once, long ago, in his hot childhood, Lancelot, spending his summer holidays at the deanery, had been so far carried away by ginger-beer and original sin as to plug a senior canon in the leg with his air-gun — only to discover, on turning, that a visiting archdeacon had been a spectator of the entire incident from his immediate rear. As he had felt then, when meeting the archdeacon's eye, so did he feel now as Webster's gaze played silently upon him.

Webster, it is true, had not actually raised his eyebrows. But this, Lancelot felt, was simply because he hadn't any.

He backed, blushing.

"Sorry!" he muttered.

There was a pause. Webster continued his steady scrutiny. Lancelot edged towards the door.

"Er — excuse me — just a moment . . ." he mumbled. And, sidling from the room, he ran distractedly upstairs.

"I say," said Lancelot.

"Now what?" asked Gladys.

"Have you finished with the mirror?"

"Why?"

"Well, I — er — I thought," said Lancelot, "that I might as well have a shave."

The girl looked at him, astonished.

"Shave? Why, you shaved only the day before yesterday."

"I know. But, all the same . . . I mean to say, it seems only respectful. That cat, I mean."

"What about him?"

"Well, he seems to expect it, somehow. Nothing actually said, don't you know, but you could tell by his manner. I thought a quick shave and perhaps a change into my blue serge suit —"

"He's probably thirsty. Why don't you give him some milk?"

"Could one, do you think?" said Lancelot, doubtfully. "I mean, I hardly seem to know him well enough." He paused. "I say, old girl," he went on, with a touch of hesitation.

"Hullo?"

"I know you won't mind my mentioning it, but you've got a few spots of ink on your nose."

"Of course I have. I always have spots of ink on my nose."

"Well . . . you don't think . . . a quick scrub with a bit of pumice stone . . . I mean to say, you know how important first impressions are . . ."

The girl stared.

"Lancelot Mulliner," she said, "if you think I'm going to skin my nose to the bone just to please a mangy cat —"

"Sh!" cried Lancelot, in agony.

"Here, let me go down and look at him," said Gladys petulantly.

As they re-entered the studio, Webster was gazing with an air of quiet distate at an illustration from *La Vie Parisienne* which adorned one of the walls. Lancelot tore it down hastily.

Gladys looked at Webster in an unfriendly way.

"So that's the blighter!"

"Sh!"

"If you want to know what I think," said Gladys, "that cat's been living too high. Doing himself a dashed sight too well. You'd better cut his rations down a bit."

In substance, her criticism was not unjustified. Certainly, there was about Webster more than a suspicion of *embonpoint*. He had that air of portly well-being which we associate with those who dwell in cathedral closes. But Lancelot winced uncomfortably. He had so hoped that Gladys would make a good impression, and here she was, starting right off by saying the tactless thing.

He longed to explain to Webster that it was only her way; that in the Bohemian circles of which she was such an ornament genial chaff of a personal order was accepted and, indeed, relished. But it was too late. The mischief had been done. Webster turned in a pointed manner and withdrew silently behind the chesterfield.

Gladys, all unconscious, was making preparations for departure.

"Well, bung-oh," she said lightly. "See you in three weeks. I suppose you and that cat'll both be out on the tiles the moment my back's turned."

"Please! Please!" moaned Lancelot. "Please!"

He had caught sight of the tip of a black tail protruding from behind the chesterfield. It was twitching slightly, and Lancelot could read it like a book. With a sickening sense of dismay, he knew that Webster had formed a snap judgment of his fiancée and condemned her as frivolous and unworthy.

It was some ten days later that Bernard Worple, the Neo-Vorticist sculptor, lunching at the Puce Ptarmigan, ran into Rodney Scollop, the powerful young Surrealist. And after talking for a while of their art —

"What's all this I hear about Lancelot Mulliner?" asked Worple. "There's a wild story going about that he was seen shaved in the middle of the week. Nothing in it, I suppose?"

Scollop looked grave. He had been on the point of mentioning Lancelot himself, for he loved the lad and was deeply exercised about him.

"It is perfectly true," he said.

"It sounds incredible."

Scollop leaned forward. His fine face was troubled.

"Shall I tell you something, Worple?"

"What?"

"I know for an absolute fact," said Scollop, "that Lancelot Mulliner now shaves every morning."

Worple pushed aside the spaghetti which he was wreathing about him, and through the gap stared at his companion.

"Every morning?"

"Every single morning. I looked in on him myself the other day, and there he was, neatly dressed in blue serge and shaved to the core. And, what is more, I got the distinct impression that he had used talcum powder afterwards."

"You don't mean that!"

"I do. And shall I tell you something else? There was a book lying open on the table. He tried to hide it, but he wasn't quick enough. It was one of those etiquette books!"

"An etiquette book!"

"*Polite Behaviour*, by Constance, Lady Bodbank."

Worple unwound a stray tendril of spaghetti from about his left ear. He was deeply agitated. Like Scollop, he loved Lancelot.

"He'll be dressing for dinner next!" he exclaimed.

"I have every reason to believe," said Scollop gravely, "that he does dress for dinner. At any rate, a man closely resembling him was seen furtively buying three stiff collars and a black tie at Hope Brothers in the King's Road last Tuesday."

Worple pushed his chair back, and rose. His manner was determined.

"Scollop," he said, "we are friends of Mulliner's, you and I. It is evident from what you tell me that subversive influences are at work and that never has he needed our friendship more. Shall we not go round and see him immediately?"

"It was what I was about to suggest myself," said Rodney Scollop.

Twenty minutes later they were in Lancelot's studio, and with a significant glance Scollop drew his companion's notice to their host's appearance. Lancelot Mulliner was neatly, even foppishly, dressed in blue serge with creases down the trouser-legs, and his chin, Worple saw with a pang, gleamed smoothly in the afternoon light.

At the sight of his friends' cigars, Lancelot exhibited unmistakable concern.

"You don't mind throwing those away, I'm sure," he said pleadingly.

Rodney Scollop drew himself up a little haughtily.

"And since when," he asked, "have the best fourpenny cigars in Chelsea not been good enough for you?"

Lancelot hastened to soothe him.

"It isn't me," he exclaimed. "It's Webster. My cat. I happen to know he objects to tobacco smoke. I had to give up my pipe in deference to his views."

Bernard Worple snorted.

"Are you trying to tell us," he sneered, "that Lancelot Mulliner allows himself to be dictated to by a blasted cat?"

"Hush!" cried Lancelot, trembling. "If you knew how he disapproves of strong language!"

"Where is this cat?" asked Rodney Scollop. "Is that the animal?" he said, pointing out of the window to where, in the yard, a tough-looking tom with tattered ears stood mewing in a hard-boiled way out of the corner of its mouth.

"Good heavens, no!" said Lancelot. "That is an alley cat which comes round here from time to time to lunch at the dust-bin. Webster is quite different. Webster has a natural dignity and repose of manner. Webster is a cat who prides himself on always being well turned out and whose high principles and lofty ideals shine from his eyes like beacon-fires . . ." And then suddenly, with an abrupt change of manner, Lancelot broke down and in a low voice added: "Curse him! Curse him! Curse him! Curse him!"

Worple looked at Scollop. Scollop looked at Worple.

"Come, old man," said Scollop, laying a gentle hand on Lancelot's bowed shoulder. "We are your friends. Confide in us."

"Tell us all," said Worple. "What's the matter?"

Lancelot uttered a bitter, mirthless laugh.

"You want to know what's the matter? Listen, then. I'm cat-pecked!"

"Cat-pecked?"

"You've heard of men being hen-pecked, haven't you?" said Lancelot with a touch of irritation. "Well, I'm cat-pecked."

And in broken accents he told his story. He sketched the history of his association with Webster from the latter's first entry into the studio. Confident now that the animal was not within earshot, he unbosomed himself without reserve.

"It's something in the beast's eye," he said in a shaking voice. "Something hypnotic. He casts a spell upon me. He gazes at me and disapproves. Little by little, bit by bit, I am degenerating under his influence from a wholesome, self-respecting artist into . . . well, I don't know what you would call it. Suffice it to say that I have given up smoking, that I have ceased to wear carpet slippers and go about without a collar, that I never dream of sitting down to my frugal evening meal without dressing, and" — he choked — "I have sold my ukulele."

"Not that!" said Worple, paling.

"Yes," said Lancelot. "I felt he considered it frivolous."

There was a long silence.

"Mulliner," said Scollop, "this is more serious than I had supposed. We must brood upon your case."

"It may be possible," said Worple, "to find a way out."

Lancelot shook his head hopelessly.

"There is no way out. I have explored every avenue. The only thing that could possibly free me from this intolerable bondage would be if once — just once — I could catch that cat unbending. If once — merely once — it would lapse in my presence from its austere dignity for but a single instant, I feel that the spell would be broken. But what hope is there of that?" cried Lancelot passionately. "You were pointing just now to that alley cat in the yard. There stands one who has strained every nerve and spared no effort to break down Webster's inhuman self-control. I have heard that animal says things to him which you would think no cat with red blood in its veins would suffer for an instant. And Webster merely looks at him like a suffragan bishop eyeing an erring choirboy and turns his head and falls into a refreshing sleep."

He broke off with a dry sob. Worple, always an optimist, attempted in his kindly way to minimize the tragedy.

"Ah, well," he said. "It's bad, of course, but still, I suppose there is no actual harm in shaving and dressing for dinner and so on. Many great artists . . . Whistler, for example —"

"Wait!" cried Lancelot. "You have not heard the worst."

He rose feverishly and, going to the easel, disclosed the portrait of Brenda Carberry-Pirbright.

"Take a look at that," he said, "and tell me what you think of her."

His two friends surveyed the face before them in silence. Miss Carberry-Pirbright was a young woman of prim and glacial aspect. One sought in vain for her reasons for wanting to have her portrait painted. It would be a most unpleasant thing to have about any house.

Scollop broke the silence.

"Friend of yours?"

"I can't stand the sight of her," said Lancelot, vehemently.

"Then," said Scollop, "I may speak frankly. I think she's a pill."

"A blister," said Worple.

"A boil and a disease," said Scollop, summing up.

Lancelot laughed hackingly.

"You have described her to a nicety. She stands for everything most alien to my artist soul. She gives me a pain in the neck. I'm going to marry her."

"What!" cried Scollop.

"But you're going to marry Gladys Bingley," said Worple.

"Webster thinks not," said Lancelot bitterly. "At their first meeting he weighed Gladys in the balance and found her wanting. And the moment he saw Brenda Carberry-Pirbright he stuck his tail up at right angles, uttered a cordial gargle, and rubbed his head against her leg. Then, turning, he looked at me. I could read that glance. I knew what was in his mind. From that moment he has been doing everything in his power to arrange the match."

"But, Mulliner," said Worple, always eager to point out the bright side, "why should this girl want to marry a wretched, scrubby, hard-up footler like you? Have courage, Mulliner. It is simply a question of time before you repel and sicken her."

Lancelot shook his head.

"No," he said. "You speak like a true friend, Worple, but you do not understand. Old Ma Carberry-Pirbright, this exhibit's mother, who chaperons her at the sittings, discovered at an early date my relationship to my Uncle Theodore, who, as you know, has got it in gobs. She knows well enough that someday I shall be a rich man. She used to know my Uncle Theodore when he was Vicar of St. Botolph's in Knightsbridge, and from the very first she assumed towards me the repellent chumminess of an old family friend. She was always trying to lure me to her At Homes, her Sunday luncheons, her little dinners. Once she actually suggested that I should escort her and her beastly daughter to the Royal Academy."

He laughed bitterly. The mordant witticisms of Lancelot Mulliner at the expense of the Royal Academy were quoted from Tite Street in the south to Holland Park in the north and eastward as far as Bloomsbury.

"To all these overtures," resumed Lancelot, "I remained firmly unresponsive. My attitude was from the start one of frigid aloofness. I did not actually say in so many words that I would rather be dead in a ditch than at one of her At Homes, but my manner indicated it. And I was just beginning to think I had choked her off when in crashed Webster and upset everything. Do you know how many times I have been to that infernal house in the last week? Five. Webster seemed to wish it. I tell you, I am a lost man."

He buried his face in his hands. Scollop touched Worple on the arm, and together the two men stole silently out.

"Bad!" said Worple.

"Very bad," said Scollop.

"It seems incredible."

"Oh, no. Cases of this kind are, alas, by no means uncommon among those who, like Mulliner, possess to a marked degree the highly-strung, ultra-sensitive artistic temperament. A friend of mine, a rhythmical interior decorator, once rashly consented to put his aunt's parrot up at his studio while she was away visiting friends in the north of England. She was a woman of strong evangelical views, which the bird had imbibed from her. It had a way of putting its head on one side, making a noise like someone drawing a cork from a bottle, and asking my friend if he was saved. To cut a long story short, I happened to call on him a month later and he had installed a harmonium in his studio and was singing hymns, ancient and modern, in a rich tenor, while the parrot, standing on one leg on its perch, took the bass. A very sad affair. We were all much upset about it."

Worple shuddered.

"You appall me, Scollop! Is there nothing we can do?"

Rodney Scollop considered for a moment.

"We might wire Gladys Bingley to come home at once. She might possibly reason with the unhappy man. A woman's gentle influence . . . Yes, we could do that. Look in at the post office on your way home and send Gladys a telegram. I'll owe you for my half of it."

In the studio they had left, Lancelot Mulliner was staring dumbly at a black shape which had just entered the room. He had the appearance of a man with his back to the wall.

"No!" he was crying. "No! I'm dashed if I do!"

Webster continued to look at him.

"Why should I?" demanded Lancelot weakly.

Webster's gaze did not flicker.

"Oh, all right," said Lancelot sullenly.

He passed from the room with leaden feet, and, proceeding upstairs, changed into morning clothes and a top hat. Then, with a gardenia in his buttonhole, he made his way to 11, Maxton Square, where Mrs. Carberry-Pirbright was giving one of her intimate little teas ("just a few friends") to meet Clara Throckmorton Stooge, authoress of *A Strong Man's Kiss*.

Gladys Bingley was lunching at her hotel in Antibes when Worple's telegram arrived. It occasioned her the gravest concern.

Exactly what it was all about, she was unable to gather, for emotion had made Bernard Worple rather incoherent. There were moments, reading it, when she fancied that Lancelot had met with a serious accident; others when the solution seemed to be that he had sprained his brain to such an extent that rival lunatic asylums were competing eagerly for his custom; others, again, when Worple appeared to be suggesting that he had gone into partnership with his cat to start a harem. But one fact emerged clearly: her loved one was in serious trouble of some kind, and his best friends were agreed that only her immediate return could save him.

Gladys did not hesitate. Within half an hour of the receipt of the telegram she had packed her trunk, removed a piece of asparagus from her right eyebrow, and was negotiating for accommodation on the first train going north.

Arriving in London, her first impulse was to go straight to Lancelot. But a natural feminine curiosity urged her, before doing so, to call upon Bernard Worple and have light thrown on some of the more abstruse passages in the telegram.

Worple, in his capacity of author, may have tended towards obscurity, but, when confining himself to the spoken word, he told a plain story well and clearly. Five minutes of his society enabled Gladys to obtain a firm grasp on the salient facts, and there appeared on her face that grim, tight-lipped expression which is seen only on the faces of fiancées who have come back from a short holiday to discover that their dear one has been straying in their absence from the straight and narrow path.

"Brenda Carberry-Pirbright, eh?" said Gladys, with ominous calm. "I'll give him Brenda Carberry-Pirbright! My gosh, if one can't go off to Antibes for the merest breather without having one's betrothed getting it up his nose and starting to act like a Mormon Elder, it begins to look a pretty tough world for a girl."

Kind-hearted Bernard Worple did his best.

"I blame the cat," he said. "Lancelot, to my mind, is more sinned against than sinning. I consider him to be acting under undue influence or duress."

"How like a man!" said Gladys. "Shoving it all off onto an innocent cat!"

"Lancelot says it has a sort of something in its eye."

"Well, when I meet Lancelot," said Gladys, "he'll find that I have a sort of something in my eye."

She went out, breathing flame quietly through her nostrils. Worple, saddened, heaved a sigh and resumed his Neo-Vorticist sculping.

It was some five minutes later that Gladys, passing through Maxton Square on her way to Bott Street, stopped suddenly in her tracks. The sight she had seen was enough to make any fiancée do so.

Along the pavement leading to Number 11 two figures were advancing. Or three, if you counted a morose-looking dog of a semi-dachshund nature which preceded them, attached to a leash. One of the figures was that of Lancelot Mulliner, natty in gray herringbone tweed and a new Homburg hat. It was he who held the leash. The other, Gladys recognized from the portrait which she had seen on Lancelot's easel as that modern Du Barry, that notorious wrecker of homes and breaker-up of love-nests, Brenda Carberry-Pirbright.

The next moment they had mounted the steps of Number 11 and had gone in to tea, possibly with a little music.

It was perhaps an hour and a half later that Lancelot, having wrenched himself with difficulty from the lair of the Philistines, sped homeward in a swift taxi. As always after an extended *tête-à-tête* with Miss Carberry-Pirbright, he felt dazed and bewildered, as if he had been swimming in a sea of glue and had swallowed a good deal of it. All he could think of clearly was that he wanted a drink and that the materials for that drink were in the cupboard behind the chesterfield in his studio.

He paid the cab and charged in with his tongue rattling dryly against his front teeth. And there before him was Gladys Bingley whom he had supposed far, far away.

"You!" exclaimed Lancelot.

"Yes, me!" said Gladys.

Her long vigil had not helped to restore the girl's equanimity. Since arriving at the studio she had had leisure to tap her foot three thousand, one hundred and forty-two times on the carpet, and the number of bitter smiles which had flitted across her face was nine hundred and eleven. She was about ready for the battle of the century.

She rose and faced him, all the woman in her flashing from her eyes.

"Well, you Casanova!" she said.

"You who?" said Lancelot.

"Don't say 'Yoo-hoo!' to me!" cried Gladys. "Keep that for your Brenda Carberry-Pirbrights. Yes, I know all about it, Lancelot Don Juan Henry the Eighth Mulliner! I saw you with her just now. I hear that you and she are inseparable. Bernard Worple says you said you were going to marry her."

"You mustn't believe everything a Neo-Vorticist sculptor tells you," quavered Lancelot.

"I'll bet you're going back to dinner there tonight," said Gladys.

She had spoken at a venture, basing the charge purely on a possessive cock of the head which she had noticed in Brenda Carberry-Pirbright at their recent encounter. There, she had said to herself at the time, had gone a girl who was about to invite — or had just invited — Lancelot Mulliner to dine quietly and take her to the pictures afterwards. But the shot went home. Lancelot hung his head.

"There was some talk of it," he admitted.

"Ah!" exclaimed Gladys.

Lancelot's eyes were haggard.

"I don't want to go," he pleaded. "Honestly I don't. But Webster insists."

"Webster!"

"Yes, Webster. If I attempt to evade the appointment, he will sit in front of me and look at me."

"Tchah!"

"Well, he will. Ask him for yourself."

Gladys tapped her foot six times in rapid succession on the carpet, bringing the total to three thousand, one hundred and forty-eight. Her manner had changed and was now dangerously calm.

"Lancelot Mulliner," she said, "you have your choice. Me, on the one hand, Brenda Carberry-Pirbright on the other. I offer you a home where you will be able to smoke in bed, spill the ashes on the floor, wear pajamas and carpet slippers all day, and shave only on Sunday mornings. From her, what have you to hope? A house in South Kensington — possibly the Brompton Road — probably with her mother living with you. A life that will be one long round of stiff collars and tight shoes, of morning coats and top hats."

Lancelot quivered, but she went on remorselessly.

"You will be at home on alternate Thursdays and will be expected to hand the cucumber sandwiches. Every day you will air the dog, till you become a confirmed dog-airer. You will dine out in Bayswater and go for the summer to Bournemouth or Dinard. Choose well, Lancelot Mulliner! I will leave you to think it over. But one last word. If by seven-thirty on the dot you have not presented yourself at 6A, Garbidge Mews ready to take me out to dinner at the Ham and Beef, I shall know what to think and shall act accordingly."

And brushing the cigarette ashes from her chin, the girl strode haughtily from the room.

"Gladys!" cried Lancelot.

But she had gone.

* * *

For some minutes Lancelot Mulliner remained where he was, stunned. Then, insistently, there came to him the recollection that he had not had that drink. He rushed to the cupboard and produced the bottle. He uncorked it, and was pouring out a lavish stream, when a movement on the floor below him attracted his attention.

Webster was standing there, looking up at him. And in his eyes was that familiar expression of quiet rebuke.

"Scarcely what I have been accustomed to at the Deanery," he seemed to be saying.

Lancelot stood paralyzed. The feeling of being bound hand and foot, of being caught in a snare from which there was no escape, had become more poignant than ever. The bottle fell from his nerveless fingers and rolled across the floor, spilling its contents in an amber river, but he was too heavy in spirit to notice it. With a gesture such as Job might have made on discovering a new boil, he crossed to the window and stood looking moodily out.

Then, turning with a sigh, he looked at Webster again — and, looking, stood spellbound.

The spectacle which he beheld was of a kind to stun a stronger man than Lancelot Mulliner. At first, he shrank from believing his eyes. Then, slowly, came the realization that what he saw was no mere figment of a disordered imagination. This unbelievable thing was actually happening.

Webster sat crouched upon the floor beside the widening pool of whisky. But it was not horror and disgust that had caused him to crouch. He was crouched because, crouching, he could get nearer to the stuff and obtain crisper action. His tongue was moving in and out like a piston.

And then, abruptly, for one fleeting instant, he stopped lapping and glanced up at Lancelot, and across his face there flitted a quick smile — so genial, so intimate, so full of jovial camaraderie, that the young man found himself automatically smiling back, and not only smiling but winking. And in answer to that wink Webster winked, too — a wholehearted, roguish wink that said as plainly as if he had spoken the words:

"How long has this been going on?"

Then with a slight hiccough he turned back to the task of getting his quick before it soaked into the floor.

Into the murky soul of Lancelot Mulliner there poured a sudden flood of sunshine. It was as if a great burden had been lifted from his shoulders. The intolerable obsession of the last two weeks had ceased to oppress him, and he felt a free man. At the eleventh hour the reprieve had come. Webster, that seeming pillar of austere virtue, was one of the boys, after all. Never again would Lancelot quail beneath his eye. He had the goods on him.

Webster, like the stag at eve, had now drunk his fill. He had left the pool of alcohol and was walking round in slow, meditative circles. From time to time he mewed tentatively, as if he were trying to say "British Constitution." His failure to articulate the syllables appeared to tickle him, for at the end of each attempt he would utter a slow, amused chuckle. It was at about this moment that he suddenly broke into a rhythmic dance, not unlike the old saraband.

It was an interesting spectacle, and at any other time Lancelot would have watched it raptly. But now he was busy at his desk, writing a brief note to Mrs. Carberry-Pirbright, the burden of which was that if she thought he was coming within a mile of her foul house that night or any other night she had vastly underrated the dodging powers of Lancelot Mulliner.

And what of Webster? The Demon Rum now had him in an iron grip. A lifetime of abstinence had rendered him a ready victim to the fatal fluid. He had now reached the stage when geniality gives way to belligerence. The rather foolish smile had gone from his face, and in its stead there lowered a fighting frown. For a few moments he stood on his hind legs, looking about him for a suitable adversary; then, losing all vestiges of self-control, he ran five times round the room at a high rate of speed and, falling foul of a small footstool, attacked it with the utmost ferocity, sparing neither tooth nor claw.

But Lancelot did not see him. Lancelot was not there. Lancelot was out in Bott Street, hailing a cab.

"6A, Garbidge Mews, Fulham," said Lancelot to the driver.

The Go-Getter

🍃On the usually unruffled brow of the Hon. Freddie
Threepwood, as he paced the gardens of Blandings Castle,
there was the slight but well-marked frown of one whose mind
is not at rest. It was high summer and the gardens were at their
loveliest, but he appeared to find no solace in their splendor.
Calceolarias, which would have drawn senile yips of ecstasy
from his father, Lord Emsworth, left him cold. He eyed the
lobelias with an unseeing stare, as if he were cutting an un-
desirable acquaintance in the paddock at Ascot.

What was troubling this young man was the continued
sales-resistance of his Aunt Georgiana. Ever since his marriage
to the only daughter of Donaldson's Dog-Biscuits, of Long
Island City, N.Y., Freddie Threepwood had thrown himself
heart and soul into the promotion of the firm's wares. And,
sent home to England to look about for likely prospects, he
had seen in Georgiana, Lady Alcester a customer who approx-
imated to the ideal. The owner of four Pekingese, two Poms,
a Yorkshire terrier, five Sealyhams, a Borzoi and an Airedale,

she was a woman who stood for something in dog-loving circles. To secure her patronage would be a big thing for him. It would stamp him as a live wire and a go-getter. It would please his father-in-law hugely. And the proprietor of Donaldson's Dog-Joy was a man who, when even slightly pleased, had a habit of spraying five-thousand dollar checks like a geyser.

And so far, despite all his eloquence, callously oblivious of the ties of kinship and the sacred obligations they involve, Lady Alcester had refused to sign on the dotted line, preferring to poison her menagerie with some degraded garbage called, if he recollected rightly, Peterson's Pup-Food.

A bitter snort escaped Freddie. It was still echoing through the gardens when he found that he was no longer alone. He had been joined by his cousin Gertrude.

"What-ho!" said Freddie, amiably. He was fond of Gertrude, and did not hold it against her that she had a mother who was incapable of spotting a good dog-biscuit when she saw one. Between him and Gertrude there had long existed a firm alliance. It was to him that Gertrude had turned for assistance when the family were trying to stop her getting engaged to good old Beefy Bingham: and he had supplied assistance in such good measure that the engagement was now an accepted fact and running along nicely.

"Freddie," said Gertrude, "may I borrow your car?"

"Certainly. Most decidedly. Going over to see old Beefers?"

"No," said Gertrude, and a closer observer than her cousin might have noted in her manner a touch of awkwardness. "Mr. Watkins wants me to drive him to Shrewsbury."

"Oh? Well, carry on, as far as I'm concerned. You haven't seen your mother anywhere, have you?"

"I think she's sitting on the lawn."

"Ah? Is she? Right-ho. Thanks."

Freddie moved off in the direction indicated and presently

came in sight of his relative, seated as described. The Airedale was lying at her feet. One of the Pekes occupied her lap. And she was gazing into the middle distance in a preoccupied manner, as if she, like her nephew, had a weight on her mind.

Nor would one who drew this inference from her demeanor have been mistaken. Lady Alcester was feeling disturbed.

A woman who stands *in loco parentis* to fourteen dogs must of necessity have her cares, but it was not the dumb friends that were worrying Lady Alcester now. What was troubling her was the disquieting behavior of her daughter Gertrude.

Engaged to the Rev. Rupert Bingham, Gertrude seemed to her of late to have become infatuated with Orlo Watkins, the Crooning Tenor, one of those gifted young men whom Lady Constance Keeble, the chatelaine of Blandings, was so fond of inviting down for lengthy visits in the summertime.

On the subject of the Rev. Rupert Bingham, Lady Alcester's views had recently undergone a complete change. In the beginning, the prospect of having him for a son-in-law had saddened and distressed her. Then, suddenly discovering that he was the nephew and heir of as opulent a shipping magnate as ever broke bread at the Adelphi Hotel, Liverpool, she had soared from the depths to the heights. She was now strongly pro-Bingham. She smiled upon him freely. Upon his appointment to the vacant Vicarage of Much Matchingham, the village nearest to Market Blandings, she had brought Gertrude to the Castle so that the young people should see one another frequently.

And, instead of seeing her betrothed frequently, Gertrude seemed to prefer to moon about with this Orlo Watkins, this Crooning Tenor. For days they had been inseparable.

Now, everybody knows what Crooning Tenors are. Dangerous devils. They sit at the piano and gaze into a girl's eyes and sing in a voice that sounds like gas escaping from a pipe about Love and the Moonlight and You: and, before you know where you are, the girl has scrapped the deserving young clergyman with prospects to whom she is affianced and is off and away with a man whose only means of livelihood consist of intermittent engagements with the British Broadcasting Corporation.

If a mother is not entitled to shudder at a prospect like that, it would be interesting to know what she is entitled to shudder at.

Lady Alcester, then, proceeded to shudder: and was still shuddering when the drowsy summer peace was broken by a hideous uproar. The Peke and the Airedale had given tongue simultaneously, and, glancing up, Lady Alcester perceived her nephew Frederick approaching.

And what made her shudder again was the fact that in Freddie's eye she noted with concern the familiar go-getter gleam, the old dog-biscuit glitter.

However, as it had sometimes been her experience, when cornered by her nephew, that she could stem the flood by talking promptly on other subjects, she made a gallant effort to do so now.

"Have you seen Gertrude, Freddie?" she asked.

"Yes. She borrowed my car to go to Shrewsbury."

"Alone?"

"No. Accompanied by Watkins. The Yowler."

A further spasm shook Lady Alcester.

"Freddie," she said, "I'm terribly worried."

"Worried?"

"About Gertrude."

Freddie dismissed Gertrude with a gesture.

"No need to worry about her," he said. "What you want to worry about is these dogs of yours. Notice how they barked at me? Nerves. They're a mass of nerves. And why? Improper feeding. As long as you mistakenly insist on giving them Peterson's Pup-Food — lacking, as it is, in many of the essential vitamins — so long will they continue to fly off the handle every time they see a human being on the horizon. Now, pursuant on what we were talking about this morning, Aunt Georgiana, there is a little demonstration I would like . . ."

"Can't you give her a hint, Freddie?"

"Who?"

"Gertrude."

"Yes, I suppose I could give her a hint. What about?"

"She is seeing far too much of this man Watkins."

"Well, so am I, for the matter of that. So is everybody who sees him more than once."

"She seems quite to have forgotten that she is engaged to Rupert Bingham."

"Rupert Bingham, did you say?" said Freddie with sudden animation. "I'll tell you something about Rupert Bingham. He has a dog named Bottles who has been fed from early youth on Donaldson's Dog-Joy, and I wish you could see him. Thanks to the bone-forming properties of Donaldson's Dog-Joy, he glows with health. A fine, upstanding dog, with eyes sparkling with the joy of living and both feet on the ground. A credit to his master."

"Never mind about Rupert's dog!"

"You've got to mind about Rupert's dog. You can't afford to ignore him. He is a dog to be reckoned with. A dog that counts. And all through Donaldson's Dog-Joy."

"I don't want to talk about Donaldson's Dog-Joy."

"I do. I want to give you a demonstration. You may not know it, Aunt Georgiana, but over in America the way we advertise this product, so rich in bone-forming vitamins, is as follows. We instruct our demonstrator to stand out in plain view before the many-headed and, when the audience is of sufficient size, to take a biscuit and break off a piece and chew it. By this means we prove that Donaldson's Dog-Joy is so superbly wholesome as actually to be fit for human consumption. Our demonstrator not only eats the biscuit — he enjoys it. He rolls it round his tongue. He chews it and mixes it with his saliva . . ."

"Freddie, please!"

"With his saliva," repeated Freddie firmly. "And so does the dog. He masticates the biscuit. He enjoys it. He becomes a bigger and better dog. I will now eat a Donaldson's Dog-Biscuit."

And before his aunt's nauseated gaze, he proceeded to attempt this gruesome feat.

It was an impressive demonstration, but it failed in one particular. To have rendered it perfect, he should not have choked. Want of experience caused the disaster. Long years of training go to the making of the seasoned demonstrators of Donaldson's Dog-Joy. They start in a small way with carpet tacks and work up through the flatirons and patent breakfast cereals till they are ready for the big effort. Freddie was a novice. Endeavoring to roll the morsel round his tongue, he allowed it to escape into his windpipe.

The sensation of having swallowed a mixture of bricks and sawdust was succeeded by a long and painful coughing fit. And when at length the sufferer's eyes cleared, no human form met their gaze. There was the Castle. There was the lawn. There were the gardens. But Lady Alcester had disappeared.

However, it is a well-established fact that good men, like Donaldson's Dog-Biscuits, are hard to keep down. Some fifty minutes later, as the Rev. Rupert Bingham sat in his study at Matchingham Vicarage, the parlormaid announced a visitor. The Hon. Freddie Threepwood limped in, looking shop-soiled.

"What-ho, Beefers," he said. "I just came to ask if I could borrow Bottles."

He bent to where the animal lay on the hearth rug and prodded it civilly in the lower ribs. Bottles waved a long tail in brief acknowledgment. He was a fine dog, though of uncertain breed. His mother had been a popular local belle with a good deal of sex appeal, and the question of his paternity was one that would have set a Genealogical College pursing its lips perplexedly.

"Oh, hullo, Freddie," said the Rev. Rupert.

The young Pastor of Souls spoke in an absent voice. He was frowning. It is a singular fact — and one that just goes to show what sort of a world this is — that of the four foreheads introduced so far to the reader of this chronicle, three have been corrugated with care. And, if girls had consciences, Gertrude's would have been corrugated, too, giving us a full hand.

"Take a chair," said the Rev. Rupert.

"I'll take a sofa," said Freddie, doing so. "Feeling a bit used up. I had to hoof it all the way over."

"What's happened to your car?"

"Gertrude took it to drive Watkins to Shrewsbury."

The Rev. Rupert sat for a while in thought. His face, which was large and red, had a drawn look. Even the massive body which had so nearly won him a Rowing Blue at Oxford gave the illusion of having shrunk. So marked was his distress that even Freddie noticed it.

"Something up, Beefers?" he inquired.

For answer the Rev. Rupert Bingham extended a hamlike hand which held a letter. It was written in a sprawling, girlish handwriting.

"Read that."

"From Gertrude?"

"Yes. It came this morning. Well?"

Freddie completed his perusal and handed the document back. He was concerned.

"I think it's the bird," he said.

"So do I."

"It's long," said Freddie, "and it's rambling. It is full of stuff about 'Are we sure?' and 'Do we know our own minds?' and 'Wouldn't it be better, perhaps?' But I think it is the bird."

"I can't understand it."

Freddie sat up.

"I can," he said. "Now I see what Aunt Georgiana was drooling about. Her fears were well founded. The snake Watkins has stolen Gertrude from you."

"You think Gertrude's in love with Watkins?"

"I do. And I'll tell you why. He's a yowler, and girls always fall for yowlers. They have a glamour."

"I've never noticed Watkins's glamour. He has always struck me as a bit of a weed."

"Weed he may be, Beefers, but, nonetheless, he knows how to do his stuff. I don't know why it should be, but there is a certain type of tenor voice which acts on girls like catnip on a cat."

The Rev. Rupert breathed heavily.

"I see," he said.

"The whole trouble is, Beefers," proceeded Freddie, "that Watkins is romantic and you're not. Your best friend couldn't call you romantic. Solid worth, yes. Romance, no."

"So it doesn't seem as if there was much to be done about it?"

Freddie reflected.

"Couldn't you manage to show yourself in a romantic light?"

"How?"

"Well — stop a runaway horse."

"Where's the horse?"

" 'Myes," said Freddie. "That's by way of being the difficulty, isn't it? The horse — where is it?"

There was silence for some moments.

"Well, be that as it may," said Freddie. "Can I borrow Bottles?"

"What for?"

"Purposes of demonstration. I wish to exhibit him to my Aunt Georgiana so that she may see for herself to what heights of robustness a dog can rise when fed sedulously on Donaldson's Dog-Joy. I'm having a lot of trouble with that woman, Beefers. I try all the artifices which win to success in salesmanship, and they don't. But I have a feeling that if she could see Bottles and poke him in the ribs and note the firm, muscular flesh, she might drop. At any rate, it's worth trying. I'll take him along, may I?"

"All right."

"Thanks. And in regard to your little trouble, I'll be giving it my best attention. You're looking in after dinner tonight?"

"I suppose so," said the Rev. Rupert, moodily.

The information that her impressionable daughter had gone off to roam the countryside in a two-seater car with the perilous Watkins had come as a grievous blow to Lady Alcester. As she sat on the terrace, an hour after Freddie had begun the weary homeward trek from Matchingham Vicarage, her heart was sorely laden.

The Airedale had wandered away upon some private ends, but the Peke lay slumbering in her lap. She envied it its calm detachment. To her the future looked black and the air seemed heavy with doom.

Only one thing mitigated her depression. Her nephew Frederick had disappeared. Other prominent local pests were present, such as flies and gnats, but not Frederick. The grounds of Blandings Castle appeared to be quite free from him.

And then even this poor consolation was taken from the stricken woman. Limping a little, as if his shoes hurt him, the Hon. Freddie came round the corner of the shrubbery, headed in her direction. He was accompanied by something having the outward aspect of a dog.

"What-ho, Aunt Georgiana!"

"Well, Freddie?" sighed Lady Alcester resignedly.

The Peke, opening one eye, surveyed the young man for a moment, seemed to be debating within itself the advisability of barking, came apparently to the conclusion that it was too hot, and went to sleep again.

"This is Bottles," said Freddie.

"Who?"

"Bottles. The animal I touched on some little time back. Note the well-muscled frame."

"I never saw such a mongrel in my life."

"Kind hearts are more than coronets," said Freddie. "The point at issue is not this dog's pedigree, which, I concede, is not all Burke and Debrett, but his physique. Reared exclusively on a diet of Donaldson's Dog-Joy, he goes his way with his chin up, frank and fearless. I should like you, if you don't mind, to come along to the stables and watch him among the rats. It will give you some idea."

He would have spoken further, but at this point something occurred, as had happened during his previous sales talk, to mar the effect of Freddie's oratory.

The dog Bottles, during this conversation, had been roaming to and fro in the inquisitive manner customary with dogs who find themselves in strange territory. He had sniffed at trees. He had rolled on the turf. Now, returning to the center of things, he observed for the first time that on the lap of the woman seated in the chair there lay a peculiar something.

What it was Bottles did not know. It appeared to be alive. A keen desire came upon him to solve this mystery. To keep the records straight, he advanced to the chair, thrust an inquiring nose against the object, and inhaled sharply.

The next moment, to his intense surprise, the thing had gone off like a bomb, had sprung to the ground, and was moving rapidly towards him.

Bottles did not hesitate. A rough-and-tumble with one of his peers he enjoyed. He, as it were, rolled it round his tongue and mixed it with his saliva. But this was different. He had never met a Pekingese before, and no one would have been more surprised than himself if he had been informed that this curious, fluffy thing was a dog. Himself, he regarded it as an Act of God, and, thoroughly unnerved, he raced three times round the lawn and tried to climb a tree. Failing in this endeavor, he fitted his ample tail if possible more firmly into its groove and vanished from the scene.

The astonishment of the Hon. Freddie Threepwood was only equalled by his chagrin. Lady Alcester had begun now to express her opinion of the incident, and her sneers, her jeers, her unveiled innuendoes, were hard to bear. If, she said, the patrons of Donaldson's Dog-Joy allowed themselves to be chased off the map in this fashion by Pekingese, she was glad she had never been weak enough to be persuaded to try it.

"It's lucky," said Lady Alcester in her hard, scoffing way, "that Susan wasn't a rat. I suppose a rat would have given that mongrel of yours heart failure."

"Bottles," said Freddie stiffly, "is particularly sound on rats. I think, in common fairness, you ought to step to the stables and give him a chance of showing himself in a true light."

"I have seen quite enough, thank you."

"You won't come to the stables and watch him dealing with rats?"

"I will not."

"In that case," said Freddie somberly, "there is nothing more to be said. I suppose I may as well take him back to the Vicarage."

"What Vicarage?"

"Matchingham Vicarage."

"Was that Rupert's dog?"

"Of course it was."

"Then have you seen Rupert?"

"Of course I have."

"Did you warn him? About Mr. Watkins?"

"It was too late to warn him. He had had a letter from Gertrude, giving him the raspberry."

"What!"

"Well, she said Was he sure and Did they know their own minds, but you can take it from me that it was tantamount to the raspberry. Returning, however, to the topic of Bottles, Aunt Georgiana, I think you ought to take into consideration the fact that, in his recent encounter with the above Peke, he was undergoing a totally new experience and naturally did not appear at his best. I repeat once more that you should see him among the rats."

"Oh, Freddie!"

"Hullo?"

"How can you babble about this wretched dog when Gertrude's whole future is at stake? It is simply vital that somehow she be cured of this dreadful infatuation . . ."

"Well, I'll have a word with her if you like, but if you ask me, I think the evil has spread too far. Watkins has yowled himself into her very soul. However, I'll do my best. Excuse me, Aunt Georgiana."

From a neighboring bush the honest face of Bottles was protruding. He seemed to be seeking assurance that the All Clear had been blown.

It was at the hour of ante-dinner cocktail that Freddie found his first opportunity of having the promised word with Gertrude. Your true salesman and go-getter is never beaten, and a sudden and brilliant idea for accomplishing the conversion of his Aunt Georgiana had come to him as he brushed his hair. He descended to the drawing-room with a certain jauntiness, and was reminded by the sight of Gertrude of his mission. The girl was seated at the piano, playing dreamy chords.

"I say," said Freddie, "a word with you, young Gertrude. What is all this bilge I hear about you and Beefers?"

The girl flushed.

"Have you seen Rupert?"

"I was closeted with him this afternoon. He told me all."

"Oh?"

"He's feeling pretty low."

"Oh?"

"Yes," said Freddie, "pretty low the poor old chap is feeling, and I don't blame him, with the girls he's engaged to rushing about the place getting infatuated with tenors. I never heard of such a thing, dash it! What do you see in this Watkins? Wherein lies his attraction? Certainly not in his ties. They're awful. And the same applies to his entire outfit. He looks as if he had bought his clothes off the peg at a second-hand gents' costumiers. And, as if that were not enough, he wears short, but distinct, side-whiskers. You aren't going to tell me that you're seriously considering chucking a sterling egg like old Beefers in favor of a whiskered warbler?"

There was a pause. Gertrude played more dreamy chords.

"I'm not going to discuss it," she said. "It's nothing to do with you."

"Pardon me!" said Freddie. "Excuse me! If you will throw your mind back to the time when Beefers was conducting his wooing, you may remember that I was the fellow who worked the whole thing. But for my resource and ingenuity you and the old bounder would never have got engaged. I regard myself, therefore, in the light of a guardian angel or something, and as such am entitled to probe the matter to its depths. Of course," said Freddie, "I know exactly how you're feeling. I see where you have made your fatal bloomer. This Watkins has cast his glamorous spell about you, and you're looking on Beefers as a piece of unromantic cheese. But mark this, girl . . ."

"I wish you wouldn't call me 'girl.' "

"Mark this, old prune," amended Freddie. "And mark it well. Beefers is tried, true and trusted. A man to be relied on. Whereas Watkins, if I have read those whiskers aright, is the sort of fellow who will jolly well let you down in a crisis. And then, when it's too late, you'll come moaning to me, weeping salt tears and saying, 'Ah, why did I not know in time?' And I shall reply, 'You unhappy little fathead . . . !' "

"Oh, go and sell your dog-biscuits, Freddie!"

Gertrude resumed her playing. Her mouth was set in an obstinate line. Freddie eyed her with disapproval.

"It's some taint in the blood," he said. "Inherited from female parent. Like your bally mother, you are constitutionally incapable of seeing reason. Pig-headed, both of you. Sell my dog-biscuits, you say? Ha! As if I hadn't boosted them to Aunt Georgiana till my lips cracked. And with what result? So far, none. But wait till tonight."

"It is tonight."

"I mean, wait till later on tonight. Watch my little experiment."

"What little experiment?"

"Ah!"

"What do you mean, 'Ah'?"

"Just 'Ah!' " said Freddie.

The hour of the after-dinner coffee found Blandings Castle apparently an abode of peace. The superficial observer, peeping into the amber drawing-room through the French windows that led to the terrace, would have said that all was well with the inmates of this stately home of England. Lord Emsworth sat in a corner absorbed in a volume dealing with the treatment of pigs in sickness and in health. His sister, Lady Constance Keeble, was sewing. His other sister, Lady Alcester, was gazing at Gertrude. Gertrude was gazing at Orlo Watkins. And Orlo Watkins was gazing at the ceiling and singing in that crooning voice of his a song of Roses.

The Hon. Freddie Threepwood was not present. And that fact alone, if one may go by the views of his father, Lord Emsworth, should have been enough to make a success of any party.

And yet beneath this surface of cozy peace troubled currents were running. Lady Alcester, gazing at Gertrude, found herself a prey to gloom. She did not like the way Gertrude was gazing at Orlo Watkins. Gertrude, for her part, as the result of her recent conversation with the Hon. Freddie, was experiencing twinges of remorse and doubt. Lady Constance was still ruffled from the effect of Lady Alcester's sisterly frankness that evening on the subject of the imbecility of hostesses who deliberately let Crooning Tenors loose in castles. And Lord Emsworth was in that state of peevish exasperation which comes to dreamy old gentlemen who, wishing to read of Pigs, find their concentration impaired by voices singing of Roses.

Only Orlo Watkins was happy. And presently he, too, was to join the ranks of gloom. For just as he started to let himself go and handle this song as a song should be handled, there came from the other side of the door the sound of eager barking. A dog seemed to be without. And, apart from the fact that he disliked and feared all dogs, a tenor resents competition.

The next moment the door had opened, and the Hon. Freddie Threepwood appeared. He carried a small sack, and was accompanied by Bottles, the latter's manner noticeably lacking in repose.

On the face of the Hon. Freddie, as he advanced into the room, there was that set, grim expression which is always seen on the faces of those who are about to put their fortune to the test, to win or lose it all. The Old Guard at Waterloo looked much the same. For Freddie had decided to stake all on a single throw.

Many young men in his position, thwarted by an aunt who resolutely declined to amble across to the stables and watch a dog redeem himself among the rats, would have resigned themselves sullenly to defeat. But Freddie was made of finer stuff.

"Aunt Georgiana," he said, holding up the sack, at which Bottles was making agitated leaps, "you refused to come to the stables this afternoon to watch this Donaldson's Dog-Joy – fed animal in action, so you have left me no alternative but to play the fixture on your own ground."

Lord Emsworth glanced up from his book.

"Frederick, stop gibbering. And take that dog out of here."

Lady Constance glanced up from her sewing.

"Frederick, if you are coming in, come in and sit down. And take that dog out of here."

Lady Alcester, glancing up from Gertrude, exhibited in even smaller degree the kindly cordiality which might have been expected from an aunt.

"Oh, do go away, Freddie! You're a perfect nuisance. And take that dog out of here."

The Hon. Freddie, with a noble look of disdain, ignored them all.

"I have here, Aunt Georgiana," he said, "a few simple rats. If you will kindly step out on to the terrace, I shall be delighted to give a demonstration which should, I think, convince even your stubborn mind."

The announcement was variously received by the various members of the company. Lady Alcester screamed. Lady Constance sprang for the bell. Lord Emsworth snorted. Orlo Watkins blenched and retired behind Gertrude. And Gertrude, watching him blench, seeing him retire, tightened her lips. A country-bred girl, she was on terms of easy familiarity with rats, and this evidence of alarm in one whom she had set on a pedestal disquieted her.

The door opened, and Beach entered. He had come in pursuance of his regular duties to remove the coffee cups but, arriving, found other tasks assigned to him.

"Beach!" The voice was that of Lady Constance. "Take away those rats."

"Rats, m'lady?"

"Take that sack away from Mr. Frederick!"

Beach understood. If he was surprised at the presence of the younger son of the house in the amber drawing-room with a sack of rats in his hand, he gave no indication of the fact. With a murmured apology, he secured the sack and started to withdraw. It was not, strictly, his place to carry rats, but a good butler is always ready to give and take. Only so can the amenities of a large country house be preserved.

"And don't drop the dashed things," urged Lord Emsworth.

"Very good, m'lord."

The Hon. Freddie had flung himself into a chair and was sitting with his chin cupped in his hands, a bleak look on his face. To an ardent young go-getter these tyrannous actions in restraint of trade are hard to bear.

Lord Emsworth returned to his book.

Lady Constance returned to her sewing.

Lady Alcester returned to her thoughts.

At the piano Orlo Watkins was endeavoring to justify the motives which had led him a few moments before to retire prudently behind Gertrude.

"I hate rats," he said. "They jar upon me."

"Oh?" said Gertrude.

"I'm not afraid of them, of course, but they give me the creeps."

"Oh?" said Gertrude.

There was an odd look in her eyes. Of what was she thinking, this idealistic girl? Was it of the evening, a few short weeks before, when, suddenly encountering a beastly bat in the gloaming, she had found in the Rev. Rupert Bingham a sturdy and intrepid protector? Was she picturing the Rev. Rupert as she had seen him then — gallant, fearless, cleaving the air with long sweeps of his clerical hat, encouraging her the while with word and gesture?

Apparently so, for a moment later she spoke.

"How are you on bats?"

"Rats?"

"Bats."

"Oh, bats?"

"Are you afraid of bats?"

"I don't like bats," admitted Orlo Watkins.

Then, dismissing the subject, he reseated himself at the

piano and sang of June and the scent of unseen flowers.

Of all the little group in the amber drawing-room, only one member has now been left unaccounted for.

An animal of slow thought-processes, the dog Bottles had not at first observed what was happening to the sack. At the moment of its transference from the custody of Freddie to that of Beach, he had been engaged in sniffing at the leg of a chair. It was only as the door began to close that he became aware of the bereavement that threatened him. He bounded forward with a passionate cry, but it was too late. He found himself faced by unyielding wood. And when he started to scratch vehemently on this wood, a sharp pain assailed him. A book on the treatment of Pigs in sickness and in health, superbly aimed, had struck him in the small of the back. Then, for a space, he, like the Hon. Freddie Threepwood, his social sponsor, sat down and mourned.

"Take that beastly, blasted, infernal dog out of here," cried Lord Emsworth.

Freddie rose listlessly.

"It's old Beefers' dog," he said. "Beefers will be here at any moment. We can hand the whole conduct of the affair over to him."

Gertrude started.

"Is Rupert coming here tonight?"

"Said he would," responded Freddie, and passed from the scene. He had had sufficient of his flesh and blood and was indisposed to linger. It was his intention to pop down to Market Blandings in his two-seater, soothe his wounded sensibilities, so far as they were capable of being soothed, with a visit to the local motion-picture house, look in at the Emsworth Arms for a spot of beer, and then home to bed, to forget.

Gertrude had fallen into a reverie. Her fair young face was

overcast. A feeling of embarrassment had come upon her. When she had written that letter and posted it on the previous night, she had not foreseen that the Rev. Rupert would be calling so soon.

"I didn't know Rupert was coming tonight," she said.

"Oh, yes," said Lady Alcester brightly.

"Like a lingering tune, my whole life through, 'twill haunt me for EV-ah, that night in June with you-oo," sang Orlo Watkins.

And Gertrude, looking at him, was aware for the first time of a curious sensation of not being completely in harmony with this young whiskered man. She wished he would stop singing. He prevented her thinking.

Bottles, meanwhile, had resumed his explorations. Dogs are philosophers. They soon forget. They do not waste time regretting the might-have-beens. Adjusting himself with composure to the changed conditions, Bottles moved to and fro in a spirit of affable inquiry. He looked at Lord Emsworth, considered the idea of seeing how he smelt, thought better of it, and advanced towards the French windows. Something was rustling in the bushes outside, and it seemed to him that this might as well be looked into before he went and breathed on Lady Constance's leg.

He had almost reached his objective, when Lady Alcester's Airedale, who had absented himself from the room some time before in order to do a bit of bone-burying, came bustling in, ready, his business completed, to resume the social whirl.

Seeing Bottles, he stopped abruptly.

Both then began a slow and cautious forward movement, of a crab-like kind. Arriving at close quarters, they stopped again. Their nostrils twitched a little. They rolled their eyes. And to the ears of those present there came, faintly at first, a low, throaty sound, like the far-off gargling of an octogenarian with bronchial trouble.

This rose to a sudden crescendo. And the next moment hostilities had begun.

In underrating Bottles's qualities and scoffing at him as a fighting force, Lady Alcester had made an error. Capable though he was of pusillanimity in the presence of female Pekingese, there was nothing of the weakling about this sterling animal. He had cleaned up every dog in Much Matchingham and was spoken of on all sides — from the Blue Boar in the High Street to the distant Cow and Caterpillar on the Shrewsbury Road — as an ornament to the Vicarage and a credit to his master's Cloth.

On the present occasion, moreover, he was strengthened by the fact that he felt he had right on his side. In spite of a certain coldness on the part of the Castle circle and a soreness about the ribs where the book on Pigs and their treatment had found its billet, there seems to be no doubt that Bottles had by this time become thoroughly convinced that this drawing-room was his official home. And, feeling that all these delightful people were relying on him to look after their interests and keep alien and subversive influences at a distance, he advanced with a bright willingness to the task of ejecting this intruder.

Nor was the Airedale disposed to hold back. He, too, was no stranger to the ring. In Hyde Park, where, when at his London residence, he took his daily airing, he had met all comers and acquitted himself well. Dogs from Mayfair, dogs from Bayswater, dogs from as far afield as the Brompton Road and West Kensington, had had experience of the stuff of which he was made. Bottles reminded him a little of an animal from Pont Street, over whom he had once obtained a decision on the banks of the Serpentine, and he joined the battle with an easy confidence.

The reactions of a country-house party to an after-dinner dog-fight in the drawing-room always vary considerably according to the individual natures of its members. Lady Alcester, whose long association with the species had made her a sort of honorary dog herself, remained tranquil. She surveyed the proceedings with unruffled equanimity through a tortoise-shell-rimmed lorgnette. Her chief emotion was one of surprise at the fact that Bottles was unquestionably getting the better of the exchanges. She liked his footwork. Impressed, she was obliged to admit that, if this was the sort of battler it turned out, there must be something in Donaldson's Dog-Joy after all.

The rest of the audience were unable to imitate her nonchalance. The two principals were giving that odd illusion, customary on these occasions, of being all over the place at the same time: and the demeanor of those in the ring-side seats was frankly alarmed. Lady Constance had backed against the wall, from which position she threw a futile cushion. Lord Emsworth, in his corner, was hunting feebly for ammunition and wishing that he had not dropped the pince-nez, without which he was no sort of use in a crisis.

And Gertrude? Gertrude was staring at Orlo Watkins, who, with a resource and presence of mind unusual in one so young, had just climbed on top of a high cabinet containing china.

His feet were on a level with her eyes, and she saw that they were feet of clay.

And it was at this moment, when a girl stood face to face with her soul, that the door opened.

"Mr. Bingham," announced Beach.

Men of the physique of the Rev. Rupert Bingham are not as a rule quick thinkers. From earliest youth, the Rev. Rupert had run to brawn rather than brain. But even the dullest-witted person could have told, on crossing that threshold, that there was a dog-fight going on. Beefy Bingham saw it in a flash, and he acted promptly.

There are numerous methods of stopping these painful affairs. Some advocate squirting water, others prefer to sprinkle pepper. Good results may be obtained, so one school of thought claims, by holding a lighted match under the nearest nose. Beefy Bingham was impatient of these subtleties.

To Beefy all this was old stuff. Ever since he had been given his Cure of Souls, half his time, it sometimes seemed to him, had been spent in hauling Bottles away from the throats of the dogs of his little flock. Experience had given him a technique. He placed one massive hand on the neck of the Airedale, the other on the neck of Bottles, and pulled. There was a rending sound, and they came apart.

"Rupert!" cried Gertrude.

Gazing at him, she was reminded of the heroes of old. And few could have denied that he made a strangely impressive figure, this large young man, standing there with bulging eyes and a gyrating dog in each hand. He looked like a statue of Right triumphing over Wrong. You couldn't place it exactly, because it was so long since you had read the book, but he reminded you of something out of *Pilgrim's Progress*.

So, at least, thought Gertrude. To Gertrude it was as if the scales had fallen from her eyes and she had wakened from some fevered dream. Could it be she, she was asking herself, who had turned from this noble youth and strayed towards one who, though on the evidence he seemed to have a future before him as an Alpine climber, was otherwise so contemptible?

"Rupert!" said Gertrude.

Beefy Bingham had now completed his masterly campaign. He had thrown Bottles out of the window and shut it behind him. He had dropped the Airedale to the carpet, where it now sat, licking itself in a ruminative way. He had produced a handkerchief and was passing it over his vermilion brow.

"Oh, Rupert!" said Gertrude, and flung herself into his arms.

The Rev. Rupert said nothing. On such occasions your knowledgeable Vicar does not waste words.

Nor did Orlo Watkins speak. He had melted away. Perhaps, perched on his eyrie, he had seen in Gertrude's eyes the look which, when seen in the eyes of a girl by any interested party, automatically induces the latter to go to his room and start packing, in readiness for the telegram which he will receive on the morrow, summoning him back to London on urgent business. At any rate, he had melted.

It was late that night when the Hon. Freddie Threepwood returned to the home of his fathers. Moodily undressing, he was surprised to hear a knock on the door.

His Aunt Georgiana entered. On her face was the unmistakable look of a mother whose daughter has seen the light and will shortly be marrying a deserving young clergyman with a bachelor uncle high up in the shipping business.

"Freddie," said Lady Alcester, "you know that stuff you're always babbling about — I've forgotten its name . . ."

"Donaldson's Dog-Joy," said Freddie. "It may be obtained either in the small (or one-and-threepenny) packets or in the half-crown (or large) size. A guarantee goes with each purchase. Unique in its health-giving properties . . ."

"I'll take two tons to start with," said Lady Alcester.

Jeeves and the Old School Chum

✜ IN THE AUTUMN of the year in which Yorkshire Pudding won the Manchester November Handicap, the fortunes of my old pal Richard (Bingo) Little seemed to have reached their — what's the word I want? He was, to all appearances, absolutely on plush. He ate well, slept well, was happily married, and, his Uncle Wilberforce having at last handed in his dinner-pail, respected by all, had come into possession of a large income and a fine old place in the country about thirty miles from Norwich. Buzzing down there for a brief visit, I came away convinced that, if ever a bird was sitting on top of the world, that bird was Bingo.

I had to come away because the family were shooting me off to Harrogate to chaperone my Uncle George, whose liver had been giving him the elbow again. But, as we sat pushing down the morning meal on the day of my departure, I readily agreed to pay a return date as soon as ever I could fight my way back to civilization.

"Come in time for the Lakenham races," urged young

Bingo. He took aboard a second cargo of sausages and bacon, for he had always been a good trencherman and the country air seemed to improve his appetite. "We're going to motor over with a luncheon basket, and more or less revel."

I was just about to say that I would make a point of it when Mrs. Bingo, who was opening letters behind the coffee-apparatus, suddenly uttered a pleased yowl.

"Oh, sweetie-lambkin!" she cried.

Mrs. B., if you remember, before her marriage was the celebrated female novelist Rosie M. Banks, and it is in some such ghastly fashion that she habitually addresses the other half of the sketch. She has got that way, I take it, from a lifetime of writing heart-throb fiction for the masses. Bingo doesn't seem to mind. I suppose, seeing that the little woman is the author of such outstanding bilge as *Mervyn Keene, Clubman,* and *Only a Factory Girl,* he is thankful it isn't anything worse.

"Oh, sweetie-lambkin, isn't that lovely?"

"What?"

"Laura Pyke wants to come here."

"Who?"

"You must have heard me speak of Laura Pyke. She was my dearest friend at school. I simply worshiped her. She always had such a wonderful mind. She wants us to put her up for a week or two.

"Right-ho. Bung her in."

"You're sure you don't mind?"

"Of course not. Any pal of yours —"

"Darling!" said Mrs. Bingo, blowing him a kiss.

"Angel!" said Bingo, going on with the sausages.

All very charming, in fact. Pleasant domestic scene, I mean. Cheery give-and-take in the home and all that. I said as much to Jeeves as we drove off.

"In these days of unrest, Jeeves," I said, "with wives yearn-

ing to fulfill themselves and husbands slipping round the corner to do what they shouldn't, and the home, generally speaking, in the melting-pot, as it were, it is nice to find a
thoroughly united couple."

"Decidedly agreeable, sir."

"I allude to the Bingos — Mr. and Mrs."

"Exactly, sir."

"What was it the poet said of couples like the Bingeese?"

" 'Two minds with but a single thought, two hearts that
beat as one,' sir."

"A dashed good description, Jeeves."

"It has, I believe, given uniform satisfaction, sir."

And yet, if I had only known, what I had been listening to
that A.M. was the first faint rumble of the coming storm. Unseen, in the background, Fate was quietly slipping the lead
into the boxing glove.

I managed to give Uncle George a miss at a fairly early date
and, leaving him wallowing in the waters, sent a wire to the
Bingos, announcing my return. It was a longish drive and I
fetched up at my destination only just in time to dress for
dinner. I had done a quick dash into the soup-and-fish and
was feeling pretty good at the prospect of a cocktail and the
well-cooked, when the door opened and Bingo appeared.

"Hullo, Bertie," he said. "Ah, Jeeves."

He spoke in one of those toneless voices; and, catching
Jeeves's eye as I adjusted the old cravat, I exchanged a ques-
tioning glance with it. From its expression I gathered that the
same thing had struck him that had struck me — viz., that our
host, the young Squire, was none too chirpy. The brow was
furrowed, the eye lacked that hearty sparkle, and the general
bearing and demeanor were those of a body discovered after
being several days in the water.

"Anything up, Bingo?" I asked, with the natural anxiety of a boyhood friend. "You have a moldy look. Are you sickening for some sort of plague?"

"I've got it."

"Got what?"

"The plague."

"How do you mean?"

"She's on the premises now," said Bingo, and laughed in an unpleasant, hacking manner, as if he were missing on one tonsil.

I couldn't follow him. The old egg seemed to me to speak in riddles.

"You seem to me, old egg," I said, "to speak in riddles. Don't you think he speaks in riddles, Jeeves?"

"Yes, sir."

"I'm talking about the Pyke," said Bingo.

"What pike?"

"Laura Pyke. Don't you remember —"

"Oh, ah. Of course. The school chum. The seminary crony. Is she still here?"

"Yes, and looks like staying forever. Rosie's absolutely potty about her. Hangs on her lips."

"The glamour of the old days still persists, eh?"

"I should say it does," said young Bingo. "This business of schoolgirl friendship beats me. Hypnotic is the only word. I can't understand it. Men aren't like that. You and I were at school together, Bertie, but, my gosh, I don't look on you as a sort of mastermind."

"You don't?"

"I don't treat your lightest utterance as a pearl of wisdom."

"Why not?"

"Yet Rosie does with this Pyke. In the hands of the Pyke she is mere putty. If you want to see what was once a first-class Garden of Eden becoming utterly ruined as a desirable residence by the machinations of a Serpent, take a look round this place."

"Why, what's the trouble?"

"Laura Pyke," said young Bingo with intense bitterness, "is a food crank, curse her. She says we all eat too much and eat it too quickly and, anyway, ought not to be eating it at all but living on parsnips and similar muck. And Rosie, instead of telling the woman not to be a fathead, gazes at her in wide-eyed admiration, taking it in through the pores. The result is that the cuisine of this house has been shot to pieces, and I am starving on my feet. Well, when I tell you that it's weeks since a beefsteak pudding raised its head in the home, you'll understand what I mean."

At this point the gong went. Bingo listened with a moody frown.

"I don't know why they still bang that damned thing," he said. "There's nothing to bang it for. By the way, Bertie, would you like a cocktail?"

"I would."

"Well, you won't get one. We don't have cocktails any more. The girl friend says they corrode the stomachic tissues."

I was appalled. I had had no idea that the evil had spread as far as this.

"No cocktails!"

"No. And you'll be dashed lucky if it isn't a vegetarian dinner."

"Bingo," I cried deeply moved, "you must act. You must assert yourself. You must put your foot down. You must take a strong stand. You must be master in the home."

He looked at me. A long, strange look.

"You aren't married, are you, Bertie?"

"You know I'm not."
"I should have guessed it, anyway. Come on."

Well, the dinner wasn't absolutely vegetarian, but when you had said that you had said everything. It was sparse, meager, not at all the jolly, chunky repast for which the old tum was standing up and clamoring after its long motor ride. And what there was of it was turned to ashes in the mouth by the conversation of Miss Laura Pyke.

In happier circs., and if I had not been informed in advance of the warped nature of her soul, I might have been favorably impressed by this female at the moment of our meeting. She was really rather a good-looking girl, a bit strong in the face but nevertheless quite reasonably attractive. But had she been a thing of radiant beauty, she could never have clicked with Bertram Wooster. Her conversation was of a kind which would have queered Helen of Troy with any right-thinking man.

During dinner she talked all the time, and it did not take me long to see why the iron had entered into Bingo's soul. Practically all she said was about food and Bingo's tendency to shovel it down in excessive quantities, thereby handing the lemon to his stomachic tissues. She didn't seem particularly interested in my stomachic tissues, rather giving the impression that if Bertram burst it would be all right with her. It was on young Bingo that she concentrated as the brand to be saved from the burning. Gazing at him like a high priestess at the favorite, though erring, disciple, she told him all the things that were happening to his inside because he would insist on eating stuff lacking in fat-soluble vitamins. She spoke freely of proteins, carbohydrates, and the physiological requirements of the average individual. She was not a girl who believed in mincing her words, and a racy little anecdote she told about a man who refused to eat prunes had the effect of causing me to be a non-starter for the last two courses.

"Jeeves," I said, on reaching the sleeping chamber that night, "I don't like the look of things."

"No, sir?"

"No, Jeeves, I do not. I view the situation with concern. Things are worse than I thought they were. Mr. Little's remarks before dinner may have given you the impression that the Pyke merely lectured on food-reform in a general sort of way. Such, I now find, is not the case. By way of illustrating her theme, she points to Mr. Little as the awful example. She criticizes him, Jeeves."

"Indeed, sir?"

"Yes. Openly. Keeps telling him he eats too much, drinks too much, and gobbles his food. I wish you could have heard a comparison she drew between him and the late Mr. Gladstone, considering them in the capacity of food chewers. It left young Bingo very much with the short end of the stick. And the sinister thing is that Mrs. Bingo approves. Are wives often like that? Welcoming criticism of the lord and master, I mean?"

"They are generally open to suggestions from the outside public with regard to the improvement of their husbands, sir."

"That is why married men are wan, what?"

"Yes, sir."

I had had the foresight to send the man downstairs for a plate of biscuits. I bit a representative specimen thoughtfully.

"Do you know what I think, Jeeves?"

"No, sir."

"I think Mr. Little doesn't realize the full extent of the peril which threatens his domestic happiness. I'm beginning to understand this business of matrimony. I'm beginning to see

how the thing works. Would you care to hear how I figure it
out, Jeeves?"

"Extremely, sir."

"Well, it's like this. Take a couple of birds. These birds get
married, and for a while all is gas and gaiters. The female regards her mate as about the best thing that ever came a girl's
way. He is her king, if you know what I mean. She looks up
to him and respects him. Joy, as you might say, reigns supreme. Eh?"

"Very true, sir."

"Then gradually, by degrees — little by little, if I may use
the expression — disillusionment sets in. She sees him eating
a poached egg, and the glamour starts to fade. She watches
him mangling a chop, and it continues to fade. And so on and
so on, if you follow me, and so forth."

"I follow you perfectly, sir."

"But mark this, Jeeves. This is the point. Here we approach
the nub. Usually it is all right, because, as I say, the disillusionment comes gradually and the female has time to adjust
herself. But in the case of young Bingo, owing to the indecent
outspokenness of the Pyke, it's coming in a rush. Absolutely
in a flash, without any previous preparation. Mrs. Bingo is
having Bingo presented to her as a sort of human boa-con-
strictor full of unpleasantly jumbled interior organs. The picture which the Pyke is building up for her in her mind is that
of one of those men you see in restaurants with three chins,
bulging eyes, and the veins starting out on the forehead. A
little more of this, and love must wither."

"You think so, sir?"

"I'm sure of it. No affection can stand the strain. Twice during dinner tonight the Pyke said things about young Bingo's
intestinal canal which I shouldn't have thought would have
been possible in mixed company even in this lax post-War era.

Well, you see what I mean. You can't go on knocking a man's intestinal canal indefinitely without causing his wife to stop and ponder. The danger, as I see it, is that after a bit more of this Mrs. Little will decide that tinkering is no use and that the only thing to do is to scrap Bingo and get a newer model."

"Most disturbing, sir."

"Something must be done, Jeeves. You must act. Unless you can find some way of getting this Pyke out of the woodwork, and that right speedily, the home's number is up. You see, what makes matters worse is that Mrs. Bingo is romantic. Women like her, who consider the day ill spent if they have not churned out five thousand words of superfatted fiction, are apt even at the best of times to yearn a trifle. The ink gets into their heads. I mean to say, I shouldn't wonder if right from the start Mrs. Bingo hasn't had a sort of sneaking regret that Bingo isn't one of those strong, curt, Empire-building kind of Englishmen she puts into her books, with sad, unfathomable eyes, lean, sensitive hands, and riding boots. You see what I mean?"

"Precisely, sir. You imply that Miss Pyke's criticisms will have been instrumental in moving the hitherto unformulated dissatisfaction from the subconscious to the conscious mind."

"Once again, Jeeves?" I said, trying to grab it as it came off the bat, but missing it by several yards.

He repeated the dose.

"Well, I daresay you're right," I said. "Anyway, the point is, P.M.G. — Pyke must go. How do you propose to set about it?"

"I fear I have nothing to suggest at the moment, sir."

"Come, come, Jeeves."

"I fear not, sir. Possibly after I have seen the lady —"

"You mean, you want to study the psychology of the individual and what-not?"

"Precisely, sir."

"Well, I don't know how you're going to do it. After all, I mean, you can hardly cluster round the dinner-table and drink in the Pyke's small talk."

"There is that difficulty, sir."

"Your best chance, it seems to me, will be when we go to the Lakenham races on Thursday. We shall feed out of a luncheon-basket in God's air, and there's nothing to stop you hanging about and passing the sandwiches. Prick the ears and be at your most observant then, is my advice."

"Very good, sir."

"Very good, Jeeves. Be there, then, with the eyes popping. And meanwhile, dash downstairs and see if you can dig up another installment of these biscuits. I need them sorely."

The morning of the Lakenham races dawned bright and juicy. A casual observer would have said that God was in His heaven and all right with the world. It was one of those days you sometimes get lateish in the autumn when the sun beams. the birds toot, and there is a bracing tang in the air that sends the blood beetling briskly through the veins.

Personally, however, I wasn't any too keen on the bracing tang. It made me feel so exceptionally fit that almost immediately after breakfast I found myself beginning to wonder what there would be for lunch. And the thought of what there probably would be for lunch, if the Pyke's influence made itself felt, lowered my spirits considerably.

"I fear the worst, Jeeves," I said. "Last night at dinner Miss Pyke threw out the remark that the carrot was the best of all vegetables, having an astonishing effect on the blood and beautifying the complexion. Now, I am all for anything that bucks up the Wooster blood. Also, I would like to give the natives a treat by letting them take a look at my rosy, glowing cheeks. But not at the expense of lunching on raw carrots. To avoid any rannygazoo, therefore, I think it will be best if you add a bit for the young master to your personal packet of sandwiches. I don't want to be caught short."

"Very good, sir."

At this point, young Bingo came up. I hadn't seen him look so jaunty for days.

"I've just been superintending the packing of the lunch-basket, Bertie," he said. "I stood over the butler and saw that there was no nonsense."

"All pretty sound?" I asked, relieved.

"All indubitably sound."

"No carrots?"

"No carrots," said young Bingo. "There's ham sandwiches," he proceeded, a strange, soft light in his eyes, "and tongue sandwiches and potted meat sandwiches and game sandwiches and hard-boiled eggs and lobster and a cold chicken and sardines and a cake and a couple of bottles of Bollinger and some old brandy —"

"It has the right ring," I said. "And if we want a bite to eat after that, of course we can go to the pub."

"What pub?"

"Isn't there a pub on the course?"

"There's not a pub for miles. That's why I was so particularly careful that there should be no funny work about the basket. The common where these races are held is a desert without an oasis. Practically a death-trap. I met a fellow the other day who told me he got there last year and unpacked his basket and found that the champagne had burst and, together with the salad dressing, had soaked into the ham, which in its turn had got mixed up with the Gorgonzola cheese, forming a sort of paste. He had had rather a bumpy bit of road to travel over."

"What did he do?"

"Oh, he ate the mixture. It was the only course. But he said he could still taste it sometimes, even now."

In ordinary circs. I can't say I should have been any too braced at the news that we were going to split up for the journey in the following order — Bingo and Mrs. Bingo in their car and the Pyke in mine, with Jeeves sitting behind in the dickey. But, things being as they were, the arrangement had its points. It meant that Jeeves would be able to study the back of her head and draw his deductions, while I could engage her in conversation and let him see for himself what manner of female she was.

I started, accordingly, directly we had rolled off and all through the journey until we fetched up at the course she gave of her best. It was with considerable satisfaction that I parked the car beside a tree and hopped out.

"You were listening, Jeeves?" I said gravely.

"Yes, sir."

"A tough baby?"

"Undeniably, sir."

Bingo and Mrs. Bingo came up.

"The first race won't be for half an hour," said Bingo. "We'd better lunch now. Fish the basket out, Jeeves, would you mind?"

"Sir?"

"The luncheon-basket," said Bingo in a devout sort of voice, licking his lips slightly.

"The basket is not in Mr. Wooster's car, sir."

"What!"

"I assumed that you were bringing it in your own, sir."

I have never seen the sunshine fade out of anybody's face as quickly as it did out of Bingo's. He uttered a sharp, wailing cry.

"Rosie!"

"Yes, sweetie-pie?"

"The bunch! The lasket!"

"What, darling?"

"The luncheon-basket!"

"What about it, precious?"

"It's been left behind!"

"Oh, has it?" said Mrs. Bingo.

I confess she had never fallen lower in my estimation. I had always known her as a woman with as healthy an appreciation of her meals as any of my acquaintance. A few years previously, when my Aunt Dahlia had stolen her French cook, Anatole, she had called Aunt Dahlia some names in my presence which had impressed me profoundly. Yet now, when informed that she was marooned on a bally prairie without bite or sup, all she could find to say was: "Oh, has it?" I had never fully realized before the extent to which she had allowed herself to be dominated by the deleterious influence of the Pyke.

The Pyke, for her part, touched an even lower level.

"It is just as well," she said, and her voice seemed to cut Bingo like a knife. "Luncheon is a meal better omitted. If taken, it should consist merely of a few muscatels, bananas, and grated carrots. It is a well-known fact —"

And she went on to speak at some length of the gastric juices in a vein far from suited to any gathering at which gentlemen were present.

"So, you see, darling," said Mrs. Bingo, "you will really feel ever so much better and brighter for not having eaten a lot of indigestible food. It is much the best thing that could have happened."

Bingo gave her a long, lingering look.

"I see," he said. "Well, if you will excuse me, I'll just go off somewhere where I can cheer a bit without exciting comment."

I perceived Jeeves withdrawing in a meaning manner, and I followed him, hoping for the best. My trust was not misplaced. He had brought enough sandwiches for two. In fact, enough for three. I whistled to Bingo, and he came slinking up, and we restored the tissues in a makeshift sort of way behind a hedge. Then Bingo went off to interview bookies about the first race, and Jeeves gave a cough.

"Swallowed a crumb the wrong way?" I said.

"No, sir, I thank you. It is merely that I desired to express a hope that I had not been guilty of taking a liberty, sir."

"How?"

"In removing the luncheon-basket from the car before we started, sir."

I quivered like an aspen. I stared at the man. Aghast. Shocked to the core.

"You, Jeeves?" I said, and I should rather think Caesar spoke in the same sort of voice on finding Brutus puncturing him with the sharp instrument. "You mean to tell me it was you who deliberately, if that's the word I want —?"

"Yes, sir. It seemed to me the most judicious course to pursue. It would not have been prudent, in my opinion, to have allowed Mrs. Little, in her present frame of mind, to witness Mr. Little eating a meal on the scale which he outlined in his remarks this morning."

I saw his point.

"True, Jeeves," I said thoughtfully. "I see what you mean. If young Bingo has a fault, it is that, when in the society of a sandwich, he is apt to get a bit rough. I've picnicked with him before, many a time and oft, and his method of approach to the ordinary tongue or ham sandwich rather resembles that of the lion, the king of beasts, tucking into an antelope. Add lobster and cold chicken, and I admit the spectacle might have been something of a jar for the consort . . . Still . . . all the same . . . nevertheless —"

"And there is another aspect of the matter, sir."

"What's that?"

"A day spent without nourishment in the keen autumnal air may induce in Mrs. Little a frame of mind not altogether in sympathy with Miss Pyke's views on diet."

"You mean, hunger will gnaw and she'll be apt to bite at the Pyke when she talks about how jolly it is for the gastric juices to get a day off?"

"Exactly, sir."

I shook the head. I hated to damp the man's pretty enthusiasm, but it had to be done.

"Abandon the idea, Jeeves," I said. "I fear you have not studied the sex as I have. Missing her lunch means little or nothing to the female of the species. The feminine attitude towards lunch is notoriously airy and casual. Where you have made your bloomer is in confusing lunch with tea. Hell, it is well known, has no fury like a woman who wants her tea and can't get it. At such times the most amiable of the sex become mere bombs which a spark may ignite. But lunch, Jeeves, no. I should have thought you would have known that — a bird of your established intelligence."

"No doubt you are right, sir."

"If you could somehow arrange for Mrs. Little to miss her tea . . . but these are idle dreams, Jeeves. By tea-time she will be back at the old home, in the midst of plenty. It only takes an hour to do the trip. The last race is over shortly after four. By five o'clock Mrs. Little will have her feet tucked under the table and will be reveling in buttered toast. I am sorry, Jeeves, but your scheme was a wash-out from the start. No earthly. A dud."

"I appreciate the point you have raised, sir. What you say is extremely true."

"Unfortunately. Well, there it is. The only thing to do seems to be to get back to the course and try to skin a bookie or two and forget."

Well, the long day wore on, so to speak. I can't say I enjoyed myself much. I was distrait, if you know what I mean. Preoccupied. From time to time assorted clusters of spavined local horses clumped down the course with farmers on top of them, but I watched them with a languid eye. To get into the spirit of one of these rural meetings, it is essential that the subject have a good, fat lunch inside him. Subtract the lunch, and what ensues? Ennui. Not once but many times during the afternoon I found myself thinking hard thoughts about Jeeves. The man seemed to me to be losing his grip. A child could have told him that that footling scheme of his would not have got him anywhere.

I mean to say, when you reflect that the average woman considers she has lunched luxuriously if she swallows a couple of macaroons, half a chocolate éclair and a raspberry vinegar, is she going to be peevish because you do her out of a midday sandwich? Of course not. Perfectly ridiculous. Too silly for words. All that Jeeves had accomplished by his bally trying to be clever was to give me a feeling as if foxes were gnawing my vitals and a strong desire for home.

It was a relief, therefore, when, as the shades of evening were beginning to fall, Mrs. Bingo announced her intention of calling it a day and shifting.

"Would you mind very much missing the last race, Mr. Wooster?" she asked.

"I am all for it," I replied cordially. "The last race means little or nothing in my life. Besides, I am a shilling and six-pence ahead of the game, and the time to leave off is when you're winning."

"Laura and I thought we would go home. I feel I should like an early cup of tea. Bingo says he will stay on. So I thought you could drive our car, and he would follow later in yours, with Jeeves."

"Right-ho."

"You know the way?"

"Oh yes. Main road as far as that turning by the pond, and then across country."

"I can direct you from there."

I sent Jeeves to fetch the car, and presently we were bowling off in good shape. The short afternoon had turned into a rather chilly, misty sort of evening, the kind of evening that sends a fellow's thoughts straying off in the direction of hot Scotch-and-water with a spot of lemon in it. I put the foot firmly on the accelerator, and we did the five or six miles of main road in quick time.

Turning eastward at the pond, I had to go a bit slower, for we had struck a wildish stretch of country where the going wasn't so good. I don't know any part of England where you feel so off the map as on the by-roads of Norfolk. Occasionally we would meet a cow or two, but otherwise we had the world pretty much to ourselves.

I began to think about that drink again, and the more I thought the better it looked. It's rummy how people differ in this matter of selecting the beverage that is to touch the spot. It's what Jeeves would call the psychology of the individual. Some fellows in my position might have voted for a tankard of ale, and the Pyke's idea of refreshing snort was, as I knew from what she had told me on the journey out, a cupful of tepid pip-and-peel water or, failing that, what she called the fruit-liquor. You make this, apparently, by soaking raisins in cold water and adding the juice of a lemon. After which, I suppose, you invite a couple of old friends in and have an orgy, burying the bodies in the morning.

Personally, I had no doubts. I never wavered. Hot Scotch-and-water was the stuff for me — stressing the Scotch, if you know what I mean, and going fairly easy on the H$_2$O. I seemed to see the beaker smiling at me across the misty fields, beckoning me on, as it were, and saying, "Courage, Bertram! It will not be long now!" And with renewed energy I bunged the old foot down on the accelerator and tried to send the needle up to sixty.

Instead of which, if you follow my drift, the bally thing flickered for a moment to thirty-five and then gave the business up as a bad job. Quite suddenly and unexpectedly, no one more surprised than myself, the car let out a faint gurgle like a sick moose and stopped in its tracks. And there we were, somewhere in Norfolk, with darkness coming on and a cold wind that smelled of guano and dead mangold-wurzels playing searchingly about the spinal column.

The back-seat drivers gave tongue.

"What's the matter? What has happened? Why don't you go on? What are you stopping for?"

I explained.

"I'm not stopping. It's the car."

"Why has the car stopped?"

"Ah!" I said, with a manly frankness that became me well. "There you have me."

You see, I'm one of those birds who drive a lot but don't know the first thing about the works. The policy I pursue is to get aboard, prod the self-starter, and leave the rest to Nature. If anything goes wrong, I scream for an A.A. scout. It's a system that answers admirably as a rule, but on the present occasion it blew a fuse owing to the fact that there wasn't an A.A. scout within miles. I explained as much to the fair cargo and received in return a "Tchah!" from the Pyke that nearly lifted the top of my head off. What with having a covey of female relations who have regarded me from childhood as about ten degrees short of a halfwit, I have become rather a connoisseur of "Tchahs," and the Pyke's seemed to me well up in Class A, possessing much of the timber and brio of my Aunt Agatha's.

"Perhaps I can find out what the trouble is," she said, becoming calmer. "I understand cars."

She got out and began peering into the thing's vitals. I thought for a moment of suggesting that its gastric juices might have taken a turn for the worse owing to lack of fat-soluble vitamins, but decided on the whole not to. I'm a pretty close observer, and it didn't seem to me that she was in the mood.

And yet, as a matter of fact, I should have been about right, at that. For after fiddling with the engine for a while in a discontented sort of way the female was suddenly struck with an idea. She tested it, and it was proved correct. There was not a drop of petrol in the tank. No gas. In other words, a complete lack of fat-soluble vitamins. What it amounted to was that the job now before us was to get the old bus home purely by will-power.

Feeling that, from whatever angle they regarded the regrettable occurrence, they could hardly blame me, I braced up a trifle — in fact, to the extent of a hearty "Well, well, well!"

"No petrol," I said. "Fancy that."

"But Bingo told me he was going to fill the tank this morning," said Mrs. Bingo.

"I suppose he forgot," said the Pyke. "He would!"

"What do you mean by that?" said Mrs. Bingo, and I noted in her voice a touch of what-is-it.

"I mean he is just the sort of man who would forget to fill the tank," replied the Pyke, who also appeared somewhat moved.

"I should be very much obliged, Laura," said Mrs. Bingo, doing the heavy loyal-little-woman stuff, "if you would refrain from criticizing my husband."

"Tchah!" said the Pyke.

"And don't say 'Tchah!' " said Mrs. Bingo.

"I shall say whatever I please," said the Pyke.

"Ladies, ladies!" I said. "Ladies, ladies, ladies!"

It was rash. Looking back, I can see that. One of the first lessons life teaches us is that on these occasions of back-chat between the delicately-nurtured a man should retire into the offing, curl up in a ball, and imitate the prudent tactics of the opossum, which, when danger is in the air, pretends to be dead, frequently going to the length of hanging out crêpe and instructing its friends to stand round and say what a pity it all is. The only result of my dash at the soothing intervention was that the Pyke turned on me like a wounded leopardess.

"Well!" she said. "Aren't you proposing to do anything, Mr. Wooster?"

"What can I do?"

"There's a house over there. I should have thought it would be well within even your powers to go and borrow a tin of petrol."

I looked. There was a house. And one of the lower windows was lighted, indicating to the trained mind the presence of a ratepayer.

"A very sound and brainy scheme," I said ingratiatingly. "I will first honk a little on the horn to show we're here, and then rapid action."

I honked, with the most gratifying results. Almost immediately a human form appeared in the window. It seemed to be waving its arms in a matey and welcoming sort of way. Stimulated and encouraged, I hastened to the front door and gave it a breezy bang with the knocker. Things, I felt, were moving.

The first bang produced no result. I had just lifted the knocker for the encore, when it was wrenched out of my hand. The door flew open, and there was a bloke with spectacles on his face and all round the spectacles an expression of strained anguish. A bloke with a secret sorrow.

I was sorry he had troubles, of course, but, having some of my own, I came right down to the agenda without delay.

"I say . . ." I began.

The bloke's hair was standing up in a kind of tousled mass, and at this juncture, as if afraid it would not stay like that without assistance, he ran a hand through it. And for the first time I noted that the spectacles had a hostile gleam.

"Was that you making that infernal noise?" he asked.

"Er — yes," I said. "I did toot."

"Toot once more — just once," said the bloke, speaking in a low, strangled voice, "and I'll shred you up into little bits with my bare hands. My wife's gone out for the evening and after hours of ceaseless toil I've at last managed to get the baby to sleep, and you come along making that hideous din with your damned horn. What do you mean by it, blast you?"

"Er —"

"Well, that's how matters stand," said the bloke, summing up. "One more toot — just one single, solitary suggestion of the faintest shadow or suspicion of anything remotely approaching a toot — and may the Lord have mercy on your soul."

"What I want," I said, "is petrol."

"What you'll get," said the bloke, "is a thick ear."

And, closing the door with the delicate caution of one brushing flies off a sleeping Venus, he passed out of my life.

Women as a sex are always apt to be a trifle down on the defeated warrior. Returning to the car, I was not well received. The impression seemed to be that Bertram had not acquitted himself in a fashion worthy of his Crusading ancestors. I did my best to smooth matters over, but you know how it is. When you've broken down on a chilly autumn evening miles from anywhere and have missed lunch and look like missing tea as well, mere charm of manner can never be a really satisfactory substitute for a tinful of the juice.

Things got so noticeably unpleasant, in fact, that after a while, mumbling something about getting help, I sidled off down the road. And, by Jove, I hadn't gone half a mile before I saw lights in the distance and there, in the middle of this forsaken desert, was a car.

I stood in the road and whooped as I had never whooped before.

"Hi!" I shouted. "I say! Hi! Half a minute! Hi! Ho! I say! Ho! Hi! Just a second if you don't mind."

The car reached me and slowed up. A voice spoke.

"Is that you, Bertie?"

"Hullo, Bingo! Is that you? I say, Bingo, we've broken down."

Bingo hopped out.

"Give us five minutes, Jeeves," he said, "and then drive slowly on."

"Very good, sir."

Bingo joined me.

"We aren't going to walk, are we?" I asked. "Where's the sense?"

"Yes, walk, laddie," said Bingo, "and warily withal. I want to make sure of something. Bertie, how were things when you left? Hotting up?"

"A trifle."

"You observed symptoms of a row, a quarrel, a parting of brass rags between Rosie and the Pyke?"

"There did seem a certain liveliness."

"Tell me."

I related what had occurred. He listened intently.

"Bertie," he said as we walked along, "you are present at a crisis in your old friend's life. It may be that this vigil in a broken-down car will cause Rosie to see what you'd have thought she ought to have seen years ago — viz., that the Pyke is entirely unfit for human consumption and must be cast into outer darkness where there is wailing and gnashing of teeth. I am not betting on it, but stranger things have happened. Rosie is the sweetest girl in the world, but, like all women, she gets edgy towards tea-time. And today, having missed lunch . . . Hark!"

He grabbed my arm, and we paused. Tense. Agog. From down the road came the sound of voices, and a mere instant was enough to tell us that it was Mrs. Bingo and the Pyke talking things over.

I had never listened in on a real, genuine female row before, and I'm bound to say it was pretty impressive. During my absence, matters appeared to have developed on rather a spacious scale. They had reached the stage now where the combatants had begun to dig into the past and rake up old scores. Mrs. Bingo was saying that the Pyke would never have got into the hockey team at St. Adela's if she hadn't flattered and fawned upon the captain in a way that it made Mrs. Bingo, even after all these years, sick to think of. The Pyke replied that she had refrained from mentioning it until now, having always felt it better to let bygones be bygones, but that if Mrs. Bingo supposed her to be unaware that Mrs. Bingo had won the Scripture prize by taking a list of the Kings of Judah into the examination room, tucked into her middy blouse, Mrs. Bingo was vastly mistaken.

Furthermore, the Pyke proceeded, Mrs. Bingo was also laboring under an error if she imagined that the Pyke proposed to remain a night longer under her roof. It had been in a moment of weakness, a moment of mistaken kindliness, supposing her to be lonely and in need of intellectual society, that the Pyke had decided to pay her a visit at all. Her intention now was, if ever Providence sent them aid and enabled her to get out of this beastly car and back to her trunks, to pack those trunks and leave by the next train, even if that train was a milk-train, stopping at every station. Indeed, rather than endure another night at Mrs. Bingo's, the Pyke was quite willing to walk to London.

To this, Mrs. Bingo's reply was long and eloquent and touched on the fact that in her last term at St. Adela's a girl named Simpson had told her (Mrs. Bingo) that a girl named Waddesley had told her (the Simpson) that the Pyke, while pretending to be a friend of hers (the Bingo's), had told her (the Waddesley) that she (the Bingo) couldn't eat strawberries and cream without coming out in spots, and, in addition, had spoken in the most catty manner about the shape of her nose. It could all have been condensed, however, into the word "Right-ho."

It was when the Pyke had begun to say that she had never had such a hearty laugh in her life as when she read the scene in Mrs. Bingo's last novel where the heroine's little boy dies of croup that we felt it best to call the meeting to order before bloodshed set in. Jeeves had come up in the car, and Bingo, removing a tin of petrol from the dickey, placed it in the shadows at the side of the road. Then we hopped on and made the spectacular entry.

"Hullo, hullo, hullo," said Bingo brightly. "Bertie tells me you've had a breakdown."

"Oh, Bingo!" cried Mrs. Bingo, wifely love thrilling in every syllable. "Thank goodness you've come."

"Now, perhaps." said the Pyke, "I can get home and do my packing. If Mr. Wooster will allow me to use his car, his man can drive me back to the house in time to catch the six-fifteen."

"You aren't leaving us?" said Bingo.

"I am," said the Pyke.

"Too bad," said Bingo.

She climbed in beside Jeeves and they popped off. There was a short silence after they had gone. It was too dark to see her, but I could feel Mrs. Bingo struggling between love of her mate and the natural urge to say something crisp about his forgetting to fill the petrol tank that morning. Eventually nature took its course.

"I must say, sweetie-pie," she said, "it was a little careless of you to leave the tank almost empty when we started today. You promised me you would fill it, darling."

"But I did fill it, darling."

"But, darling, it's empty."

"It can't be, darling."

"Laura said it was."

"The woman's an ass," said Bingo. "There's plenty of petrol. What's wrong is probably that the sprockets aren't running true with the differential gear. It happens that way sometimes.

I'll fix it in a second. But I don't want you to sit freezing out here while I'm doing it. Why not go to that house over there and ask them if you can't come in and sit down for ten minutes? They might give you a cup of tea, too."

A soft moan escaped Mrs. Bingo.

"Tea!" I heard her whisper.

I had to bust Bingo's daydream.

"I'm sorry, old man," I said, "but I fear the old English hospitality which you outline is off. That house is inhabited by a sort of bandit. As unfriendly a bird as I ever met. His wife's out and he's just got the baby to sleep, and this has darkened his outlook. Tap even lightly on his front door, and you take your life into your hands."

"Nonsense," said Bingo. "Come along."

He banged the knocker, and produced an immediate reaction.

"Hell!" said the Bandit, appearing as if out of a trap.

"I say," said young Bingo, "I'm just fixing our car outside. Would you object to my wife coming in out of the cold for a few minutes?"

"Yes," said the Bandit, "I would."

"And you might give her a cup of tea."

"I might," said the Bandit, "but I won't."

"You won't?"

"No. And for heaven's sake don't talk so loud. I know that baby. A whisper sometimes does it."

"Let us get this straight," said Bingo. "You refuse to give my wife tea?"

"Yes."

"You would see a woman starve?"

"Yes."

"Well, you jolly well aren't going to," said young Bingo.

"Unless you go straight to your kitchen, put the kettle on, and start slicing bread for the buttered toast, I'll yell and wake the baby."

The Bandit turned ashen.

"You wouldn't do that?"

"I would."

"Have you no heart?"

"No."

"No human feeling?"

"No."

The Bandit turned to Mrs. Bingo. You could see his spirit was broken.

"Do your shoes squeak?" he asked humbly.

"No."

"Then come on in."

"Thank you," said Mrs. Bingo.

She turned for an instant to Bingo, and there was a look in her eyes that one of those damsels in distress might have given the knight as he shot his cuffs and turned away from the dead dragon. It was a look of adoration, of almost reverent respect. Just the sort of look, in fact, that a husband likes to see.

"Darling!" she said.

"Darling!" said Bingo.

"Angel!" said Mrs. Bingo.

"Precious!" said Bingo. "Come along, Bertie, let's get at that car."

He was silent till he had fetched the tin of petrol and filled the tank and screwed the cap on again. Then he drew a deep breath.

"Bertie," he said, "I am ashamed to admit it, but occasionally in the course of a lengthy acquaintance there have been moments when I have temporarily lost faith in Jeeves."

"My dear chap!" I said, shocked.

"Yes, Bertie, there have. Sometimes my belief in him has wobbled. I have said to myself: 'Has he the old speed, the ancient vim?' I shall never say it again. From now on, childlike trust. It was his idea, Bertie, that if a couple of women headed for tea suddenly found the cup snatched from their lips, so to speak, they would turn and rend one another. Observe the result."

"But, dash it, Jeeves couldn't have known that the car would break down."

"On the contrary. He let all the petrol out of the tank when you sent him to fetch the machine — all except just enough to carry it well into the wilds beyond the reach of human aid. He foresaw what would happen. I tell you, Bertie, Jeeves stands alone."

"Absolutely."

"He's a marvel."

"A wonder."

"A wizard."

"A stout fellow," I agreed. "Full of fat-soluble vitamins."

"The exact expression," said young Bingo. "And now let's go and tell Rosie the car is fixed, and then home to the tankard of ale."

"Not the tankard of ale, old man," I said firmly. "The hot Scotch-and-water with a spot of lemon in it."

"You're absolutely right," said Bingo. "What a flair you have in these matters, Bertie. Hot Scotch-and-water it is."

Uncle Fred Flits By

In order that they might enjoy their after-luncheon coffee in peace, the Crumpet had taken the guest whom he was entertaining at the Drones Club to the smaller and less frequented of the two smoking rooms. In the other, he explained, though the conversation always touched an exceptionally high level of brilliance, there was apt to be a good deal of sugar thrown about.

The guest said he understood.

"Young blood, eh?"

"That's right. Young blood."

"And animal spirits."

"And animal, as you say, spirits," agreed the Crumpet. "We get a fairish amount of those here."

"The complaint, however, is not, I observe, universal."

"Eh?"

The other drew his host's attention to the doorway, where a young man in form-fitting tweeds had just appeared. The aspect of this young man was haggard. His eyes glared wildly, and he sucked at an empty cigarette holder. If he had a mind, there was something on it. When the Crumpet called to him to come and join the party, he merely shook his head in a distraught sort of way and disappeared, looking like a character out of a Greek tragedy pursued by the Fates.

The Crumpet sighed.

"Poor old Pongo!"

"Pongo?"

"That was Pongo Twistleton. He's all broken up about his Uncle Fred."

"Dead?"

"No such luck. Coming up to London again tomorrow. Pongo had a wire this morning."

"And that upsets him?"

"Naturally. After what happened last time."

"What was that?"

"Ah!" said the Crumpet.

"What happened last time?"

"You may well ask."

"I do ask."

"Ah!" said the Crumpet.

Poor old Pongo (said the Crumpet) has often discussed his Uncle Fred with me, and if there weren't tears in his eyes when he did so, I don't know a tear in the eye when I see one. In round numbers the Earl of Ickenham, of Ickenham Hall, Ickenham, Hants, he lives in the country most of the year, but from time to time has a nasty way of slipping his collar and getting loose and descending upon Pongo at his flat in Albany. And every time he does so, the unhappy young blighter is subjected to some soul-testing experience. Because the trouble with this uncle is that, though sixty if a day, he becomes on arriving in the metropolis as young as he feels — which is, apparently, a youngish twenty-two. I don't know if you happen to know what the word "excesses" means, but those are what Pongo's Uncle Fred from the country, when in London, invariably commits.

It wouldn't so much matter, mind you, if he would confine his activities to the club premises. We're pretty broad-minded here, and if you stop short of smashing the piano, there isn't much that you can do at the Drones that will cause the raised eyebrow and the sharp intake of breath. The snag is that he will insist on lugging Pongo out in the open and there, right in the public eye, proceeding to step high, wide and plentiful.

So when, on the occasion to which I allude, he stood pink and genial on Pongo's hearth-rug, bulging with Pongo's lunch and wreathed in the smoke of one of Pongo's cigars, and said: "And now, my boy, for a pleasant and instructive afternoon," you will readily understand why the unfortunate young clam gazed at him as he would have gazed at twopenn'orth of dynamite, had he discovered it lighting up in his presence.

"A what?" he said, giving at the knees and paling beneath the tan a bit.

"A pleasant and instructive afternoon," repeated Lord Ickenham, rolling the words round his tongue. "I propose that you place yourself in my hands and leave the program entirely to me."

Now, owing to Pongo's circumstances being such as to necessitate his getting into the aged relative's ribs at intervals and shaking him down for an occasional much-needed tenner or what-not, he isn't in a position to use the iron hand with the old buster. But at these words he displayed a manly firmness.

"You aren't going to get me to the dog races again."

"No, no."

"You remember what happened last June."

"Quite," said Lord Ickenham, "quite. Though I still think that a wiser magistrate would have been content with a mere reprimand."

"And I won't —"

"Certainly not. Nothing of that kind at all. What I propose to do this afternoon is to take you to visit the home of your ancestors."

Pongo did not get this.

"I thought Ickenham was the home of my ancestors."

"It is one of the homes of your ancestors. They also resided rather nearer the heart of things, at a place called Mitching Hill."

"Down in the suburbs, do you mean?"

"The neighborhood is now suburban, true. It is many years since the meadows where I sported as a child were sold and cut up into building lots. But when I was a boy Mitching Hill was open country. It was a vast, rolling estate belonging to your Great-uncle, Marmaduke, a man with whiskers of a nature which you with your pure mind would scarcely credit, and I have long felt a sentimental urge to see what the hell the old place looks like now. Perfectly foul, I expect. Still, I think we should make the pious pilgrimage."

Pongo absolutely-ed heartily. He was all for the scheme. A great weight seemed to have rolled off his mind. The way he looked at it was that even an uncle within a short jump of the loony bin couldn't very well get into much trouble in a suburb. I mean, you know what suburbs are. They don't, as it were, offer the scope. One follows his reasoning, of course.

"Fine!" he said. "Splendid! Topping!"

"Then put on your hat and rompers, my boy," said Lord

Ickenham, "and let us be off. I fancy one gets there by omnibuses and things."

Well, Pongo hadn't expected much in the way of mental uplift from the sight of Mitching Hill, and he didn't get it. Alighting from the bus, he tells me, you found yourself in the middle of rows and rows of semidetached villas, all looking exactly alike, and you went on and you came to more semidetached villas, and those all looked exactly alike, too. Nevertheless, he did not repine. It was one of those early spring days which suddenly change to midwinter, and he had come out without his overcoat, and it looked like rain and he hadn't an umbrella, but despite this his mood was one of sober ecstasy. The hours were passing and his uncle had not yet made a goat of himself. At the dog races the other had been in the hands of the constabulary in the first ten minutes.

It began to seem to Pongo that with any luck he might be able to keep the old blister pottering harmlessly about here till nightfall, when he could shoot a bit of dinner into him and put him to bed. And as Lord Ickenham had specifically stated that his wife, Pongo's Aunt Jane, had expressed her intention of scalping him with a blunt knife if he wasn't back at the Hall by lunchtime on the morrow, it really looked as if he might get through this visit without perpetrating a single major outrage on the public weal. It is rather interesting to note that as he thought this Pongo smiled, because it was the last time he smiled that day.

All this while, I should mention, Lord Ickenham had been stopping at intervals like a pointing dog and saying that it must have been just about here that he plugged the gardener in the trousers seat with his bow and arrow and that over there he had been sick after his first cigar, and he now paused in front of a villa which for some unknown reason called itself The Cedars. His face was tender and wistful.

"On this very spot, if I am not mistaken," he said, heaving a bit of a sigh, "on this very spot, fifty years ago come Lammas Eve, I . . . Oh, blast it!"

The concluding remark had been caused by the fact that the rain, which had held off until now, suddenly began to buzz down like a shower bath. With no further words, they leaped into the porch of the villa and there took shelter, exchanging glances with a gray parrot which hung in a cage in the window.

Not that you could really call it shelter. They were protected from above all right, but the moisture was now falling with a sort of swivel action, whipping in through the sides of the porch and tickling them up properly. And it was just after Pongo had turned up his collar and was huddling against the door that the door gave way. From the fact that a female of general-servant aspect was standing there he gathered that his uncle must have rung the bell.

This female wore a long mackintosh, and Lord Ickenham beamed upon her with a fairish spot of suavity.

"Good afternoon," he said.

The female said good afternoon.

"The Cedars?"

The female said yes, it was The Cedars.

"Are the old folks at home?"

The female said there was nobody at home.

"Ah? Well, never mind. I have come," said Lord Ickenham, edging in, "to clip the parrot's claws. My assistant, Mr. Walkinshaw, who applies the anesthetic," he added, indicating Pongo with a gesture.

"Are you from the bird shop?"

"A very happy guess."

"Nobody told me you were coming."

"They keep things from you, do they?" said Lord Ickenham, sympathetically. "Too bad."

Continuing to edge, he had got into the parlor by now, Pongo following in a sort of dream and the female following Pongo.

"Well, I suppose it's all right," she said. "I was just going out. It's my afternoon."

"Go out," said Lord Ickenham, cordially. "By all means go out. We will leave everything in order."

And presently the female, though still a bit on the dubious side, pushed off, and Lord Ickenham lit the gas-fire and drew a chair up.

"So here we are, my boy," he said. "A little tact, a little address, and here we are, snug and cozy and not catching our deaths of cold. You'll never go far wrong if you leave things to me."

"But, dash it, we can't stop here," said Pongo.

Lord Ickenham raised his eyebrows.

"Not stop here? Are you suggesting that we go out into that rain? My dear lad, you are not aware of the grave issues involved. This morning, as I was leaving home, I had a rather painful disagreement with your aunt. She said the weather was treacherous and wished me to take my woolly muffler. I replied that the weather was not treacherous and that I would be dashed if I took my woolly muffler. Eventually, by the exercise of an iron will, I had my way, and I ask you, my dear boy, to envisage what will happen if I return with a cold in the head. I shall sink to the level of a fifth-class power. Next time I came to London, it would be with a liver pad and a respirator. No! I shall remain here, toasting my toes at this really excellent fire. I had no idea that a gas-fire radiated such warmth. I feel all in a glow."

So did Pongo. His brow was wet with honest sweat. He is reading for the Bar, and while he would be the first to admit that he hasn't yet got a complete toe-hold on the Law of Great Britain, he had a sort of notion that oiling into a perfect stranger's semidetached villa on the pretext of pruning the parrot was a tort or misdemeanor, if not actual barratry or soccage in fief or something like that. And apart from the legal aspect of the matter there was the embarrassment of the thing. Nobody is more of a whale on correctness and not doing what's not done than Pongo, and the situation in which he now found himself caused him to chew the lower lip and, as I say, perspire a goodish deal.

"But suppose the blighter who owns this ghastly house comes back?" he asked. "Talking of envisaging things, try that one over on your pianola."

And, sure enough, as he spoke, the front-door bell rang.

"There!" said Pongo.

"Don't say 'There!' my boy," said Lord Ickenham reprovingly. "It's the sort of thing your aunt says. I see no reason for alarm. Obviously this is some casual caller. A ratepayer would have used his latchkey. Glance cautiously out of the window and see if you can see anybody."

"It's a pink chap," said Pongo, having done so.

"How pink?"

"Pretty pink."

"Well, there you are, then. I told you so. It can't be the big chief. The sort of fellows who own houses like this are pale and sallow, owing to working in offices all day. Go and see what he wants."

"You go and see what he wants."

"We'll both go and see what he wants," said Lord Ickenham.

So they went and opened the front door, and there, as Pongo had said, was a pink chap. A small young pink chap, a bit moist about the shoulder-blades.

"Pardon me," said this pink chap, "is Mr. Roddis in?"

"No," said Pongo.

"Yes," said Lord Ickenham. "Don't be silly, Douglas — of course I'm in. I am Mr. Roddis," he said to the pink chap. "This, such as he is, is my son Douglas. And you?"

"Name of Robinson."

"What about it?"

"My name's Robinson."

"Oh, *your* name's Robinson? Now we've got it straight. Delighted to see you, Mr. Robinson. Come right in and take your boots off."

They all trickled back to the parlor, Lord Ickenham pointing out objects of interest by the wayside to the chap, Pongo gulping for air a bit and trying to get himself abreast of this new twist in the scenario. His heart was becoming more and more bowed down with weight of woe. He hadn't liked being Mr. Walkinshaw the anesthetist, and he didn't like it any better being Roddis Junior. In brief, he feared the worst. It was only too plain to him by now that his uncle had got it thoroughly up his nose and had settled down to one of his big afternoons, and he was asking himself, as he had so often asked himself before, what would the harvest be?

Arrived in the parlor, the pink chap proceeded to stand on one leg and look coy.

"Is Julia here?" he asked, simpering a bit, Pongo says.

"Is she?" said Lord Ickenham to Pongo.

"No," said Pongo.

"No," said Lord Ickenham.

"She wired me she was coming here today."

"Ah, then we shall have a bridge four."

The pink chap stood on the other leg.

"I don't suppose you've ever met Julia. Bit of trouble in the family, she gave me to understand."

"It is often the way."

"The Julia I mean is your niece Julia Parker. Or, rather, your wife's niece Julia Parker."

"Any niece of my wife is a niece of mine," said Lord Ickenham heartily. "We share and share alike."

"Julia and I want to get married."

"Well, go ahead."

"But they won't let us."

"Who won't?"

"Her mother and father. And Uncle Charlie Parker and Uncle Henry Parker and the rest of them. They don't think I'm good enough."

"The morality of the modern young man is notoriously lax."

"Class enough, I mean. They're a haughty lot."

"What makes them haughty? Are they earls?"

"No, they aren't earls."

"Then why the devil," said Lord Ickenham warmly, "are they haughty? Only earls have a right to be haughty. Earls are hot stuff. When you get an earl, you've got something."

"Besides, we've had words. Me and her father. One thing led to another, and in the end I called him a perishing old — Coo!" said the pink chap, breaking off suddenly.

He had been standing by the window, and he now leaped lissomely into the middle of the room, causing Pongo, whose nervous system was by this time definitely down among the wines and spirits and who hadn't been expecting this *adagio* stuff, to bite his tongue with some severity.

"They're on the doorstep! Julia and her mother and father.
I didn't know they were all coming."

"You do not wish to meet them?"

"No, I don't!"

"Then duck behind the settee, Mr. Robinson," said Lord
Ickenham, and the pink chap, weighing the advice and finding
it good, did so. And as he disappeared the door bell rang.

Once more, Lord Ickenham led Pongo out into the hall.

"I say!" said Pongo, and a close observer might have noted
that he was quivering like an aspen.

"Say on, my dear boy."

"I mean to say, what?"

"What?"

"You aren't going to let these bounders in, are you?"

"Certainly," said Lord Ickenham. "We Roddises keep open
house. And as they are presumably aware that Mr. Roddis has
no son, I think we had better return to the old layout. You are
the local vet, my boy, come to minister to my parrot. When I
return, I should like to find you by the cage, staring at the bird
in a scientific manner. Tap your teeth from time to time with
a pencil and try to smell of iodoform. It will help to add
conviction."

So Pongo shifted back to the parrot's cage and stared so
earnestly that it was only when a voice said, "Well!" that he
became aware that there was anybody in the room. Turning,
he perceived that Hampshire's leading curse had come back,
bringing the gang.

It consisted of a stern, thin, middle-aged woman, a middle-
aged man and a girl.

You can generally accept Pongo's estimate of girls, and
when he says that this one was a pippin, one knows that he
uses the term in its most exact sense. She was about nineteen,
he thinks, and she wore a black beret, a dark-green leather

coat, a shortish tweed skirt, silk stockings and high-heeled shoes. Her eyes were large and lustrous and her face like a dewy rosebud at daybreak on a June morning. So Pongo tells me. Not that I suppose he has ever seen a rosebud at daybreak on a June morning, because it's generally as much as you can do to lug him out of bed in time for nine-thirty breakfast. Still, one gets the idea.

"Well," said the woman, "you don't know who I am, I'll be bound. I'm Laura's sister Connie. This is Claude, my husband. And this is my daughter Julia. Is Laura in?"

"I regret to say, no," said Lord Ickenham.

The woman was looking at him as if he didn't come up to her specifications.

"I thought you were younger," she said.

"Younger than what?" said Lord Ickenham.

"Younger than you are."

"You can't be younger than you are, worse luck," said Lord Ickenham. "Still, one does one's best, and I am bound to say that of recent years I have made a pretty good go of it."

The woman caught sight of Pongo, and he didn't seem to please her, either.

"Who's that?"

"The local vet, clustering round my parrot."

"I can't talk in front of him."

"It is quite all right," Lord Ickenham assured her. "The poor fellow is stone deaf."

And with an imperious gesture at Pongo, as much as to bid him stare less at girls and more at parrots, he got the company seated.

"Now, then," he said.

There was silence for a moment, then a sort of muffled sob, which Pongo thinks proceeded from the girl. He couldn't see, of course, because his back was turned and he was looking at the parrot, which looked back at him — most offensively, he says, as parrots will, using one eye only for the purpose. It also asked him to have a nut.

The woman came into action again.

"Although," she said, "Laura never did me the honor to invite me to her wedding, for which reason I have not communicated with her for five years, necessity compels me to cross her threshold today. There comes a time when differences must be forgotten and relatives must stand shoulder to shoulder."

"I see what you mean," said Lord Ickenham. "Like the boys of the old brigade."

"What I say is, let bygones be bygones. I would not have intruded on you, but needs must. I disregard the past and appeal to your sense of pity."

The thing began to look to Pongo like a touch, and he is convinced that the parrot thought so, too, for it winked and cleared its throat. But they were both wrong. The woman went on.

"I want you and Laura to take Julia into your home for a week or so, until I can make other arrangements for her. Julia is studying the piano, and she sits for her examination in two weeks' time, so until then she must remain in London. The trouble is, she has fallen in love. Or thinks she has."

"I know I have," said Julia.

Her voice was so attractive that Pongo was compelled to slew round and take another look at her. Her eyes, he says, were shining like twin stars and there was a sort of Soul's Awakening expression on her face, and what the dickens there was in a pink chap like the pink chap, who even as pink chaps go wasn't much of a pink chap, to make her look like that, was frankly, Pongo says, more than he could understand. The thing baffled him. He sought in vain for a solution.

"Yesterday, Claude and I arrived in London from our Bex-hill home to give Julia a pleasant surprise. We stayed, natu-rally, in the boarding house where she has been living for the past six weeks. And what do you think we discovered?"

"Insects."

"Not insects. A letter. From a young man. I found to my horror that a young man of whom I knew nothing was ar-ranging to marry my daughter. I sent for him immediately, and found him to be quite impossible. He jellies eels!"

"Does what?"

"He is an assistant at a jellied-eel shop."

"But surely," said Lord Ickenham, "that speaks well for him. The capacity to jelly an eel seems to me to argue intelligence of a high order. It isn't everybody who can do it, by any means. I know if someone came to me and said 'Jelly this eel!' I should be nonplussed. And so, or I am very much mistaken, would Ramsay MacDonald and Winston Churchill."

The woman did not seem to see eye to eye.

"Tchah!" she said. "What do you suppose my husband's brother Charlie Parker would say if I allowed his niece to marry a man who jellies eels?"

"Ah!" said Claude, who, before we go any further, was a tall, drooping bird with a red soup-strainer mustache.

"Or my husband's brother, Henry Parker."

"Ah!" said Claude. "Or Cousin Alf Robbins, for that matter."

"Exactly. Cousin Alfred would die of shame."

The girl Julia hiccoughed passionately, so much so that Pongo says it was all he could do to stop himself nipping across and taking her hand in his and patting it.

"I've told you a hundred times, Mother, that Wilberforce is only jellying eels till he finds something better."

"What is better than an eel?" asked Lord Ickenham, who

had been following this discussion with the close attention it deserved. "For jellying purposes, I mean."

"He is ambitious. It won't be long," said the girl, "before Wilberforce suddenly rises in the world."

She never spoke a truer word. At this very moment, up he came from behind the settee like a leaping salmon.

"Julia!" he cried.

"Wilby!" yipped the girl.

And Pongo says he never saw anything more sickening in his life than the way she flung herself into the blighter's arms and clung there like the ivy on the old garden wall. It wasn't that he had anything specific against the pink chap, but this girl had made a deep impression on him and he resented her glueing herself to another in this manner.

Julia's mother, after just that brief moment which a woman needs in which to recover from her natural surprise at seeing eel-jelliers pop up from behind sofas, got moving and plucked her away like a referee breaking a couple of welter-weights.

"Julia Parker," she said. "I'm ashamed of you!"

"So am I," said Claude.

"I blush for you."

"Me, too," said Claude. "Hugging and kissing a man who called your father a perishing old bottle-nosed Gawd-help-us."

"I think," said Lord Ickenham, shoving his oar in, "that before proceeding any further we ought to go into that point. If he called you a perishing old bottle-nosed Gawd-help-us, it seems to me that the first thing to do is to decide whether he was right, and frankly, in my opinion . . ."

"Wilberforce will apologize."

"Certainly I'll apologize. It isn't fair to hold a remark passed in the heat of the moment against a chap . . ."

"Mr. Robinson," said the woman, "you know perfectly well

that whatever remarks you may have seen fit to pass don't matter one way or the other. If you were listening to what I was saying you will understand . . ."

"Oh, I know, I know. Uncle Charlie Parker and Uncle Henry Parker and Cousin Alf Robbins and all that. Pack of snobs!"

"What!"

"Haughty, stuck-up snobs. Them and their class distinctions. Think themselves everybody just because they've got money. I'd like to know how they got it."

"What do you mean by that?"

"Never mind what I mean."

"If you are insinuating —"

"Well, of course, you know, Connie," said Lord Ickenham mildly, "he's quite right. You can't get away from that."

I don't know if you have ever seen a bull-terrier embarking on a scrap with an Airedale and just as it was getting down nicely to its work suddenly having an unexpected Kerry Blue sneak up behind it and bite it in the rear quarters. When this happens, it lets go of the Airedale and swivels round and fixes the butting-in animal with a pretty nasty eye. It was exactly the same with the woman Connie when Lord Ickenham spoke these words.

"What!"

"I was only wondering if you had forgotten how Charlie Parker made his pile."

"What are you talking about?"

"I know it is painful," said Lord Ickenham, "and one doesn't mention it as a rule, but, as we are on the subject, you must admit that lending money at two hundred and fifty per cent interest is not done in the best circles. The judge, if you remember, said so at the trial."

"I never knew that!" cried the girl Julia.

"Ah," said Lord Ickenham. "You kept it from the child? Quite right, quite right."

"It's a lie!"

"And when Henry Parker had all that fuss with the bank it was touch and go they didn't send him to prison. Between ourselves, Connie, has a bank official, even a brother of your husband, any right to sneak fifty pounds from the till in order to put it on a hundred-to-one shot for the Grand National? Not quite playing the game, Connie. Not the straight bat. Henry, I grant you, won five thousand of the best and never looked back afterwards, but, though we applaud his judgment of form, we must surely look askance at his financial methods. As for Cousin Alf Robbins . . ."

The woman was making rummy stuttering sounds. Pongo tells me he once had a Pommery Seven which used to express itself in much the same way if you tried to get it to take a hill on high. A sort of mixture of gurgles and explosions.

"There is not a word of truth in this," she gasped at length, having managed to get the vocal cords disentangled. "Not a single word. I think you must have gone mad."

Lord Ickenham shrugged his shoulders.

"Have it your own way, Connie. I was only going to say that, while the jury were probably compelled on the evidence submitted to them to give Cousin Alf Robbins the benefit of the doubt when charged with smuggling dope, everybody knew that he had been doing it for years. I am not blaming him, mind you. If a man can smuggle cocaine and get away with it, good luck to him, say I. The only point I am trying to make is that we are hardly a family that can afford to put on the dog and sneer at honest suitors for our daughters' hands. Speaking for myself, I consider that we are very lucky to have the chance of marrying even into eel-jellying circles."

"So do I," said Julia firmly.

"You don't believe what this man is saying?"

"I believe every word."

"So do I," said the pink chap.

The woman snorted. She seemed overwrought.

"Well," she said, "goodness knows I have never liked Laura, but I would never have wished her a husband like you!"

"Husband?" said Lord Ickenham, puzzled. "What gives you the impression that Laura and I are married?"

There was a weighty silence, during which the parrot threw out a general invitation to the company to join it in a nut. Then the girl Julia spoke.

"You'll have to let me marry Wilberforce now," she said. "He knows too much about us."

"I was rather thinking that myself," said Lord Ickenham. "Seal his lips, I say."

"You wouldn't mind marrying into a low family, would you, darling?" asked the girl, with a touch of anxiety.

"No family could be too low for me, dearest, if it was yours," said the pink chap.

"After all, we needn't see them."

"That's right."

"It isn't one's relations that matter; it's oneselves."

"That's right, too."

"Wilby!"

"Julia!"

They repeated the old ivy-on-the-garden-wall act. Pongo says he didn't like it any better than the first time, but his distaste wasn't in it with the woman Connie's.

"And what, may I ask," she said, "do you propose to marry on?"

This seemed to cast a damper. They came apart. They looked at each other. The girl looked at the pink chap, and the pink chap looked at the girl. You could see that a jarring note had been struck.

"Wilberforce is going to be a very rich man some day."

"Some day!"

"If I had a hundred pounds," said the pink chap, "I could buy a half-share in one of the best milk walks in South London tomorrow."

"If!" said the woman.

"Ah!" said Claude.

"Where are you going to get it?"

"Ah!" said Claude.

"Where," repeated the woman, plainly pleased with the snappy crack and loath to let it ride without an encore, "are you going to get it?"

"That," said Claude, "is the point. Where are you going to get a hundred pounds?"

"Why, bless my soul," said Lord Ickenham jovially, "from me, of course. Where else?"

And before Pongo's bulging eyes he fished out from the recesses of his costume a crackling bundle of notes and handed it over. And the agony of realizing that the old bounder had had all that stuff on him all this time and that he hadn't touched him for so much as a tithe of it was so keen, Pongo says, that before he knew what he was doing he had let out a sharp, whinnying cry which rang through the room like the yowl of a stepped-on puppy.

"Ah," said Lord Ickenham. "The vet wishes to speak to me. Yes, vet?"

This seemed to puzzle the cerise bloke a bit.

"I thought you said this chap was your son."

"If I had a son," said Lord Ickenham, a little hurt, "he would be a good deal better-looking than that. No, this is the local veterinary surgeon. I may have said I *looked* on him as a son. Perhaps that was what confused you."

He shifted across to Pongo and twiddled his hands inquiringly. Pongo gaped at him, and it was not until one of the hands caught him smartly in the lower ribs that he remembered he was deaf and started to twiddle back. Considering that he wasn't supposed to be dumb, I can't see why he should have twiddled, but no doubt there are moments when twiddling is about all a fellow feels himself equal to. For what seemed to him at least ten hours Pongo had been undergoing great mental stress, and one can't blame him for not being chatty. Anyway, be that as it may, he twiddled.

"I cannot quite understand what he says," announced Lord Ickenham at length, "because he sprained a finger this morning and that makes him stammer. But I gather that he wishes to have a word with me in private. Possibly my parrot has got something the matter with it which he is reluctant to mention even in sign language in front of a young unmarried girl. You know what parrots are. We will step outside."

"*We* will step outside," said Wilberforce.

"Yes," said the girl Julia. "I feel like a walk."

"And you?" said Lord Ickenham to the woman Connie, who was looking like a female Napoleon at Moscow. "Do you join the hikers?"

"I shall remain and make myself a cup of tea. You will not grudge us a cup of tea, I hope?"

"Far from it," said Lord Ickenham cordially. "This is Liberty Hall. Stick around and mop it up till your eyes bubble."

Outside, the girl, looking more like a dewy rosebud than ever, fawned on the old buster pretty considerably.

"I don't know how to thank you!" she said. And the pink chap said he didn't, either.

"Not at all, my dear, not at all," said Lord Ickenham.

"I think you're simply wonderful."

"No, no."

"You are. Perfectly marvelous."

"Tut, tut," said Lord Ickenham. "Don't give the matter another thought."

He kissed her on both cheeks, the chin, the forehead, the right eyebrow, and the tip of the nose, Pongo looking on the while in a baffled and discontented manner. Everybody seemed to be kissing this girl except him.

Eventually the degrading spectacle ceased and the girl and the pink chap shoved off, and Pongo was enabled to take up the matter of that hundred quid.

"Where," he asked, "did you get all that money?"

"Now, where did I?" mused Lord Ickenham. "I know your aunt gave it to me for some purpose. But what? To pay some bill or other, I rather fancy."

This cheered Pongo up slightly.

"She'll give you the devil when you get back," he said, with not a little relish. "I wouldn't be in your shoes for something. When you tell Aunt Jane," he said, with confidence, for he knew his Aunt Jane's emotional nature, "that you slipped her entire roll to a girl, and explain, as you will have to explain, that she was an extraordinarily pretty girl — a girl, in fine, who looked like something out of a beauty chorus of the better sort, I should think she would pluck down one of the ancestral battle-axes from the wall and jolly well strike you on the mazzard."

"Have no anxiety, my dear boy," said Lord Ickenham. "It is like your kind heart to be so concerned, but have no anxiety. I shall tell her that I was compelled to give the money to you to enable you to buy back some compromising letters from a Spanish *demi-mondaine*. She will scarcely be able to blame me for rescuing a fondly-loved nephew from the clutches of an adventuress. It may be that she will feel a little vexed with you for a while, and that you may have to allow a certain time to elapse before you visit Ickenham again, but then I shan't be wanting you at Ickenham till the ratting season starts, so all is well."

At this moment, there came toddling up to the gate of The Cedars a large red-faced man. He was just going in when Lord Ickenham hailed him.

"Mr. Roddis?"

"Hey?"

"Am I addressing Mr. Roddis?"

"That's me."

"I am Mr. J. G. Bulstrode from down the road," said Lord Ickenham. "This is my sister's husband's brother, Percy Frensham, in the lard-and-imported-butter business."

The red-faced bird said he was pleased to meet them. He asked Pongo if things were brisk in the lard-and-imported-butter business, and Pongo said they were all right, and the red-faced bird said he was glad to hear it.

"We have never met, Mr. Roddis," said Lord Ickenham, "but I think it would be only neighborly to inform you that a short while ago I observed two suspicious-looking persons in your house."

"In my house? How on earth did they get there?"

"No doubt through a window at the back. They looked to me like cat burglars. If you creep up, you may be able to see them."

The red-faced bird crept, and came back not exactly foaming at the mouth but with the air of a man who for two pins would so foam.

"You're perfectly right. They're sitting in my parlor as cool as dammit, swigging my tea and buttered toast."

"I thought as much."

"And they've opened a pot of my raspberry jam."

"Ah, then you will be able to catch them red-handed. I should fetch a policeman."

"I will. Thank you, Mr. Bulstrode."

"Only too glad to have been able to render you this little service, Mr. Roddis," said Lord Ickenham. "Well, I must be moving along. I have an appointment. Pleasant after the rain, is it not? Come, Percy."

He lugged Pongo off.

"So that," he said, with satisfaction, "is that. On these visits of mine to the metropolis, my boy, I always make it my aim, if possible, to spread sweetness and light. I look about me, even in a foul hole like Mitching Hill, and I ask myself — How can I leave this foul hole a better and happier foul hole than I found it? And if I see a chance, I grab it. Here is our omnibus. Spring aboard, my boy, and on our way home we will be sketching out rough plans for the evening. If the old Leicester Grill is still in existence, we might look in there. It must be fully thirty-five years since I was last thrown out of the Leicester Grill. I wonder who is the bouncer there now."

Such (concluded the Crumpet) is Pongo Twistleton's Uncle Fred from the country, and you will have gathered by now a rough notion of why it is that when a telegram comes announcing his impending arrival in the great city Pongo blenches to the core and calls for a couple of quick ones.

The whole situation, Pongo says, is very complex. Looking at it from one angle, it is fine that the man lives in the country most of the year. If he didn't, he would have him in his midst all the time. On the other hand, by living in the country he generates, as it were, a store of loopiness which expends itself with frightful violence on his rare visits to the center of things.

What it boils down to is this — Is it better to have a loopy uncle whose loopiness is perpetually on tap but spread out thin, so to speak, or one who lies low in distant Hants for three hundred and sixty days in the year and does himself proud in London for the other five? Dashed moot, of course, and Pongo has never been able to make up his mind on the point.

Naturally, the ideal thing would be if someone would chain the old hound up permanently and keep him from Jan. One to Dec. Thirty-one where he wouldn't do any harm — viz., among the spuds and tenantry. But this, Pongo admits, is a Utopian dream. Nobody could work harder to that end than his Aunt Jane, and she has never been able to manage it.

The Mixer

🐾 LOOKING BACK, I always consider that my career as a dog proper really started when I was bought for the sum of half a crown by the Shy Man. That event marked the end of my puppyhood. The knowledge that I was worth actual cash to somebody filled me with a sense of new responsibilities. It sobered me. Besides, it was only after that half-crown changed hands that I went out into the great world; and, however interesting life may be in an East End public-house, it is only when you go out into the world that you really broaden your mind and begin to see things.

Within its limitations, my life had been singularly full and vivid. I was born, as I say, in a public-house in the East End, and however lacking a public-house may be in refinement and the true culture, it certainly provides plenty of excitement. Before I was six weeks old, I had upset three policemen by getting between their legs when they came round to the side-door, thinking they had heard suspicious noises; and I can still recall the interesting sensation of being chased seventeen times round the yard with a broom-handle after a well-planned and completely successful raid on the larder. These and other happenings of a like nature soothed for the moment but could not cure the restlessness which has always been so marked a trait in my character. I have always been restless, unable to settle down in one place and anxious to get on to the next thing. This may be due to a gipsy strain in my ancestry — one of my uncles traveled with a circus — or it may be the Artistic Temperament, acquired from a grandfather who, before dying of a surfeit of paste in the property-room of the Bristol Coliseum, which he was visiting in the course of a professional tour, had an established reputation on the music-hall stage as one of Professor Pond's Performing Poodles.

I owe the fullness and variety of my life to this restlessness of mine, for I have repeatedly left comfortable homes in order to follow some perfect stranger who looked as if he were on his way to somewhere interesting. Sometimes I think I must have cat blood in me.

The Shy Man came into our yard one afternoon in April, while I was sleeping with mother in the sun on an old sweater which we had borrowed from Fred, one of the barmen. I heard Mother growl, but I didn't take any notice. Mother is what they call a good watch-dog, and she growls at everybody except Master. At first when she used to do it, I would get up and bark my head off, but not now. Life's too short to bark at everybody who comes into our yard. It is behind the public-house, and they keep empty bottles and things there, so people are always coming and going.

Besides, I was tired. I had had a very busy morning, helping the men bring in a lot of cases of beer and running into the saloon to talk to Fred and generally looking after things. So I was just dozing off again when I heard a voice say, "Well, he's ugly enough." Then I knew that they were talking about me.

I have never disguised it from myself, and nobody has ever disguised it from me, that I am not a handsome dog. Even Mother never thought me beautiful. She was no Gladys Cooper herself, but she never hesitated to criticize my appearance. In fact, I have yet to meet anyone who did. The first thing strangers say about me is "What an ugly dog!"

I don't know what I am. I have a bull-dog kind of a face, but the rest of me is terrier. I have a long tail which sticks straight up in the air. My hair is wiry. My eyes are brown. I am jet black with a white chest. I once overheard Fred saying that I was a Gorgonzola cheese-hound, and I have generally found Fred reliable in his statements.

When I found that I was under discussion, I opened my eyes. Master was standing there, looking down at me, and by his side the man who had just said I was ugly enough. The man was a thin man, about the age of a barman and smaller than a policeman. He had patched brown shoes and black trousers.

"But he's got a sweet nature," said Master.

This was true, luckily for me. Mother always said, "A dog without influence or private means, if he is to make his way in the world, must have either good looks or amiability." But, according to her, I overdid it. "A dog," she used to say, "can have a good heart without chumming with every Tom, Dick, and Harry he meets. Your behavior is sometimes quite un-dog-like." Mother prided herself on being a one-man dog. She kept herself to herself, and wouldn't kiss anybody except Master — not even Fred.

Now, I'm a mixer. I can't help it. It's my nature. I like men. I like the taste of their boots, the smell of their legs, and the sound of their voices. It may be weak of me, but a man has only to speak to me, and a sort of thrill goes right down my spine and sets my tail wagging.

I wagged it now. The man looked at me rather distantly. He didn't pat me. I suspected — what I afterwards found to be the case — that he was shy, so I jumped up at him to put him at his ease. Mother growled again. I felt that she did not approve.

"Why, he's took quite a fancy to you already," said Master.

The man didn't say a word. He seemed to be brooding on something. He was one of those silent men. He reminded me of Joe, the old dog down the street at the grocer's shop, who lies at the door all day, blinking and not speaking to anybody.

Master began to talk about me. It surprised me, the way he praised me. I hadn't a suspicion he admired me so much. From what he said you would have thought I had won prizes and ribbons at the Crystal Palace. But the man didn't seem to be impressed. He kept on saying nothing.

When Master had finished telling him what a wonderful dog I was till I blushed, the man spoke.

"Less of it," he said. "Half a crown is my bid, and if he was an angel from on high you couldn't get another ha'penny out of me. What about it?"

A thrill went down my spine and out at my tail, for of course I saw now what was happening. The man wanted to buy me and take me away. I looked at Master hopefully.

"He's more like a son to me than a dog," said Master, sort of wistful.

"It's his face that makes you feel that way," said the man, unsympathetically. "If you had a son that's just how he would look. Half a crown is my offer, and I'm in a hurry."

"All right," said Master, with a sigh, "though it's giving him away, a valuable dog like that. Where's your half-crown?"

The man got a bit of rope and tied it round my neck.

I could hear Mother barking advice and telling me to be a credit to the family, but I was too excited to listen.

"Good-bye, Mother," I said. "Good-bye, Master. Good-bye, Fred. Good-bye, everybody. I'm off to see life. The Shy Man has bought me for half a crown. Wow!"

I kept running round in circles and shouting, till the man gave me a kick and told me to stop it.

So I did.

I don't know where we went, but it was a long way. I had never been off our street before in my life and I didn't know the whole world was half as big as that. We walked on and on, and the man jerking at my rope whenever I wanted to stop and look at anything. He wouldn't even let me pass the time of the day with dogs we met.

When we had gone about a hundred miles and were just going to turn in at a dark doorway, a policeman suddenly stopped the man. I could feel by the way the man pulled at my rope and tried to hurry on that he didn't want to speak to the policeman. The more I saw of the man, the more I saw how shy he was.

"Hi!" said the policeman, and we had to stop.

"I've got a message for you, old pal," said the policeman. "It's from the Board of Health. They told me to tell you you needed a change of air. See?"

"All right!" said the man.

"And take it as soon as you like. Else you'll find you'll get it given you. See?"

I looked at the man with a good deal of respect. He was evidently someone very important, if they worried so about his health.

"I'm going down to the country tonight," said the man.

The policeman seemed pleased.

"That's a bit of luck for the country," he said. "Don't go changing your mind."

And we walked on, and went in at the dark doorway, and climbed about a million stairs, and went into a room that smelt of rats. The man sat down and swore a little, and I sat and looked at him.

Presently I couldn't keep it in any longer.

"Do we live here?" I said. "Is it true we're going to the country? Wasn't that policeman a good sort? Don't you like policemen? I knew lots of policemen at the public-house. Are there any other dogs here? What is there for dinner? What's in that cupboard? When are you going to take me out for another run? May I go out and see if I can find a cat?"

"Stop that yelping," he said.

"When we go to the country, where shall we live? Are you going to be a caretaker at a house? Fred's father is a caretaker at a big house in Kent. I've heard Fred talk about it. You didn't meet Fred when you came to the public-house, did you? You would like Fred. I like Fred. Mother likes Fred. We all like Fred."

I was going on to tell him a lot more about Fred, who had always been one of my warmest friends, when he suddenly got hold of a stick and walloped me with it.

"You keep quiet when you're told," he said.

He really was the shyest man I had ever met. It seemed to hurt him to be spoken to. However, he was the boss, and I had to humor him, so I didn't say any more.

We went down to the country that night, just as the man had told the policeman we would. I was all worked up, for I had heard so much about the country from Fred that I had always wanted to go there. Fred used to go off on a motor-bicycle sometimes to spend the night with his father in Kent, and once he brought back a squirrel with him, which I thought was for me to eat, but Mother said no. "The first thing a dog has to learn," Mother used often to say, "is that the whole world wasn't created for him to eat."

It was quite dark when we got to the country, but the man seemed to know where to go. He pulled at my rope, and we began to walk along a road with no people in it at all. We walked on and on, but it was all so new to me that I forgot how tired I was. I could feel my mind broadening with every step I took.

Every now and then we would pass a very big house which looked as if it was empty, but I knew that there was a caretaker inside, because of Fred's father. These big houses belong to very rich people, but they don't want to live in them till the summer, so they put in caretakers, and the caretakers have a dog to keep off burglars. I wondered if that was what I had been brought here for.

"Are you going to be a caretaker?" I asked the man.

"Shut up," he said.

So I shut up.

After we had been walking a long time, we came to a cottage. A man came out. My man seemed to know him, for he called him Bill. I was quite surprised to see the man was not at all shy with Bill. They seemed very friendly.

"Is that him?" said Bill, looking at me.

"Bought him this afternoon," said the man.

"Well," said Bill, "he's ugly enough. He looks fierce. If you want a dog, he's the sort of dog you want. But what do you want one for? It seems to me it's a lot of trouble to take, when there's no need of any trouble at all. Why not do what I've always wanted to do? What's wrong with just fixing the dog, same as it's always done, and walking in and helping yourself?"

"I'll tell you what's wrong," said the man. "To start with,

you can't get at the dog to fix him except by day, when they let him out. At night he's shut up inside the house. And suppose you do fix him during the day, what happens then? Either the bloke gets another before night, or else he sits up all night with a gun. It isn't like as if these blokes was ordinary blokes. They're down here to look after the house. That's their job, and they don't take any chances."

It was the longest speech I had ever heard the man make, and it seemed to impress Bill. He was quite humble.

"I didn't think of that," he said. "We'd best start in to train this tyke at once."

Mother often used to say, when I went on about wanting to go out into the world and see life, "You'll be sorry when you do. The world isn't all bones and liver." And I hadn't been living with the man and Bill in their cottage long before I found out how right she was.

It was the man's shyness that made all the trouble. It seemed as if he hated to be taken notice of.

It started on my very first night at the cottage. I had fallen asleep in the kitchen, tired out after all the excitement of the day and the long walks I had had, when something woke me with a start. It was somebody scratching at the window, trying to get in.

Well, I ask you, I ask any dog, what would you have done in my place? Ever since I was old enough to listen, Mother had told me over and over again what I must do in a case like this. It is the ABC of a dog's education. "If you are in a room and you hear anyone trying to get in," mother used to say, "bark. It may be some one who has business there, or it may not. Bark first, and inquire afterwards. Dogs were made to be heard and not seen."

I lifted my head and yelled. I have a good, deep voice, due to a hound strain in my pedigree, and at the public-house, when there was a full moon, I have often had people leaning out of the windows and saying things all down the street. I took a deep breath and let it go.

"Man!" I shouted. "Bill! Man! Come quick! Here's a burglar getting in!"

Then somebody struck a light, and it was the man himself. He had come in through the window.

He picked up a stick, and he walloped me. I couldn't understand it. I couldn't see where I had done the wrong thing. But he was the boss, so there was nothing to be said.

If you'll believe me, that same thing happened every night. Every single night! And sometimes twice or three times before morning. And every time I would bark my loudest, and the man would strike a light and wallop me. The thing was baffling. I couldn't possibly have mistaken what Mother had said to me. She said it too often for that. Bark! Bark! Bark! It was the main plank of her whole system of education. And yet, here I was, getting walloped every night for doing it.

I thought it out till my head ached, and finally I got it right. I began to see that Mother's outlook was narrow. No doubt, living with a man like Master at the public-house, a man without a trace of shyness in his composition, barking was all right. But circumstances alter cases. I belonged to a man who was a mass of nerves, who got the jumps if you spoke to him. What I had to do was to forget the training I had had from Mother, sound as it no doubt was as a general thing, and to adapt myself to the needs of the particular man who had happened to buy me. I had tried Mother's way, and all it had brought me was walloping, so now I would think for myself.

So next night, when I heard the window go, I lay there without a word, though it went against all my better feelings. I didn't even growl. Someone came in and moved about in the dark, with a lantern, but, though I smelt that it was the man,

I didn't ask him a single question. And presently the man lit a light and came over to me and gave me a pat, which was a thing he had never done before.

"Good dog!" he said. "Now you can have this."

And he let me lick out the saucepan in which the dinner had been cooked.

After that, we got on fine. Whenever I heard anyone at the window I just kept curled up and took no notice, and every time I got a bone or something good. It was easy, once you had got the hang of things.

It was about a week after that the man took me out one morning, and we walked a long way till we turned in at some big gates and went along a very smooth road till we came to a great house, standing all by itself in the middle of a whole lot of country. There was a big lawn in front of it, and all round there were fields and trees, and at the back a great wood.

The man rang a bell, and the door opened, and an old man came out.

"Well?" he said, not very cordially.

"I thought you might want to buy a good watch-dog," said the man.

"Well, that's queer, your saying that," said the caretaker. "It's a coincidence. That's exactly what I do want to buy. I was just thinking of going along and trying to get one. My old dog picked up something this morning that he oughtn't to have, and he's dead, poor feller."

"Poor feller," said the man. "Found an old bone with phosphorus on it, I guess."

"What do you want for this one?"

"Five shillings."

"Is he a good watch-dog?"

"He's a grand watch-dog."

"He looks fierce enough."

"Ah!"

So the caretaker gave the man his five shillings, and the man went off and left me.

At first the newness of everything and the unaccustomed smells and getting to know the caretaker, who was a nice old man, prevented my missing the man, but as the day went on and I began to realize that he had gone and would never come back, I got very depressed. I pattered all over the house, whining. It was a most interesting house, bigger than I thought a house could possibly be, but it couldn't cheer me up. You may think it strange that I should pine for the man, after all the wallopings he had given me, and it is odd, when you come to think of it. But dogs are dogs, and they are built like that. By the time it was evening I was thoroughly miserable. I found a shoe and an old clothes-brush in one of the rooms, but could eat nothing. I just sat and moped.

It's a funny thing, but it seems as if it always happened that just when you are feeling most miserable, something nice happens. As I sat there, there came from outside the sound of a motor-bicycle, and somebody shouted.

It was dear old Fred, my old pal Fred, the best old boy that ever stepped. I recognized his voice in a second, and I was scratching at the door before the old man had time to get up out of his chair.

Well, well, well! That was a pleasant surprise! I ran five times round the lawn without stopping, and then I came back and jumped up at him.

"What are you doing down here, Fred?" I said, "Is this caretaker your father? Have you seen the rabbits in the wood? How long are you going to stop? How's Mother? I like the country. Have you come all the way from the public-house? I'm living here now. Your father gave five shillings for me.

That's twice as much as I was worth when I saw you last."

"Why, it's young Blackie!" That was what they called me at the saloon. "What are you doing here? Where did you get this dog, Father?"

"A man sold him to me this morning. Poor old Bob got poisoned. This one ought to be just as good a watch-dog. He barks loud enough."

"He should be. His mother is the best watch-dog in London. This cheese-hound used to belong to the boss. Funny him getting down here."

We went into the house and had supper. And after supper we sat and talked. Fred was only down for the night, he said, because the boss wanted him back next day.

"And I'd sooner have my job than yours, Dad," he said. "Of all the lonely places! I wonder you aren't scared of burglars."

"I've got my shot-gun, and there's the dog. I might be scared if it wasn't for him, but he kind of gives me confidence. Old Bob was the same. Dogs are a comfort in the country."

"Get many tramps here?"

"I've only seen one in two months, and that's the feller who sold me the dog here."

As they were talking about the man, I asked Fred if he knew him. They might have met at the public-house, when the man was buying me from the boss.

"You would like him," I said. "I wish you could have met."

They both looked at me.

"What's he growling at?" asked Fred. "Think he heard something?"

The old man laughed.

"He wasn't growling. He was talking in his sleep. You're nervous, Fred. It comes of living in the city."

"Well, I am. I like this place in the daytime, but it gives me the pip at night. It's so quiet. How you can stand it here all the time, I can't understand. Two nights of it would have me seeing things."

His father laughed.

"If you feel like that, Fred, you had better take the gun to bed with you. I shall be quite happy without it."

"I will," said Fred. "I'll take six if you've got them."

And after that they went upstairs. I had a basket in the hall, which had belonged to Bob, the dog who had got poisoned. It was a comfortable basket, but I was so excited at having met Fred again that I couldn't sleep. Besides, there was a smell of mice somewhere, and I had to move around, trying to place it.

I was just sniffing at a place in the wall when I heard a scratching noise. At first I thought it was the mice working in a different place, but, when I listened, I found that the sound came from the window. Somebody was doing something to it from outside.

If it had been Mother, she would have lifted the roof off right there, and so should I, if it hadn't been for what the man had taught me. I didn't think it possible that this could be the man come back, for he had gone away and said nothing about ever seeing me again. But I didn't bark. I stopped where I was and listened. And presently the window came open, and somebody began to climb in.

I gave a good sniff, and I knew it was the man.

I was so delighted that for a moment I nearly forgot myself and shouted with joy, but I remembered in time how shy he was, and stopped myself. But I ran to him and jumped up quite quietly, and he told me to lie down. I was disappointed that he didn't seem more pleased to see me. I lay down.

It was very dark, but he had brought a lantern with him, and I could see him moving about the room, picking things up and putting them in a bag which he had brought with him. Every now and then he would stop and listen, and then he would start moving round again. He was very quick about it, but very quiet. It was plain that he didn't want Fred or his father to come down and find him.

I kept thinking about this peculiarity of his while I watched him. I suppose, being chummy myself, I find it hard to understand that everybody else in the world isn't chummy too. Of course, my experience at the public-house had taught me that men are just as different from each other as dogs. If I chewed Master's shoe, for instance, he used to kick me, but if I chewed Fred's, Fred would tickle me under the ear. And, similarly, some men are shy and some men are mixers. I quite appreciated that, but I couldn't help feeling that the man carried shyness to a point where it became morbid. And he didn't give himself a chance to cure himself of it. That was the point. Imagine a man hating to meet people so much that he never visited their houses till the middle of the night, when they were in bed and asleep. It was silly. Shyness had always been something so outside my nature that I suppose I have never really been able to look at it sympathetically. I have always held the view that you can get over it if you make an effort. The trouble with the man was that he wouldn't make an effort. He went out of his way to avoid meeting people.

I was fond of the man. He was the sort of person you never get to know very well, but we had been together for quite a while, and I wouldn't have been a dog if I hadn't got attached to him.

As I sat and watched him creep about the room, it suddenly came to me that here was a chance of doing him a real good turn in spite of himself. Fred was upstairs, and Fred, as I knew by experience, was the easiest man to get along with in the world. Nobody could be shy with Fred. I felt that if only I could bring him and the man together, they would get along splendidly, and it would teach the man not to be silly and avoid people. It would help to give him the confidence which he needed. I had seen him with Bill, and I knew that he could be perfectly natural and easy when he liked.

It was true that the man might object at first, but after a while he would see that I had acted simply for his good, and would be grateful.

The difficulty was, how to get Fred down without scaring the man. I knew that if I shouted he wouldn't wait, but would be out of the window and away before Fred could get there. What I had to do was to go to Fred's room, explain the whole situation quietly to him, and ask him to come down and make himself pleasant.

The man was far too busy to pay any attention to me. He was kneeling in a corner with his back to me, putting something in his bag. I seized the opportunity to steal softly from the room.

Fred's door was shut, and I could hear him snoring. I scratched gently, and then harder, till I heard the snores stop. He got out of bed and opened the door.

"Don't make a noise," I whispered. "Come on downstairs. I want you to meet a friend of mine."

At first he was quite peevish.

"What's the idea," he said, "coming and spoiling a man's beauty-sleep? Get out."

He actually started to go back into the room.

"No, honestly, Fred," I said, "I'm not fooling you. There *is* a man downstairs. He got in through the window. I want you to meet him. He's very shy, and I think it will do him good to have a chat with you."

"What are you whining about?" Fred began, and then he

broke off suddenly and listened. We could both hear the man's footsteps as he moved about.

Fred jumped back into the room. He came out, carrying something. He didn't say any more but started to go downstairs, very quiet, and I went after him.

There was the man, still putting things in his bag. I was just going to introduce Fred, when Fred, the silly ass, gave a great yell.

I could have bitten him.

"What did you want to do that for, you chump?" I said. "I told you he was shy. Now you've scared him."

He certainly had. The man was out of the window quicker than you would have believed possible. He just flew out. I called after him that it was only Fred and me, but at that moment a gun went off with a tremendous bang, so he couldn't have heard me.

I was pretty sick about it. The whole thing had gone wrong. Fred seemed to have lost his head entirely. He was behaving like a perfect ass. Naturally the man had been frightened with him carrying on in that way. I jumped out of the window to see if I could find the man and explain, but he was gone. Fred jumped out after me, and nearly squashed me.

It was pitch dark out there. I couldn't see a thing. But I knew the man could not have gone far, or I should have heard him. I started to sniff round on the chance of picking up his trail. It wasn't long before I struck it.

Fred's father had come down now, and they were running about. The old man had a light. I followed the trail, and it ended at a large cedar tree, not far from the house. I stood underneath it and looked up, but of course I could not see anything.

"Are you up there?" I shouted. "There's nothing to be

scared at. It was only Fred. He's an old pal of mine. He works at the place where you bought me. His gun went off by accident. He won't hurt you."

There wasn't a sound. I began to think I must have made a mistake.

"He's got away," I heard Fred say to his father, and just as he said it I caught a faint sound of someone moving in the branches above me.

"No he hasn't!" I shouted. "He's up this tree."

"I believe the dog's found him, Dad!"

"Yes, he's up here. Come along and meet him."

Fred came to the foot of the tree.

"You up there," he said, "come along down."

Not a sound from the tree.

"It's all right," I explained, "he *is* up there, but he's very shy. Ask him again."

"All right," said Fred, "stay there if you want to. But I'm going to shoot off this gun into the branches just for fun."

And then the man started to come down. As soon as he touched the ground I jumped up at him.

"This is fine!" I said. "Here's my friend Fred. You'll like him."

But it wasn't any good. They didn't get along together at all. They hardly spoke. The man went into the house, and Fred went after him, carrying his gun. And when they got into the house it was just the same. The man sat in one chair, and Fred sat in another, and after a long time some men came in a motor-car, and the man went away with them. He didn't say good-bye to me.

When he had gone, Fred and his father made a great fuss of me. I couldn't understand it. Men are so odd. The man wasn't a bit pleased that I had brought him and Fred together, but Fred seemed as if he couldn't do enough for me for having introduced him to the man. However, Fred's father produced some cold ham — my favorite dish — and gave me quite a lot of it, so I stopped worrying over the thing. As Mother used to say, "Don't bother your head about what doesn't concern you. The only thing a dog need concern himself with is the bill of fare. Eat your bun, and don't make yourself busy about other people's affairs." Mother's was in some ways a narrow outlook, but she had a great fund of sterling common sense.

D. R. Bensen is the editor of *Fore! The Best of Wodehouse on Golf* and *Wodehouse on Crime,* as well as a volume of essays on Wodehouse which was published in 1981 in conjunction with the Pierpont Morgan Library's centennial exhibition. He lives in Croton-on-Hudson, New York.